AMERICAN MONOGRAPH SERIES

Addison Mizner (1872–1933), c. 1920.

MIZNER'S FLORIDA

American Resort Architecture

Donald W. Curl

THE ARCHITECTURAL HISTORY FOUNDATION, NEW YORK
THE MIT PRESS, CAMBRIDGE, MASSACHUSETTS,
and LONDON, ENGLAND

Donald W. Curl is Professor of History at Florida Atlantic University.
Modern photography by Craig Kuhner.

Library of Congress Cataloging-in-Publication Data

Curl, Donald Walter, 1935–
  Mizner's Florida.

  (American monograph series)
  Bibliography: p. 225
  Includes index.
  1. Mizner, Addison, 1872–1933—Criticism and
interpretation. 2. Eclecticism in architecture—
Florida. 3. Architecture, Spanish—Florida—
Influence. 4. Vacation homes—Florida.
5. Architecture—Florida. 6. Architecture,
Modern—20th century—Florida. I. Title.
II. Series: American monograph series (Architectural
History Foundation (New York, N.Y.))
[NA737.M59C87   1987]   720′.92′4   86-33763
ISBN 0-262-53068-6 (pbk.)

Designed by Gilbert Etheredge

CONTENTS

ACKNOWLEDGMENTS

Although much has been written on Addison Mizner, many of his commissions remained unknown, unlocated, and undocumented. His last associate retained most of the firm's office tracings, but the office records have all disappeared. The years of mythmaking since his death have meant that much of the readily available information on his career is inaccurate or incomplete. Thus it was necessary to reconstruct Mizner's professional practice from the beginning. In this job I have had the aid of many individuals and institutions. For their knowledge and time I am grateful to: Richard Plack, librarian for Palm Beach Newspapers; Carole Traylor of the Long Island Society for the Preservation of Antiquities; Gay Wagner of the Huntington Historical Society; Mrs. Howard McCall and Stanford Smith of the Boca Raton Historical Society; Maxine Banash of the Historical Society of Palm Beach County; Neil Surprenant of Paul Smith's College; Alfred Jones, Sr., and Sig Kaufman of the Cloisters of Sea Island, Georgia; Robert Nayer of Fountain Valley School; Mrs. Clorice Keats of the Boynton Woman's Club; Mr. and Mrs. L. Bert Stephens of the Boca Raton Hotel and Club; Gary Parsons and Dahrl Moore of the Wimberly Library, Florida Atlantic University; and Ashley Abel and William Watkins of the university's photography department, and the staffs of the Society of the Four Arts Library, the Historical Association of Southern Florida, the Town of Palm Beach Building Department, the West Palm Beach Chamber of Commerce, and the Eleutherian Mills-Hagley Foundation Library.

Mrs. Henry Petronis, Mr. and Mrs. Persifor Frazer III, Sidney K. Neill, the late Marion Sims Wyeth, Irene Saxe, Ronald Miller, x / MIZNER'S FLORIDA

Robert Eigelberger, Judge James R. Knott, Mack Ritchie, James Mannion, Karl Riddle, Andrew Blanda, Mr. and Mrs. Kim Mizner Hollins, Nancy Dubner, Phillip and Susan Federspiel, Edward Brown, F. Martin Brown, Richard A. Winsche, Jerry Gold, James Nichols, Delores Jenkins, Stella Suberman, and Ralph Howell, Sr., supplied photographs, information, and encouragement. Steven Seiden allowed me to use his Yale senior thesis with its invaluable photographs of Playa Riente taken just before its destruction. The current owners of Mizner's houses deserve special thanks for their unfailing graciousness in allowing inspection, photography, and measurements.

I am particularly in debt to Mrs. Alice Mizner Lewitin (the daughter of the Reverend and Mrs. Henry Mizner), the late Miss Alice De Lamar, Mrs. H. Halpine Smith, Mrs. Vilma Richardson Townby, and Draper Babcock for their first-hand memories, their long and detailed letters, and, in general, for the insights that could be found nowhere else. Their good-humored responses to what must have seemed like unending questions will always be appreciated.

Professor Craig Kuhner's dedication to his art can readily be seen in the modern photography and I thank him. Thelma Spangler and Phyllis Surbaugh deserve great credit for being able to decipher my handwriting and my editing techniques.

Finally, without the constant help, interest, and resources of Jon von Gunst-Andersen and Frederick L. Eckel this book could never have been completed. "Andy's" enthusiasm for Mizner's architecture is unequaled. As a volunteer he devotes full time to the Mizner Collection of the Historical Society of Palm Beach County. He participated in many of the interviews and helped arrange tours and photography sessions. Fred Eckel aided in the research from the beginning. Without his perseverance and sense of direction, most of the houses from Mizner's New York years would remain unlocated. His work in Miami led to the discovery of the Harris brokerage office and the only known photograph of it in a contractor's advertisement. Perhaps his most valuable aid came from his lists, which told me what I had forgotten.

FOREWORD

The architects of the Western world have for centuries maintained an ambivalent attitude towards history. On the one hand, they have used it for their own generalized intellectual enrichment, like other members of the literate, book-reading public. But, on the other hand, architects have put the specialized histories of their own field to quite other uses—namely, as a kind of visual sperm bank or warehouse of design concepts from which they could borrow bits and pieces of the past, *disjecta membra*, at will. This phenomenon of historicizing eclecticism, so unlike contemporaneous use of the past in other fields (for example, science, technology, engineering), was the product of literacy. It could not have appeared before the printed book, with its woodcuts, etchings, lithographs, and photoengravings. It dominated Western architecture from the appearance of Alberti's *de re Aedificatoria* (1485) until the beginning of the present century.

The American architect, Addison Cairns Mizner, stands as one of the last and more spectacular exemplars of this centuries-old tradition. Although, as Professor Curl points out, Mizner worked in a number of the then-fashionable historicizing modes, his reputation rested on his astonishing repertory of Venetian, Spanish, and Latin American architectural styles. His freewheeling virtuosity in all these modes gave his work in them a grace and skill unmatched by any of his eclectic contemporaries.

His preparation for this career was, as Curl points out in fascinating detail, extracurricular in the most literal sense of the word. He finished no schools, gained no degrees, and only won a

license to practice under the so-called "grandfather clause" of registration at the age of forty-seven. But long before his death in 1933,
he had built some of the grandest houses in the country for some of
its wealthiest men and women. What he might have lacked in formal
training, he more than compensated for in many areas of expertise.
He was a world traveler and a leading connoisseur and dealer in
antique art and furnishings. He was his own general contractor and
real estate dealer. At the same time he was proud of his skills as a
cabinetmaker, plasterer, electrician, and plumber. He was the planner of several towns (Palm Beach, Boca Raton) until the collapse of
the Florida land boom in 1927.

He died, with almost poetic precision, in February 1933, just
as the particular world wealth and fashion for which he was such
an eloquent spokesman, was foundering in the depths of the Great
Depression. Thereafter, like most of the eclectic architects of his
generation, his work—indeed, his very name—was submerged in
the rising tide of modern architecture. Professor Curl thus does us a
great service in disinterring Mizner from obloquy, in this notably
informative and comprehensive biography.

I especially admire the distinction the author makes between
straightforward description of an event or a building and the sort of
hyperbolic, self-indulgent criticism which marks (and mars) so much
of the putative historiography of Curl's generation. Curl has selected
as his subject a man who epitomizes a very narrow band of American *nouveaux riches* in the brief period of their ascendency between
World War I and the Great Depression. His handling of this clientele
is admirably cool and restrained. He places minimal emphasis on
the broader sociopolitical setting, and avoids the lush, antihistorical
polemics of the post-modernist celebrations of this period.

As it happens, my own career touched Mizner's at just the
time of his death, when, as an apprentice draftsman, I was handed
the folio-sized publication of his Florida houses and told to prepare
working drawings for the duplication of one of his Venetian Gothic
windows in a house which my office was just then designing. I did
my best, being much impressed by the felicity of his designs. But,
as it turned out, this was my last contact with his work. Our clients,
hard hit by the same Depression, abandoned the project and my
own involvement with historicizing eclecticism was being eclipsed
by an increasing commitment to modern design. Mizner dropped
quite out of my field of vision and only resurfaces now, half a century later, in Professor Curl's study. It is a pleasure to meet this
fascinating man once more.

James Marston Fitch, D. Arts, D.H.L.

MIZNER'S FLORIDA

INTRODUCTION

The Career of a Society Architect

On 15 April 1925, Addison Mizner announced that he, his brother Wilson, and a group of Palm Beach associates had formed the Mizner Development Corporation to build "the world's most architecturally beautiful playground" at Boca Raton. The company had acquired 16,000 acres of land, including two miles of beach front at the Boca Raton Inlet. Coming at the very height of the Florida land boom, Mizner's planned development quickly captured national attention for the project and for its architect.

By 1925 Mizner already ranked as one of the country's most prominent architects. Dixon Wecter, the social historian, placed him with Richard M. Hunt and Stanford White as America's "great society architects." Mizner gained this reputation from his work in Palm Beach. His design for Paris Singer's Everglades Club in 1918 revolutionized Palm Beach architecture. In just seven years he transformed the shingle cottage, bungalow, and yellow hotel town of Henry M. Flagler into a resort of fashion and elegance in the "Spanish style." His town buildings included the club, dozens of mansions scattered across the island, the Via Mizner and Via Parigi, office buildings, apartments, and shops. When he found that barrel tiles and other decorative items needed for his buildings were unavailable, he established his own factories. Soon Mizner Industries even manufactured the furniture, both new and "antique," used in decorating his houses.

Although Mizner had no formal university training in architecture, he spent many years studying design, first in Guatemala,

1

where his father served as the American minister, and later in Spain at the University of Salamanca. From 1893 to 1896 he apprenticed in the San Francisco office of architect Willis Polk, a principal proponent of the Spanish "mission" style and the designer of the Hallidie Building in San Francisco. Here he received his practical training in the profession, eventually becoming Polk's partner. Later, in New York City, Stanford White befriended him by passing on a few minor commissions. His New York success allowed him to establish an office on Park Avenue. When he first arrived in Florida in 1918 to convalesce from an accident, he had already won recognition for his northern work.

The first settlers had come to Palm Beach in the late 1870s. Along with Flagler and later real estate promoters, they laid out streets and determined the character of the town development. Although Mizner transformed the architectural style of Palm Beach, he worked within this framework. And, of course, there were other architects, with other visions, who added buildings of their own to the town. The development of Boca Raton gave Mizner the opportunity to become a city planner. His Palm Beach buildings reflected his unique interpretation of Spanish architecture; his plans for Boca Raton called for a complete Spanish city. Mizner took responsibility for the layout of Boca Raton and the design of its most important buildings, and he retained artistic and architectural approval of all construction. Mizner the architect, and now city planner, envisioned Boca Raton as the ultimate achievement of his career.

Backed by some of the nation's most wealthy and powerful men, Mizner had every reason to be optimistic about the success of Boca Raton. Unfortunately, by the time he announced the project the confidence needed to sustain a land boom had been stretched to the breaking point. Boca Raton sales totaled over $16 million in less than six months; then came the collapse, putting an end to Mizner's dreams for the city. The bust also saw the decline in the fashion for Spanish architecture; new architects and new architectural styles appeared on the Palm Beach scene.

Mizner's reputation as an architect suffered after his death in 1933. Although serious about his work, in his personal life Mizner cultivated the impression of the sophisticated man-about-town, unbothered by the details of his profession. His autobiography, *The Many Mizners*, a breezy account of his life as a world traveler, bon vivant, and social lion, barely mentioned his architectural training or practice. All of this gave rise to the Palm Beach myths that he copied his building facades from his large collection of pictures and sketches. According to these stories, only the facades interested him, and since he had little training in architecture, he often forgot to include bathrooms, kitchens, and stairways. In reality, Mizner's architectural training rivaled that of many in the profession of his day. Moreover, he always employed well-trained people in his office and drafting rooms. The legends, nonetheless, have long since been accepted as fact. Alva Johnston, Mizner's only biographer, retold the myths and discounted the architectural accomplishments.

Changes in architectural styles also damaged his reputation. Mizner designed picturesque buildings. His clients had wealth and presumed social position. Thus boom-time developers thought they could ensure the success of their projects by using Spanish architecture. The results, often ludicrous caricatures of Mizner's houses, ill-proportioned and with garish decoration, dotted the Florida landscape. Fashionable Palm Beach believed they cheapened all work in the Spanish style, and a reaction set in against its use.

Moreover, by the beginning of the 1930s architectural critics in America had come to accept the validity of modernism in architecture. Mizner's work, as compared to that of Wright or the architects of the International Style, appeared overdecorated and dated. Consequently, his architecture remained largely forgotten for the next fifty years. Most surveys of American architectural history either omit Mizner or deprecate his work as unimportant or entirely derivative. Burchard and Bush-Brown, in *The Architecture of America: A Social and Cultural History*, spare one condescending sentence, "Addison Mizner built the J. S. Phipps house in Palm Beach in 1922, a lesser version of the greatest Florida villa, Vizcaya." Thus Mizner's story remained the property of the social historians who continued to tell of the missing bathrooms.

In 1977, a Palm Beach exhibition mounted by Christina Orr for the Norton Gallery, the Henry Morrison Flagler Museum, and the Society of the Four Arts, focused attention on Mizner, the architect and his architecture, for the first time in fifty years. This new examination of Mizner's work captured wide attention. Preservationists, concerned about the proposed destruction of one of Mizner's finest Palm Beach houses, received needed support. Environmentalists, worried about the energy crisis, realized that fifty years earlier Mizner had designed his houses for the climate of south Florida. Finally, architects, bored with utilitarian architecture and willing to experiment with historical styles, saw Mizner's work with new respect. Mizner's architecture once again appeared fresh and innovative and worthy of consideration.

1

Training

During the first thirty-two years of Addison Cairns Mizner's life he prepared for the career of a society architect. The son of prominent California pioneers, he spent his youth among the best families of San Francisco. From his earliest days, knowing "the right people" became one of the important ambitions of his life. His father's appointment as United States minister to Central America gave increased stature to his family, and also introduced the young Addison to Spanish culture. A year at the University of Salamanca deepened his appreciation of Spanish architecture and determined his professional career. After an apprenticeship with the San Francisco architect Willis Polk, in 1904 he combined his love of society and architecture and started a practice in New York City.

The Mizners were the first family of Benicia, California, and one of the first families of the state. Addison's father, Lansing Bond Mizner, who arrived in 1849, qualified for membership in the Society of California Pioneers and remained active in the organization throughout his life. Lansing's father, Illinois lawyer Henry Caldwell Mizner, died in 1829 when Lansing was four. In 1833 Addison's paternal grandmother married General James Semple, an Illinois politician and commander of the state militia. In 1837 Semple received appointment as minister to New Granada (the present-day Colombia and Panama), and the family lived in Bogotá for five years. During this period young Lansing became fluent in Spanish, an ability that profoundly affected his future career and that of his son.

Lansing returned to Illinois in 1843 to study law. When war broke out between Mexico and the United States in 1846, he left his studies to join a regiment of volunteers. His knowledge of Spanish allowed him to serve as an interpreter and prompted his rapid rise as an officer. At the end of the war, Lansing received a letter from Robert Baylor Semple, his stepfather's brother, inviting him to come to California. Telling of his purchase of a site for a city on San Francisco Bay in partnership with General Mariano Guadalupe Vallejo, "the wealthiest and best educated man in California," Semple concluded: "Now, my dear boy, if you have finished your studies and can get to this country, with a small library and your knowledge of the Spanish language, and my influence, you can make ten thousand dollars a year in the practice of law." Lansing accepted the invitation and arrived in California in May 1849.[1]

Addison's mother, Ella Watson Mizner, came with her family to San Francisco in 1853. The Watsons, originally from Ireland's County Clare, migrated to Pennsylvania in the eighteenth century. The family claimed a distant kinship to the painter Joshua Reynolds which in later years Addison liked to emphasize by saying, "I josh and I paint." Tragedy struck the Watsons on their way to California. The *Independence,* the steamship they took from Panama to San Francisco, struck a reef off Santa Margarita Island and sank. Ella's only brother, Asa, died in the wreck. Although the seventeen-year-old Ella met Lansing shortly after her arrival in San Francisco, they waited until 26 May 1856 to marry.[2]

Lansing brought his bride to Benicia, the site of Semple's new city on the Carquinez Straits, thirty miles northeast of San Francisco. Semple had actively promoted Benicia, hoping to make it the state capital. As president of the California constitutional convention, he used his political influence to bring the state legislature to Benicia for a brief session in 1853/54. Legislators believed the city failed to furnish the promised facilities and after this one session moved the capital permanently to Sacramento. By the time of Lansing and Ella's marriage Semple had died, leaving Benicia's future development in his stepnephew's hands. Although the city did attract several schools, including one that later developed into Mills College, and a small army arsenal, at Addison's birth it was a backwater of little importance. Addison later said that whenever he mentioned his birthplace someone always asked, "For God's sake, where was your mother going?"[3]

Addison's birth on 12 December 1872 added the sixth son and seventh child to the Mizner family. His names came from Addison Leech, uncle-in-law on his mother's side, and his paternal great-grandfather, Caldwell Cairns. Finding names for their offspring must have become a task for his parents, whose family already included sons Murray McLaughlin, a junior Lansing, Edgar Ames, William Garrison, and Henry Watson, and a daughter Mary Isabella. When their last child was born, four years after Addison, they named him simply Wilson.

From the beginning, Ella Mizner, or "Mama" Mizner to her children, stood at the heart of the Benicia household. "Papa" Mizner's legal and political career (he served two terms in the California Senate) often meant long separations from his family. The original Mizner house, a prefabricated six-room cottage, had been brought around Cape Horn. As the family grew, more rooms were added until, according to Addison, "from the air it must have looked like a telescope." Besides the many children, the household also included Ying Lee, the Chinese cook, and Mary Hamilton, a maid-of-all-work. Both served the family for over twenty-five years.

Addison said the children paired off according to their ages, making Addison and Wilson childhood companions and playmates. With Wilson's birth, Ella Mizner relaxed the strong discipline of the earlier household, and "Angel Birdie," her youngest, became the family terror, aided and abetted by Addison. As children and throughout their entire lives, Addison felt a need to protect and defend his younger brother.

Two events during Addison's childhood had a marked effect on his later life. The first involved his older brother Edgar, who fell in love with Tessie Fair, the daughter and heiress of James G. Fair, the Silver Bonanza King. Although she and Edgar never married, in later years her friendship with the Mizners helped Addison establish his New York career as a society architect. The second event occurred on the evening of 4 July 1888. Addison's parents invited "fifty kids" for fireworks, ice cream, and cake. To conclude the evening they lighted a bonfire in honor of the holiday and the more boisterous of the boys followed the tradition of "jumping over the fire." Addison caught his foot in a root, twisting his ankle, and several other boys landed on top of him. Although at first judged only a sprain, the injury failed to heal and new doctors consulted by his worried parents called for amputation. Finally, older brother William, a medical student, took him to a doctor in San Francisco who saved the leg, although Addison was confined to bed for almost a year. To help him pass the time, brother Henry gave him a set of watercolors, thus awaking his interest in painting and design.

During 1888 Lansing Mizner campaigned throughout California for successful presidential candidate Benjamin Harrison. After the election he went to Washington, seeking a diplomatic post. Although Mizner preferred Mexico, Harrison awarded him with appointment as Envoy Extraordinary and Minister Plenipotentiary to Central America. The appointment, which the Senate confirmed on 30 March 1889, made Mizner the highest ranking American diplomat in the five Central American nations of Guatemala, Honduras, El Salvador, Nicaragua, and Costa Rica. Although credited to all five republics, the United States minister lived in Guatemala City. Since Addison had yet to recover the full use of his leg, his parents decided he should come with them to Guatemala. Thus the sixteen-year-old Addison's introduction to Spanish culture also resulted from the bonfire injury.[4]

By the spring of 1889 Murray Mizner had died and Addison's older brothers and sister had left the family home: the younger Lansing to become an attorney and William, a doctor; Henry attended West Point, though later he entered the church; and Mary Isabella—or Min to her family—had married Horace Blanchard Chase and gone to live at Stag's Leap, his northern California vineyard. Only Addison, Wilson, and Edgar, who served as Secretary of the Legation, accompanied their parents to Guatemala City. Addison spent only a year in Central America, yet this short visit provided the foundation for his future life. An indifferent student at best, he learned Spanish in this year, "for without the language we could make no friends." He and Wilson attended the Instituto Nacional, though his travels throughout the five republics with his father probably contributed more to his education and appreciation of Spanish art and architecture.[5]

In August Addison went to Managua, when his father presented his credentials to the Nicaraguan government. Later they journeyed by river to San José, Costa Rica. On this trip the American party missed a steamer and was forced to travel by dugout canoe. The minister's arrival took the Costa Rican official committee by surprise, and their reception turned into a near riot when a spider monkey, given to Addison in Nicaragua, jumped onto the general's hat. In the confusion that followed, "Duty," the first of Addison's many pet monkeys, fell into the harbor and drowned. The elder Mizner's diplomatic problems also began on this trip. On taking his leave of Costa Rica, he called for a union of all five Central American republics for protection against the more powerful Mexico to the north and Colombia to the south. Both Mexico and Colombia immediately protested. Washington disavowed Mizner's statement; his remarks, wrote an Acting Secretary of State, "indicate a failure to

appreciate the impartial attitude of the United States." This became
the first of several rebukes Mizner was to receive from his government.[6]

Addison said his father had a particular interest in pre-Span-
ish civilization. After their return from Costa Rica he accompanied
his father on an expedition to rediscover the Mayan ruins at Copán,
just across the Guatemala border in Honduras. The enormous ruins
kindled the young Addison's romanticism: "It has left an indelible
picture on my mind of what was once the glory of a great and
vanished civilization—a city that must have housed a half million
souls, with all its pomp of royalty, and priesthood." In three days of
"climbing and hacking" they only saw a fraction of the once great
city.[7]

Addison returned from Copán in time to celebrate Christmas
in Guatemala City where Wilson and Edgar added to their father's
problems by their unruly behavior. As for Addison, his interest in
the culture and art of Central America helped him lead what was,
by his standards, an exemplary life. Alva Johnston said that Addison
met a young Guatemalan priest who awakened his love for Spanish
art and architecture. His autobiography suggests that the entire culture captured his enthusiasm.[8]

Addison was in California preparing for college when his
father's short diplomatic career ended as a result of General Carlos
Ezeta's violent early July 1890 *coup d'état* in El Salvador. After Ezeta
seized power Guatemala declared martial law. A week later the Guatemalan government informed Mizner that an American ship in San
José harbor was carrying arms destined for El Salvador. It demanded
that Mizner order the arms deposited at a "neutral port." When
Mizner telegraphed Washington for instructions he discovered that
El Salvador had closed the cable.[9]

The next four weeks proved critical for his diplomatic career.
All communications with the State Department passed through Mexico
where they were "either delayed, garbled, intercepted, or lost." Mizner was forced to decide questions without consultation with his
government and showed what Mary Patricia Chapman called "an
uncanny knack of making the wrong decision at the wrong time."
Although he agreed to Guatemalan demands, the government still
seized the arms. To further complicate the diplomatic situation, Guatemala learned that General J. Martin Barrundia, an exiled former
member of the government who had earlier attempted several inva-
sions from Mexico, was aboard an American ship scheduled to stop
at Guatemalan ports. The government ordered him seized and Miz-

ner gave his approval. The Guatemalan police then killed Barrundia in a gun battle while attempting to arrest him.[10]

Added to the protests over Mizner's Costa Rican speech and the belief that he had mishandled the arms issue, the Barrundia incident led Secretary of State James G. Blaine to end his appointment, directing him on 18 November "to leave your post with convenient dispatch." Mizner, his spirit broken by the dismissal, never attempted to reestablish his old law practice. The family lived in San Francisco where ill health plagued the former minister for the next three years. He died in December 1893 and was buried on Addison's twenty-first birthday.[11]

Addison had returned home in the early summer of 1890 to prepare for college entrance examinations. He attended Bates and another preparatory school before flunking the University of California examination. Admitting he "had no foundation to build an education on," he attached no blame to the schools. Denied admission to the University of California, he was prompted by his fluency in Spanish and his love of Spanish culture to study at the University of Salamanca. Addison stayed in Spain less than a year, and probably never formally enrolled in a degree program. Nonetheless, the experience became central to his life and future career. He was profoundly affected by his exposure to the diversity of periods and styles that comprise the unique beauty of Spanish architecture. In his later buildings he sought to capture this quality. As he said:

Most modern architects have spent their lives carrying out a period to the last letter and producing a characterless copybook effect. My ambition has been to take the reverse stand—to make a building look traditional and as though it had fought its way from a small unimportant structure to a great rambling house that took centuries of different needs and ups and downs of wealth to accomplish. I sometimes start a house with a Romanesque corner, pretend that it has fallen into disrepair and been added to in the Gothic spirit, when suddenly the great wealth of the New World has poured in and the owner has added a very rich Renaissance addition.[12]

If the Salamanca experience produced no degrees, it did help mold the artist's sense of beauty and fitness. Like many before him, he began studying architecture by seeing and sketching great examples of the art.[13]

When Addison returned to California his brother William was about to embark on a trip to China as a ship's doctor. His parents sent him along to keep him from becoming an artist, "the lowest form of long-haired, flowing-cravat ass extant." Nonetheless, his sketchbook also made the trip. As in Spain, the young man sketched examples of Eastern buildings which later supplied inspiration for his own work. He became particularly interested in Japanese gardens, believing their techniques had many applications for American landscaping. In the first years of his career he designed a number of gardens, and always insisted that he be consulted on the landscape design of his later houses.[14]

Addison made the decision to become an architect after the Far East trip. "I went in to Willis Polk, who was a young architect of great taste and little work, and applied as an apprentice draftsman." Polk, just five years older than Addison, apprenticed in Saint Louis and came to San Francisco as an assistant to Arthur Page Brown, the designer of the Ferry Building. Variously described as "a near genius with irresistible personal charm," and "an intolerable egomaniac," Polk proved a good teacher for the young Mizner, now seriously interested in the profession. The older architect had no commitment to a specific style. He completed his own house on the top of Russian Hill in simple "shingle style." He had helped design the Ferry Building with its spire modeled on Seville's Giralda Tower, and showed his willingness to experiment when he designed the Hallidie Building with its glass curtain wall in 1918. Moreover, Polk took pride in being a master builder, involving himself in all aspects of construction.[15]

Mizner began his apprenticeship in 1893. His previous training and travels had schooled his eye and given him some background in history; with Polk he learned the fundamentals of the profession. As Polk's office remained very small during this period, Mizner became involved in the entire design process. Moreover, he received his training as a draftsman.

I was working hard, and took architecture very seriously. Willis had a good, though small library; and wherein I had not been a worker in school, I became an absorbed student. Even through later frivolities, I put in a specified amount of labor at the drawing board, and at odd moments you could find me with a book in my hand.[16]

Under Polk's tutelage Mizner also learned the building trades. This early training allowed the mature Mizner to call himself "as good a bricklayer as any man I ever had. I can plaster as well as any plasterer I have seen. I am a fairly good carpenter, a better than ordinary electrician. I know how to wipe a joint in plumbing." During this period Mizner also maintained an active party schedule. His amiability, easy wit, and family position gave him access to San Francisco's highest society. Setting the pattern for his later career, he combined work with pleasure, meeting clients through social contacts. Nonetheless, the practice remained small and Mizner's "microscopic" salary often went unpaid, so after two years Polk made him a partner.[17]

Mizner left Polk's office in 1897. In his autobiography he said that he received a commission for a $2 million presidential palace from Guatemalan dictator Refino Barriose. The nephew of a former president, Barriose had become "very popular" with the Guatemalan people while the architect's father was minister. The government, fearing a *coup d'etat*, had arrested him and ordered his execution. Mizner, acting for his father, had secured his release and spirited him across the border to Mexico. Later Barriose seized power. The commission was a reward to Mizner for saving the dictator's life. Anticipating a $25,000 retainer, Mizner bought a new wardrobe, entertained, and generally incurred bills all over San Francisco. According to his account, when the boat from Guatemala arrived, Mizner found that instead of his retainer, it brought news of Barriose's assassination. Now insolvent, and with numerous creditors demanding payment, he left town to work brother William's gold mine in the Sierras.

Although probably a true description of Mizner's financial condition, Alva Johnston points out that Barriose actually remained in power a year after the architect left San Francisco. Mizner's commissions simply had failed to match the expenses of his life as the debonair man-about-town.[18]

Mizner had spent only a few weeks in the Sierras when he received a letter from William. Brother Edgar, now head of the Alaska Commercial Company for the Yukon district, reported a great gold strike in the Klondike. William told Addison to close down the Sierra mine and join Wilson in a rush for the new gold fields. The brothers arrived in Dawson in early spring 1898. Word of the gold strike had spread and prospectors soon overwhelmed the small town. Like the other new arrivals, Mizner had hoped to make a Klondike fortune. With thousands of prospectors descending on Dawson, he despaired of finding gold and instead became a grocery clerk for the Alaska Commercial Company. Through his job he made a friend who gave him an early tip of a strike on the Dominion Creek. Leaving Dawson immediately and traveling through the night, he beat the other prospectors and staked a 200-foot claim.

During the winter of 1898/99 Mizner sunk a shaft with the aid of three helpers. The mine immediately proved rich, and he removed a quantity of gold. When he accidentally overheard the helpers plotting to murder him for the claim, he hid part of his dust in an old boot stashed under his bed. Mizner foiled the murder plot by confronting the men, but then corrupt Canadian officials accused him of allowing the mine shaft to drift into the "Queen's Fraction." The government surveyed each claim after it had been registered. The official surveyors almost always found the claim larger than allowed by law. The additional land then reverted to the Crown. Mizner had fashioned a 6-foot rule using his watch chain as a measure and knew he had a legal claim. Nonetheless, government officials decided to confiscate his gold and take possession of his mine. After months of backbreaking work, only the gold concealed in the old boot remained. Although convinced the Canadian authorities had no case, Mizner feared years of costly litigation. Instead of fighting for his claim, he smuggled the hidden gold from the country and returned to San Francisco.[19]

Mizner arrived in California in the autumn of 1899. He had shipped gold worth $27,000 out of the Klondike. Upon paying his debts, he placed the rest in a trust. After he had bought new clothing and had "given presents to everybody," he needed an income until the trust matured. Mizner naturally thought of an architectural practice. His plans seemed to be realized when he met a man from Honolulu who headed a syndicate that proposed to build a hotel at Waikiki. His new friend listed other island projects that could keep Mizner busy for two years. Unfortunately, Mizner arrived in Honolulu only to discover that his friend "had about as much influence as a Protestant in the Vatican."

Without a job or even the prospect of one, Mizner decided to tour the islands. On a visit to the former royal palace, which served as the territorial capitol, he found the royal portrait collection on the walls of an open gallery. The collection contained "huge canvases, flapping on their shrunken stretchers" in the wind. A chance meeting with President Sanford B. Dole secured Mizner the job of restoring the portraits. Finding many of the canvases unidentified, he appealed to ex-Queen Liliuokalani for help in naming and dating the pictures. They became fast friends after he convinced her of his interest in preserving the historical record of the dynasty. Also, while searching the capitol attics for portraits, Mizner came across boxes of medals the ex-queen had lost during the revolution. He later claimed that she knighted him in appreciation for the return of her decorations.[20]

Mizner spent two years in Hawaii, supporting himself by his artwork. He painted miniature portraits on ivory, leaving "a trail of atrocities for future generations to wonder at," and charcoal and pastel portraits on photographic enlargements. Although he did no building in the islands, this period helped hone his sketching skills. In later years Mizner's beautifully drawn and colored house sketches became prized possessions of his clients.[21]

Always interested in knowing the right people, Mizner secured introductions to Hawaiian society. Family friendships and his own high spirits and wit soon made him a regular member of the local party scene. He also met and became friendly with Ethel Watts Mumford, a young divorcee living at Waikiki. To entertain themselves they twisted old adages to give them contemporary meanings. They decided to have a calendar made of their aphorisms to give to friends as Christmas gifts. When they sent their manuscript to a San Francisco printer, he asked to publish it commercially. The little bound volume, called the *Cynic's Calendar,* went through several editions and earned Mizner $1,500 in royalties in the first year. Mizner's contributions included: "Be hailed truthful that your lies may count," "People who live in glass houses should pull down the blinds," and "A word to the wise is resented." According to Johnston, the little almanacs made Mizner a literary figure in the States.[22]

Mizner spent two years in Hawaii waiting for his trust to mature. Anticipating a comfortable income, he moved on to Samoa where he received word that his investments had been unsuccessful. Once more seeking a means of livelihood, he agreed to color lantern slides for a "second-rate" English professor who was preparing for a lecture tour. After ten days in Samoa he accompanied the professor to Australia where the two men argued and Mizner found himself again broke and without a job.

In Australia he became friendly with a boxing crowd who constantly talked of the coming match between The Pride of Australia and the Brisbane Kid. Mizner, who stood over six feet tall and had a large upper torso, looked like a prizefighter, and occasionally he boxed a few rounds with his new friends. On the day before the fight the promoter told Mizner that the Brisbane Kid had "turned yellow" and he needed a substitute. The promoter chose Mizner because the Australian crowd would enjoy seeing their fighter defeat an American. Mizner, who needed the money, agreed to the bout. On the night of the fight Mizner "took [his] corner and kept it the twenty rounds." The infuriated crowd demanded a return bout and Mizner accepted the challenge when the promoter promised the winner one-third of the gate receipts and the loser $150.

Seeing that a ship was due to sail for San Francisco at one in the morning following the fight, Mizner decided to return home, and booked passage with money from the loser's purse. Once in the ring, he succeeded in keeping away from The Pride for the first three rounds, then in the fourth he received a clip on the end of his nose. "It had always annoyed me to be hit on the end of my nose that way, so I reached out and picked one up off the floor and slammed him one on the chin." After collecting his winnings Mizner ran for the docks, only to find that the ship he boarded was headed for Shanghai. He had missed the San Francisco steamer by minutes. When he discovered that $2,000 in winnings remained after paying his fare he decided to continue his travels. He stopped at Manila and then visited Siam and India, ending his Far Eastern travels in Shanghai when his money ran out.[23]

Mizner returned to San Francisco in 1902 or 1903. In his autobiography he hints of employment as a draftsman; without question he resumed his highly social life as a man-about-town. He also fell in love. The object of his affections was Bertha Dolber, who had inherited several million dollars on her father's death. She agreed to consider his proposal of marriage provided he found a position that commanded a good salary. Now just over thirty, Mizner despaired of becoming a successful architect, claiming that every architect he knew "was a doddering old man." He decided to make his fortune by importing Guatemalan coffee, which he considered to be of far better quality than the blends sold in American stores. After securing a few investors for the venture, he left for Guatemala early in 1904 to buy coffee beans.[24]

The Guatemalan trip saw the beginning of another business venture far more congenial to Mizner's temperament than importing coffee. While waiting to sign the coffee contracts he traveled to Antigua. Many years earlier the government had confiscated the church's property and expelled the religious orders. As capital of Guatemala, Antigua had supported many magnificent churches. After earthquakes convinced the government to move the capital to Guatemala City, Antigua's population greatly declined. With its lands gone, the churches often stood vacant, tended only by a few impoverished priests. These churches

had vast treasures in old velvet, damask, and embroideries, together with silver and furniture. All of these things were going to rack and ruin, . . . so I decided on a looting expedition. . . . I mean no disrespect to the church, and it should be understood that it was legitimate at this time for priests to sell, and that they were near starvation.[25]

Mizner purchased hundreds of items from the cathedral and then paid $600 for an entire monastery on the edge of town. He bought the monastery for the eight side chapels in the church, each with carved and gilded wooden altars. Mizner later sold the altars for $6,000. As his client wanted the altars without the gilding, Mizner had them scraped, salvaging several thousand dollars in gold.[26]

While still in Guatemala, Mizner received word that Bertha Dolber, still mourning her dead father, had either fallen or jumped from a window at the Waldorf-Astoria Hotel. Her death may also have decided Mizner against the "respectable" business of coffee trading. Instead, he resolved to go to New York City, sell his Guatemalan plunder, and with the profits establish an architectural practice. Without question, he chose to launch his career among "the right people," and New York, as the center of American fashion and society, offered him this opportunity.[27]

Even before Mizner decided on his profession, the experiences of his early life had laid the foundation for his career. The year in Central America awakened his interest in Spanish art and architecture and allowed him to learn the Spanish language. Study at the University of Salamanca, and additional travel in Europe, helped broaden his knowledge of history and architecture. His lifelong travel habit of sketching buildings and details helped train his eye, providing the basis for his later mastery of proportion.

Few American universities offered formal architectural training in the late nineteenth century. Once the choice was made, Mizner, like many of his colleagues, acquired the training for the profession through apprenticeship. Mizner's three years in the San Francisco office of Willis Polk taught him draftsmanship as well as the practical aspects of construction. In this era, his apprenticeship, self-study, and travel experiences all combined to give him impressive credentials for the practice of architecture. Mizner's family position, well-placed San Francisco friends, cosmopolitan outlook, and ready wit also helped prepare him for the role of society architect.

2

The New York Years

Mizner spent the next fourteen years in New York. In this period he began his architectural practice and established himself among the cream of New York society. Through family connections and friends he received invitations from the leading hostesses. With these introductions he used his wit and unquestioned intelligence to gain a place as an extra man much in demand at the best parties. Authorship of the *Cynic's Calendar* had helped to make him a minor celebrity. By 1911 his commissions for Long Island country houses for members of the social set that he so carefully cultivated show the start of a successful architectural career; the completed houses also mark the beginnings of an architectural style that finds fulfillment in his Florida work.

In 1904 Mrs. O.H.P. Belmont, Mrs. Stuyvesant Fish, and Mrs. Hermann Oelrichs reigned as America's three great society hostesses. Mizner's first New York call went to Mrs. Oelrichs, the former Tessie Fair of San Fransicso. She and her sister Birdie, who had married Mrs. Belmont's son, William K. Vanderbilt, Jr., launched the newly arrived architect into New York and Newport society. Through the efforts of the sisters he met the other great hostesses. He told of Mrs. Fish questioning the originality of some of his quips from the *Cynic's Calendar*, quoting long passages from both Racine and Confucius to prove her point. Mizner replied: "You must admit that at least I paraphrased it into one line." Mrs. Fish then changed the subject and the architect concluded: "I had crossed swords with the greatest wit in society and had gotten away with it." Mizner's friendship with Mrs. Belmont developed as a result of the waltz craze that struck New York society with the opening of the light opera *The Merry Widow.* He arranged for the male lead, Donald Brian, to teach Mrs. Belmont and her friends the new dance.[1]

At the same time Mizner was meeting the right people, he was also developing friendships among the New York theatrical world. He joined The Lambs, a club for those "engaged professionally in the drama, music, authorship, and the fine arts," and Wilson Mizner, who had returned from the gold fields to begin a career as a theatrical agent and playwright, provided additional contacts. Mizner claimed to have introduced the comedienne Marie Dressler to Mrs. Fish, starting the trend of popular entertainers performing at society parties. No mention of his help appeared in Dressler's autobiography, though she later came to Florida to promote the architect's real estate ventures. Her accompanist, Jerome Kern, also became Mizner's friend at this time. Mizner's niece remembered Kern's visit to Florida years later when as an old man he performed handstands in the architect's living room.[2]

Mrs. Oelrichs introduced Mizner to Stanford White, the architect of Rosecliff, her white marble palace at Newport. She also convinced White to give Mizner "a few small jobs, which were too unimportant to go through his office." Mizner said he and White became friends and often discussed architecture: "I worshipped him, for he was my god." Mizner knew White for only a short period, since Harry Thaw murdered the older architect in 1906; nonetheless, Mizner said White had influenced his career. Certainly the two men shared similar approaches in decorating their houses. White's biographer tells of a trip to Italy in which the architect bought "everything that caught his fancy" and "anything that would add to the beauty of the town and country houses he was then designing"; he compared White to a modern Ulysses, coming home with the treasures of Troy. In later years Mizner, too, made European looting raids, returning with "half a ship load." Without doubt, White contributed to the young architect's education.[3]

During his first years in New York Mizner spent most of his time making the social contacts that later supplied his commissions. With Mrs. Oelrichs's help, he sold part of his Guatemalan purchases at a good profit. His San Francisco investments also began paying. Thus he could support an active social life and also indulge his desire for travel. In the spring and early summer he went to Italy with Mrs. Oelrichs, visiting Venice for the first time. The city had a profound influence on his design, and detailing from Venetian palaces appeared often on his later houses. After Italy he and another friend toured Spain and then spent several weeks in Morocco. As always Mizner kept his sketchbook at hand. He also added to his collection of architectural photographs and postcards. When he returned to the United States in the late summer he went to Newport, where "a few of the best people" sponsored Mizner, making him a success there, too. In 1906 he went to Mardi Gras in New Orleans with a party of friends in a private railroad car. The host received an urgent call to an important meeting in the north and the rest of the group returned on their own. Their route took them through Florida, where they decided to see Palm Beach. The resort failed to impress Mizner who later recalled, "there was nothing but two old wooden Flagler hotels."[4]

When Mizner first arrived in New York he moved into an apartment at the Livingston House on West 24th Street. In 1906 he moved to a small town house near Washington Square, and then later in the year to an East Side apartment on 44th Street. In New York, as later in the houses he built for himself in Florida, Mizner always demanded a large drawing room for entertaining. He also began the practice of decorating his apartments and houses with Guatemalan and Spanish antiques and using huge church candles for light. In this period Wilson Mizner married Myra Yerkes, the widow of Charles T. Yerkes, the traction magnate. In Mizner's account of the marriage Mrs. Yerkes became "the second richest widow in America." Her Fifth Avenue mansion with its galleries of Old Masters belied the fact that Yerkes's millions had been spent before his death. Although Wilson's marriage lasted only a few months, the notoriety probably helped his brother's career.[5]

Mizner described his first New York commissions as "a few old brownstone fronts . . . made over into apartments . . . and a brick front warehouse." These jobs held little interest for the architect whose ambitions lay in designing elegant houses for the rich and fashionable. His first commission from this set came through the recommendation of a California friend. In 1907 the Stephen Howland Browns fired the architect of their partially built town house on 70th Street. Mizner finished the construction and "did all the interiors." Brown, a governor of the New York Stock Exchange and a partner in the prestigious firm of Vernon C. Brown and Company, collected medieval art. The *New York Times* called the collegiate Gothic style house "one of the city's show places."[6]

Mizner's last New York City apartment had only one bedroom. Since the San Francisco earthquake of April 1906 he had thought of finding a house so that his mother might live with him. In the spring of 1907 he spent a weekend at the Port Washington, Long Island estate of former Congressman William Bourke Cockran. During the visit he found the Baxter Homestead, "an old house on the edge of the village, on the Sands Point side." Although the house had neither central heat nor indoor plumbing, and needed much work, it faced directly on Manhasset Bay with Baxter Pond to the south. The earliest part of the house dated from the 1670s and had housed Hessian troops during the Revolutionary War. Oliver Baxter, a shipbuilder, added the main section with its "beautifully proportioned neo-classical rooms" in 1795. Between 1892 and 1903 it housed the Port Washington library. Mizner leased the house, probably with the understanding that he might later purchase it, and added bathrooms and central heating. In the spring of 1914 he bought the house from Mrs. Elizabeth Perry and spent $5,000 for further renovations and the addition of a new kitchen wing.[7]

In 1917 the *Architectural Record* published an eight-page article on the remodeling of the house. Mizner made few changes to the exterior, retaining its colonial character. Moving the principal entrance to the rear allowed him to add an 18-foot-wide terrace, surrounded by a low stone wall, overlooking the bay (Fig. 1). On the north wall of the terrace he installed a small fountain fashioned from

1. Chateau Myscene, Addison Mizner house in Port Washington, New York. Mizner remodeled it and added the terraces, 1907–1915.

2. Chateau Myscene, dining room.

an iron panel of a Spanish stove. He left the columns and roof of the original porch, and the elaborate 1812 doorway with sidelights in place. Viewed from the street the facade appeared unaltered. His interior alterations included new bathrooms and the removal of a wall between the two small parlors to create a living room more suitable to his style of furnishing and entertaining. While Mizner continued to lease a New York City office, he lived and worked in this house until he moved to Florida.[8]

Mizner enjoyed his years in Port Washington. Since his first trip to China he usually owned a Chow dog. Now he established a kennel and sold "forty to fifty puppies each year." Indulging his passion for pets, Mizner's household also included Miko, a monkey; Kazy Kat, a Maltese; an Angora rabbit; and on the practical side, a coop full of prize-winning chickens. His growing collection of antiques also found a home in Port Washington. Eighth-century porcelain Fu dogs, sixteenth-century carved wooden candlesticks, ancient hand-illuminated manuscripts, and a 200-year old bier made for a pope (Mizner removed the four corner crucifixes and installed electric lamps in their place), all showed the architect's eclectic taste (Fig. 2).[9]

Until her death in 1915, Ella Mizner spent several months each year in Port Washington. Her letters to the family give a picture of life in the household. The gregarious Mizner filled his house with guests. Former clients and prospective clients came for weekends, Mrs. Oelrichs motored out from the city for lunch, the Shane Leslies came to call, and birthdays and anniversaries brought parties at the now-christened Chateau Myscene. When a friend suffered financial difficulties in the 1907 panic, Mizner took in his two eldest sons, Merwyn and Wyburn Lee, who lived with him for the next eight years. Many of Mizner's friends had country houses in the area around Port Washington. Ella Mizner described a constant round of dinners, parties, and balls. They celebrated the Fourth of July in 1912 at the Frank Hoffstots' "magnificent" Sands Point estate, and dined with the George Bakers and the John Alley Parkers. When they attended a costume ball the architect dressed as a Santa Barbara monk, "wearing that lovely brown thing he wore in the mornings here," with a rosary, a rope around his waist, and sandals. Mizner's hosts and his guests belonged "to the smart set of New York," the set that now asked him to design their country houses.[10]

In the second decade of the century, Port Washington and the surrounding area underwent a building boom somewhat similar to Florida's in the first years of the 1920s. Mizner's residence in Port Washington placed him in the right place at the right time. From 1911 to 1914, H. K. Landis published a small biweekly newspaper in the town to promote natural gas interests. *Plain Talk,* with its subtitle "Stands for Port Washington and Progress," combined heavy-handed articles on the advantages of natural gas with local gossip and real estate boosterism. Landis, a neighbor and friend of Mizner's, at times seemed to act as the architect's press agent within the columns of his newspaper. Almost every issue contained a story of Mizner's latest commission or a fanciful account of the activities at the "Chateau Mizner."

With the exception of his autobiography, in which he rarely discussed his architectural work, and a few drawings and plans from his office files in Palm Beach, almost nothing is known of Mizner's New York career until Landis began publishing *Plain Talk.* In 1911 alone, Landis mentioned seven different Mizner commissions. From the number and variety of these commissions, Mizner obviously had established a flourishing practice with well-to-do businessmen, actors, politicians, and socialites as his clients.

In 1911/1912 Mizner's projects ranged geographically from the Adirondacks to Maine; Connecticut; and Huntington, Long Island, though they centered in the Port Washington area. Stylistically an eclectic period, the architect produced Japanese houses and gardens, Norman mansions and tennis pavilions, "Alaskan mining towns," and, of course, Spanish villas. Mizner personally supervised construction for his various commissions, with Landis reporting his many trips to upstate New York and Connecticut.

Mizner gained a reputation for his landscaping abilities and usually insisted on designing the gardens for his houses. On moving to Port Washington he said, "Being a Californian and a godson of Burbank's, I had a garden going in no time." He believed that a successful garden design resulted from having a definite motive in mind. "The day of gardens planted helter-skelter, without any preconcerted idea of the ultimate result, is over. . . . Things that have merit must also have a reason." Mizner demonstrated this view in the landscaping of William Bourke Cockran's estate. To provide a vista from the house Mizner removed a privet hedge and created a series of thirty turfed steps down to a small dry lake bed which he converted into a miniature amphitheater. He replanted the privet to form wings for the stage, the hedge acting as a frame for the distant view of hills and trees. Cockran, a noted orator, thus had a magnificent setting from which to launch his 1912 campaign for reelection to Congress as a Progressive. The small amphitheater also served for the glittering international wedding of Cockran's sister-in-law to Shane Leslie, the nephew of the orator's close friend, Lady Randolph Churchill.[11]

During this period Mizner also received a landscaping commission from the comedian Raymond Hitchcock for his Kings Point estate, which sat on a narrow sloping strip of land between Sunset Road and Little Neck Bay at Elms Point. According to Alva Johnston, Mizner terraced and planted the grounds and built a baroque staircase down to the water. The architect of the Hitchcock house, a large two-and-a-half-story colonial revival building, is unknown.[12]

Mizner combined his interest in landscaping and his experience in the Far East in the commission for a Japanese house and garden for Sarah Cowen Monson in Huntington, Long Island. The architect particularly admired the way the Japanese merged their interior spaces with the outside "so that it is hard to say whether this people live more in their houses or in their gardens." He believed the Japanese idea of planning the garden "in miniature" so that "the view seemed of unlimited extent, though the grounds no more than an acre," an idea for owners of summer and weekend houses.[13]

In this case, the house sat on high ground overlooking the Chateau des Beaux Arts, a café on Huntington Bay. The site allowed

3. Sketch of proposed house for Mrs. Sarah Cowen Monson, Huntington, New York, 1911.

vistas over the treetops of the bay and Long Island Sound in the distance. Although Mizner oriented the house to this view, he landscaped the immediately surrounding grounds with small plants, stone lanterns for candles, fountains, a variety of stepping-stone paths through the lawns, and a miniature lake.

Mrs. Monson dictated the choice of architecture, since she had traveled extensively in the Far East and owned a large collection of Japanese furniture, screens, and other decorative items. Mizner said his inspiration came from a seventeenth-century house built by a Japanese nobleman in Nikko, a city eighty miles west of Tokyo. The architect's design called for a series of pavilions stretching for 150 feet along the crest of the hill (Fig. 3). Green-tiled roofs with "pug-nosed," upturned ends topped each of the semidetached sections, creating the effect of a small oriental village. A brick entrance court led to a 30-foot-square central hall which extended upward 17 feet to exposed wooden rafters. A gallery over the hall gave access to Mrs. Monson's second-floor rooms above the dining room and butler's pantry. A separate wing on the other side of the hall contained guest rooms.

In his design Mizner adapted a Japanese house to the climate and living conditions of America. He used glass windows in place of sliding paper screens and installed modern heating equipment, bathrooms, and lighting fixtures. Nonetheless, Mizner strived for authenticity, installing oriental wall hangings and furniture, and Japanese mats on the floors of the major rooms. He even apologized for the fireplace in the hall, explaining that the Japanese always used charcoal braziers.[14]

While he supervised construction of Mrs. Monson's Japanese house, Mizner completed a half-timbered Norman country residence and tennis pavilion for Ralph Thomas. The Thomas estate was south of the lighthouse grounds at the tip of Sands Point. In 1911 *Plain Talk* published an article on the tennis house. Mrs. Thomas, an amateur championship tennis player, asked Mizner to include a court in his plans. Middle Neck Road ran through the center of the Thomases' long, narrow, and hilly lot. After placing the residence on the west side of the road, no room remained for a court. Locating the court on the east side of the road made it inconvenient to the house. Mizner solved the problem with a tennis pavilion.

The half-timbered brick and stucco building included changing and shower rooms and a large lounge with folding doors that opened onto the court and commanded a view of the Long Island Sound (Fig. 4). Its 7-foot-wide fireplace kept players warm on chilly days. Mizner used red brick tiles for the floor, chestnut paneling for the walls, and rough-hewn rafters for the ceiling. Rough-cut timbers joined by wooden pins, small diamond-paned casement windows, and uneven wooden roof shingles completed the Norman decor. Mizner said he based his design on an inn where William the Conqueror stopped while raising troops for his invasion of England.[15]

4. Sketch of Ralph Thomas tennis house, Sands Point, New York, 1911.

In 1911 Mizner also completed work on an Adirondack camp near Paul Smiths, New York, for Archibold S. White, multimillionaire president of the Columbia Gas Company. Although White first engaged William G. Massarene, a New York City architect who "had grown tired of building skyscrapers," to design his mountain retreat, local tradition holds that White rejected his plans as inappropriate for the wilderness setting and called instead upon Ben Muncil, a builder who designed several camps in the area, including Marjorie Merriweather Post's Topridge, for the job. Actually, Massarene planned and supervised the construction for the first group of buildings completed. In a 1926 interview he recalled using stones and timbers from the vicinity to "achieve harmony between building and site," and told how he patterned the cabins after the "curious shaped houses one sees in Italy." He also "put dormer windows in here and there to get special lighting effects." Muncil probably acted as contractor.[16]

In 1910 White asked Mizner to enlarge the camp and add refinements. Mizner said he took his inspiration from a "typical mining town." Massarene had placed a line of guest cabins along the top of a rise overlooking Osgood Lake. Mizner sited a service building opposite the cabins to form a "street." He designed this building to represent "the grocery store, used as a sort of provision storehouse; a post office where the numerous guests received their mail; blacksmith shop; saloon, etc." Untypical of mining towns, the street ended in a tennis court, where Mizner placed a "tea house and lockers" similar in design to that for the Thomas estate. He also added the large living room cabin with its two fireplaces, a bowling alley and billiards cabin, and a tea house at the end of a peninsula jutting out into the lake. Although Mizner gave the tea house roof a distinctive oriental silhouette, his other camp buildings had plain, unadorned rooflines. All the camp buildings achieved unity from the barnstorm siding used by both Massarene and Mizner. The rough-hewn green siding, developed by Muncil and Charles Nichols, a millwright for the Paul Smith's Hotel Company, also accounted for the camp's rustic appearance. When completed, White Pine Camp contained thirty buildings and accommodations for twenty-four guests.[17]

Mizner worked in a variety of styles in this period, and several houses show his interest in Spanish architecture. In October 1911 *Plain Talk* reported Mizner's trip to Winsted, Connecticut to superintend the building of the $150,000 country house of Jerome Alexandre, "whose city residence is near the Plaza." Although nei-

5. Jerome Alexandre house, Colebrook, Connecticut, 1911.

ther the plan nor the massing could be termed Spanish, Rock Hall had many of the characteristics found in Mizner's later work (Fig. 5). The architect obviously lavished his attentions on the first floor and the major rooms of the house. On this floor he used random Connecticut rock for the exterior walls punctuated by large leaded windows with expansive views of the countryside. Stucco covered the walls of the second and third floors, and the standard double-hung windows appeared haphazardly placed. The H-shaped plan consisted of a center section of two-and-a-half stories with two wings of three-and-a-half stories. Mizner echoed the outlining of the strongly articulated eaves on the three-story fronts in the eaves of the dormers on the center section, giving the only visual interest to the top floors. He also used red tile for the roof.

In this plan (Fig. 6), as in the Monson house, the 32-foot-long reception hall served as the principal living room. Perhaps Mizner had the living hall of the English country house in mind. A small sheltered porch on the western facade provided entry to the hall, which was lighted by a large stepped window that followed the outline of the staircase. Mizner placed the library and porch in the

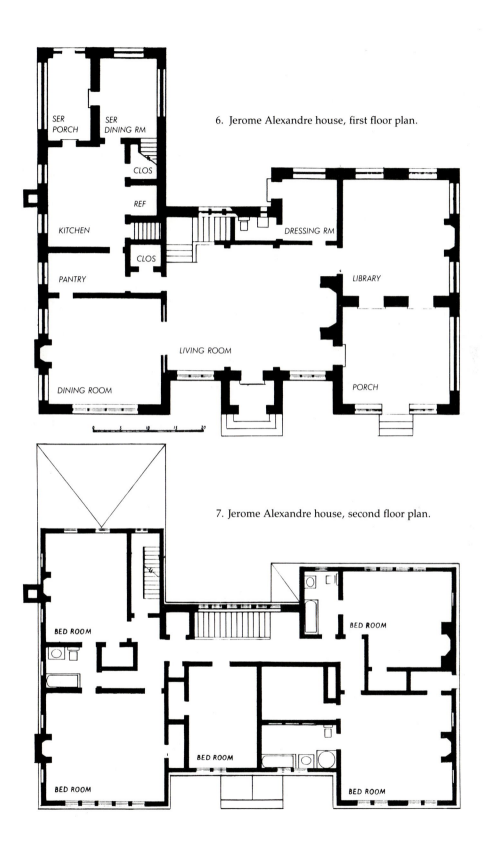

SER
PORCH

SER
DINING RM

CLOS

REF

KITCHEN

CLOS

PANTRY

DRESSING RM

LIBRARY

LIVING ROOM

DINING ROOM

PORCH

6. Jerome Alexandre house, first floor plan.

BED ROOM

BED ROOM

BED ROOM

BED ROOM

BED ROOM

7. Jerome Alexandre house, second floor plan.

south wing and the dining room and service rooms in the north wing. As the exterior fenestration hinted, the second floor contained five utilitarian bedrooms (Fig. 7) and the third floor, a maze of very small servants' rooms.[18]

The fall of 1911 also saw construction begin on the "Spanish type of residence" which Mizner designed for the William A. Primes. The Primes owned one hundred acres along Northern Boulevard in Brookville. Mizner sited the house on the crest of a hill, giving the main rooms a distant vista to the west. The lawns and grounds occupied twenty acres, "having swimming pools and other features of a landscape and architectural character that will make the place unusually attractive." Only first floor plans for the Prime house remained in Mizner's Palm Beach files. Once more he made the reception hall the main room of the house. The hall, 40 feet long and 27 feet wide, remains the most impressive room of Mizner's New York career. Stairs rose on the north wall to a gallery that ran over the entry and turned the corner on the south wall (Fig. 8). Large rafters formed the ceiling. He centered the entry on the west wall directly opposite the 7-foot-wide fireplace. Large windows on both the east and west walls and on the gallery level flooded the room with light.

8. William Prime house, Brookville, New York, 1911, plan.

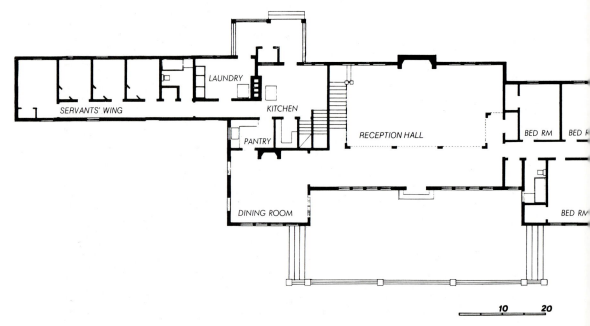

As so often happened, Mizner spent his energy on the creation of the magnificent reception hall. The rest of the first floor rooms were small and of little interest. Three bedrooms and a bath formed the south wing, while the dining room and kitchen occupied the asymmetrical northern wing.

Without second-floor plans or facade drawings, it is impossible to visualize the appearance of the original house. What remains has no hint of a Spanish origin. In the early twenties the Primes sold their estate to Edward F. Hutton. Hutton and his wife, Marjorie Merriweather Post, brought in the architectural firm of Hart & Shape to plan Hillwood, a great Tudor mansion. The firm incorporated the Prime house into the new plans, making Mizner's reception room Hillwood's Great Hall (Fig. 9), while the Primes' dining room became the new entry and the three small bedrooms the new living room. Work on Hillwood began in 1922 and continued for almost a decade. Through all the changes and additions, the heart of the house remained Mizner's reception hall.[19]

9. William Prime house, reception hall.

10. John Alley Parker house,
Sands Point, New York, 1912, plan.

Mizner's Palm Beach files contained the original detailed floor plans and facade drawings for the third Spanish house of these years. In February 1912, John Alley Parker purchased thirty acres on Sands Point Road and asked Mizner to plan "a handsome villa . . . after the Spanish style of architecture." Mizner designed a very large U-shaped house which enclosed a 90-by-75-foot courtyard (Fig. 10). Because of the small size of the hilltop site, he built up the court on the fourth side with a retaining wall. The site allowed vistas of the countryside through the court to the east and of Hempstead Bay to the west. This location also allowed Mizner to place the kitchen and servants' rooms on ground level, yet a floor below the courtyard.

A 50-foot-long living room and a smaller library made up the central section of the Parker house. A large open porch formed the north wing. The south wing contained the service rooms on the ground floor; a reception hall and 29-by-24-foot dining room with passage, stairway, and butler's pantry on the courtyard level; and on the second floor, three small bedrooms and a bath over the dining room and an owner's suite of bedroom, den, bath, and lavatory over the hall. Along the second floor passage Mizner placed closets with sliding pocket doors and a shower bath. In 1912 the Parkers built the south wing of the house, the retaining wall, and foundations for the living room-library wing which included wine cellars and basement areas to store coal (Fig. 11). Although Mizner even labeled a small porch projecting into the court "temporary" on the plans, the Parkers never completed the house.

The Parker house parti, with its large, airy rooms placed only one deep around the courtyard, resembled many of Mizner's later Palm Beach plans, although the asymmetrical massing of the long, low central section, the two-story south wing, and the elaborate pillared door-surround produced a house closer in design to the Spanish colonial than to the usual style of his later work.[20]

One other commission of this period can also be identified from the pages of *Plain Talk*. An article on Wampage Shores, a Port Washington real estate development, said Mizner designed two speculative houses in the project for a local contractor. The extent and variety of the known commissions of these two years naturally

11. John Alley Parker house.

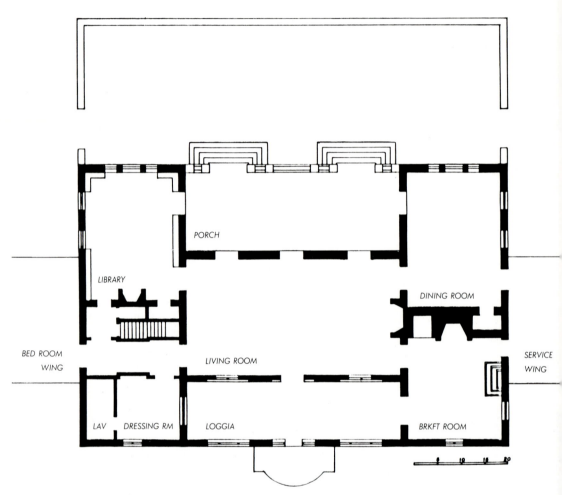

12. Alfred E. Dieterich house, Dutchess County, New York, 1912, plan.

lead to the assumption that Mizner had a large, profitable practice
and continued to produce work on this level in the following years.
Unfortunately, when the articles in *Plain Talk* no longer detail his
commissions, the only remaining records are from his mother's letters and his office files. These contain references to only five more
projects in the next five years. However, since these years find Mizner purchasing his Port Washington house and spending $5,000
additional in remodeling, supporting a household that included his
mother, two young men, and several servants, and continuing his
active social life, there must have been many more.[21]

Ella Mizner's letters identify Alfred E. Dieterich as a Mizner
client in this period. The house for Dieterich, on his father's 3,500-

acre estate in Dutchess County, New York, related closely in plan to Mizner's other northern work, although the scope, architectural detailing, and decor approached his later designs in Palm Beach. Mizner placed the long, low house on the crest of a hill, allowing an expansive vista to the west. A central pavilion contained the principal rooms, while symmetrical, 69-foot-long angled wings provided space for bedrooms on the south and a two-story kitchen and servants' section on the north. The terrain allowed the architect to place a lower story on the service wing without disturbing the entrance court's formal design. Known variously as the Bungalow, the Stone Bungalow, and the Million-Dollar Bungalow, it held Mizner's most elegantly detailed Spanish interiors of the New York years (Fig. 12). A vaulted stone loggia gave entrance to a lofty 45-foot-long living room with a heavily beamed wooden ceiling and a massive fireplace. A 20-by-20-foot room off both the loggia and the living room, used for hunt breakfasts (Mrs. Dieterich was an avid horsewoman), contained a stone fountain and an elaborate vaulted and groined stone ceiling similar to those Mizner would use many times in his later work.[22]

In 1914 Mizner designed a large country house for I. Townsend Burden, Jr., whose grandfather, Henry Burden, had founded a Troy, New York, steel company and the family fortune. Burden owned land along Northern Boulevard in Greenvale, just to the west of the Prime estate. The U-shaped house rose around an entry courtyard which opened on to the west. The courtyard, stucco walls, tiled roof, and elaborate entrance doorway-surround defined the mansion as Spanish, although the nearly symmetrical fenestration, projecting facade, and centered entry approached Georgian formality (Fig. 13). The main section of the house contained a brick-floored entry hall, a large living room and dining room, an open porch, and guest suite on the ground floor, and an owners' suite and five other bedrooms on the second floor.

Burden asked Mizner to incorporate an old stable and carriage house into his plan (Fig. 14). The use of the older building created a design problem for the architect. The stable sat on the crest of a rise with the only real vista to the north. Mizner placed the main section of the house on the hillside, connecting it to the stable with a wing of service and servants' rooms. This solution allowed him an impressive formal entry court, though all the major living rooms faced north. To provide enough light, he replaced the formality of the courtyard facade with large, almost unbroken expanses of glass.[23]

Of Tessie Oelrichs's many friends whom Mizner met in his

13. I. Townsend Burden, Jr., house, Greenvale, New York, 1916.

14. I. Townsend Burden, Jr., house, plan.

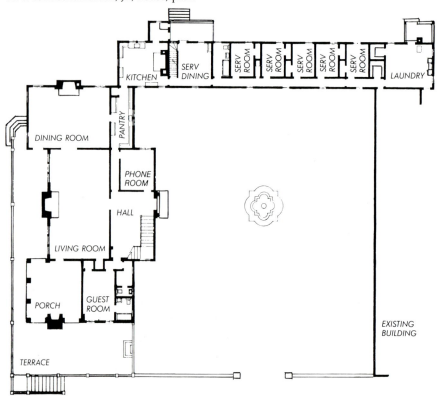

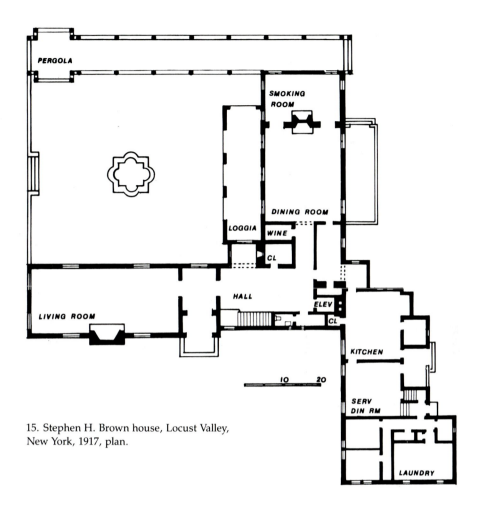

PERGOLA

SMOKING ROOM

DINING ROOM

LOGGIA WINE

CL

HALL

ELEV

CL

LIVING ROOM

10   20

KITCHEN

SERV DIN RM

15. Stephen H. Brown house, Locust Valley, New York, 1917, plan.

LAUNDRY

early New York years, the most impressive must have been Mrs. O. H. P. Belmont. As an architect, Mizner recognized her potential as a client. Since she and her first husband, William K. Vanderbilt, Sr., built their great Fifth Avenue chateau in 1879, hardly a year went by without "Miss Alva" beginning a new project. In fact, her unmatched building activity led ultimately to membership in the American Institute of Architects.[24]

Drawings for two 1915 Belmont projects remained in Mizner's Palm Beach files. Although Mizner labeled his drawings "Great Neck, Long Island," Mrs. Belmont owned waterfront property in 1915 at Sands Point, having purchased from the government land south of the old lighthouse at the very tip of the point. Now having one of the most magnificent sites on Long Island, she decided to build a replica of a small French chateau. Mizner proposed a design for a large waterfront house that in outline resembled Beacon Towers, the house she built. Although baronial in scale, with an 80-foot great

hall and a 60-foot drawing room, Mizner's proposal lacked the grandeur demanded by America's premier society client. She then turned
to the sons of Richard Morris Hunt, the designer of her Fifth Avenue
mansion and her Newport palace, who completed the great castel-
lated chateau in 1916.[25]

Mizner's office files also contained a set of plans for a Belmont
beach house. Mizner placed the small, one-room pavilion at the top
of a cliff with an elaborate stairway giving access to the beach. Since
he included no changing or shower rooms, the little house must
have been intended for tea. Alva Johnston said that Mizner built a
Chinese tea house for Mrs. Belmont at Sands Point, and that Ethel
Watts Mumford, the architect's collaborator on the *Cynic's Calendar*,
later used it as a studio. Although the plans show no Chinese influence, perhaps Mrs. Belmont built the small beach house as consola-
tion for failing to accept Mizner's plans for the larger house.[26]

Mizner completed his last New York house for his former
clients, the Stephen H. Browns. The Browns purchased a fifteen-
acre estate in Locust Valley adjoining the Piping Rock Club in January 1917. They asked Mizner to design a large Spanish-style house
which they planned to furnish with their growing collection of antiques. Mizner centered his plan on a three-story tower from which
three wings radiated in a pinwheel (Fig. 15). On the first floor the
tower contained the hall and stairway. The 40-foot living room to the
east of the hall, and the dining room, loggia, and library to the south
formed an ell around a courtyard. A trellised pergola enclosed the
south side of the court, which also contained a fountain. A large
kitchen and service wing projected to the north and west of the hall,
sheltering an entry court. On the second floor Mizner included five
master bedrooms and baths, and a sitting room. The tower held a
sixth bedroom.

The Brown house marked a transition between Mizner's other
northern, Spanish designs and his Florida work. In its free and
rambling plan he departed from the tighter massing found in many
of his earlier houses. The small windows and understated arched
entry on the motor court gave little hint of the great expanse of glass
that opened the house to the patio, a device Mizner often used in
Palm Beach. He provided visual interest to a flat and plain facade
with the tower and the strongly articulated roofline, a technique
often used in Florida to overcome the flatness of the terrain. Finally,
the interior stone walls, beamed and paneled ceilings, tiled floors,
vaulted stairhalls, and particularly, the loggia, became trademarks
of later Mizner design.[27]

One further indication of the extent of the Mizner practice in this era comes from the pages of *House and Garden*. The April 1916 issue contained a picture of the boudoir in the New York City house of William H. Earhardt showing a corner of a comfortable room with a daybed and armchair covered in matching chintz. The caption explained that the daybed "has become an almost indispensable adjunct to the boudoir." A second picture in October 1916 illustrated a formal oval Adam dining room, and a third in January 1917, a Jacobean paneled library with a tapestry lambrequin hanging from the mantel. The magazine credited all three rooms to "Addison Mizner, architect." None of the rooms related to other known commissions.[28]

Mizner said his practice began to suffer with the coming of World War I in Europe: "People were so intent on Belgian relief they didn't think about building." It collapsed when the United States entered the war. Building materials became scarce, and when available, it seemed unpatriotic to use them for the construction of luxurious country houses. The flourishing practice that Mizner enjoyed just a few years before disappeared. Since the architect's social life demanded a full income, he soon was forced to mortgage his house. And money was not his only worry. Late one night during the spring of 1917, Mizner gave a ride to three hitchhikers as he returned home after a party. When he stopped the car to let them out, they jumped him. In the fight that followed one of the hitchhikers kicked the ankle that Mizner had injured almost thirty years before. Once more the doctors feared he might lose his leg. Although an operation saved it, he was still bedridden in December. In this, the first year of the war, Americans faced an exceptionally cold winter and a severe fuel shortage. With his practice limited by the war, the damp and cold hampering his recovery, and his mother's death in 1915, he saw little reason to remain in New York.[29]

By December 1917 and his forty-fifth birthday, Mizner had fulfilled his youthful dreams. Still far from being a "doddering old man," he had also established an architectural career, executing commissions for members of the social set he had so arduously cultivated since arriving in the city. Mizner also grew as an architect in the New York period. In slightly over a decade, his earlier tightly contained and eclectic approach to commissions gave way to the randomly massed and romantic Spanish-styled buildings that established the reputation of the mature architect. Nonetheless, the coming of the war marked the end of an era for Mizner. His injury called for a milder climate and so, too, did his architecture.

3

The Everglades Club

Mizner's Florida career began in January 1918, when he arrived in Palm Beach as the house guest of Paris Singer. For the next fifteen years Mizner made Palm Beach his home, his workplace, and ultimately his creation. Beginning with his design for the Everglades Club, Mizner added countless mansions, shops, offices, and additional clubs. His buildings set a new architectural style, transforming the town and making Mizner the era's prime regional architect.

Although Mizner had known Paris Singer, the sewing machine heir, only a few months, a mutual interest in architecture had made them close friends. Singer believed a warmer climate might help speed the architect's recovery. Mizner's stories about his Central American adventures sparked Singer's interest, and he proposed a trip to Guatemala. When an earthquake hit Guatemala City, Singer then suggested going to Palm Beach, where he owned a small cottage near the ocean. Mizner agreed and Singer insisted on engaging a nurse to care for the architect during the trip.[1]

Singer, one of four sons and two daughters of Isabella Singer, Isaac M. Singer's last wife, inherited an immense fortune on his father's death. The family had lived in Europe, and most of the children had been born there; both daughters married into the French nobility, one becoming the Duchesse Decazes, the other the Princesse de Polignac. Paris's three brothers settled into the life of the English country gentry, and one achieved knighthood. Of the children, Paris most resembled his father, combining, in the view of one author, "artistic inclinations" and a "taste for pretty women." Miz-

ner described Singer as 6 feet 3 or 4 inches tall and as "the finest
looking man I ever saw." Married at nineteen, Paris was separated
from his wife when in 1909 he met the dancer Isadora Duncan; their
almost decade-long affair produced stormy scenes on several continents. Isadora, who bore Paris's son, told the entire story in her
memoirs, calling Singer "Lohengrin" for fear he might stop publication. By the winter of 1917 their affair had ended and Singer had
chosen a replacement.[2]

With the outbreak of World War I, Singer turned Paignton,
his estate in the south of England, into a military hospital, placing
Joan Bates, an English nurse who had cared for him during an ill-
ness, in charge of converting the house. Before coming to the United
States in 1917, Singer established two hospitals in France. In each
case, Mrs. Bates managed the conversion. Respect for Mrs. Bates's
abilities grew into love, and Mizner's injury provided the excuse for
Singer to bring Mrs. Bates to Palm Beach.[3]

Local legend states that both Mizner and Singer came to Palm
Beach to die. Both men came south rather to recover: Singer from
physical exhaustion, Mizner from his injury. Warm days, the sunny
beach, and the ministrations of Mrs. Bates had their effect. The two
men recovered but grew bored, even though many of Mizner's New
York friends spent the season at the resort participating in events
like Tessie Oelrichs's "Fête Champêtre," organized that year to ben-
efit Good Samaritan Hospital in West Palm Beach. The restless convalescents needed more than social activities to occupy their time.
Singer had tired of the Peruvian Avenue cottage, a typical white-
painted resort bungalow of the era, and asked Mizner to make it
more distinguished. The result was the Chinese Villa, and it remained a town landmark throughout the twenties. One writer described the house as "a beautiful Chinese pagoda painted in many
wonderful Chinese colors with a pagoda roof sweeping down to the
porch and carvings of quaint design." A woven bamboo fence and
Chinese gate and garden completed the new design. Unmentioned
in this description was the 5-foot long stuffed alligator Singer placed
on the roof "to defy good taste."[4]

Mizner and Singer found Palm Beach social life in 1918 cen-
tered on its hotels. Because the season lasted only from the end of
December to the Washington's Birthday Ball on 22 February, few
resorters became "cottagers"; the major exception to this rule was
Henry Morrison Flagler, who had created Palm Beach's role as
America's great winter resort. Flagler, an original partner in John D.
Rockefeller's Standard Oil Company, first became interested in Flor-

ida when he and the second Mrs. Flagler honeymooned in Jacksonville and Saint Augustine in the winter of 1883/84. Enchanted by
Spanish Florida's oldest city but deploring its lack of adequate tourist
facilities, he commissioned the young firm of Carrère & Hastings to
design the Spanish-style Ponce de Leon Hotel in 1885. Realizing the
need for more convenient railroad connections between Jacksonville
and Saint Augustine to make his hotel venture successful, in 1886
Flagler bought the Jacksonville, Saint Augustine, and Halifax line.
This purchase marked the beginning of the Florida East Coast Railway; together with new Flagler hotels it moved down the east coast
of the state. In 1893 Flagler decided to develop a resort in Palm
Beach, intended as the terminus of his railroad. Purchasing the estate of Robert R. McCormick, a Denver businessman, and the home-
steads of other pioneer settlers, Flagler directed work to begin immediately on the Royal Poinciana Hotel. Construction crews soon
overran Palm Beach's small population; to house these workers a
city of shacks and tents known as "The Styx" arose. Believing that
"The Styx" spoiled the tropical setting, Flagler decided to build West
Palm Beach across Lake Worth to house workers, service facilities,
and business enterprises, leaving Palm Beach for the winter tourists.
In February 1894 the railroad reached West Palm Beach and the
Royal Poinciana opened its doors.[5]

The new hotel rose six stories high on the shores of Lake
Worth; it was a vast sprawling wooden structure with miles of hallways radiating from a central rotunda, eventually housing 1,200 guests
and seating 1,600 in its cavernous dining room. "Flagler yellow"
with white trim covered the hotel's exterior walls, acres of emerald
green carpets cushioned its floors, and white-painted wicker furnished its rooms. The simplicity of its decor belied its $1 million cost.
McDonald & McGuire, the designers, made no attempt to relate the
hotel, like the Ponce de Leon, to the romance of Spain.[6]

In 1896 Flagler opened the Palm Beach Inn, another wooden
hotel designed by McDonald & McGuire, across the island from the
Royal Poinciana and directly on the ocean; he later changed its name
to The Breakers. Although Flagler extended his railroad south to
Miami and then to Key West, Palm Beach retained its position as the
most fashionable Florida resort. On the shore of Lake Worth, south
of the Royal Poinciana, Flagler commissioned Carrère & Hastings to
build Whitehall, Palm Beach's first large mansion, as a wedding gift
for his third wife, Mary Lily Kenan. Its severe white exterior only
hinted at the opulent marbled, gilded, and paneled rooms grouped
around an interior patio. Although at Whitehall only a few months

each year, the Flaglers lavished over a $1.5 million on its furnishings.[7]

From the first, Palm Beach served as a winter Newport, playing host to the nation's most fashionable, wealthy, and powerful citizens. After Flagler built a railway spur across Lake Worth to the Royal Poinciana, as many as sixty luxurious private palace cars might be found parked along the golf course.[8]

When Mizner arrived in 1918, life revolved around the hotels and the Beach Club, Colonel Edward R. Bradley's casino. Bradley and his brother John, shortly after the building of the Ponce de Leon, opened Saint Augustine's Bacchus Club, Florida's answer to Monte Carlo. While Flagler personally objected to gambling, he realized that many guests demanded that form of entertainment in a resort; thus in 1898 the Bradley brothers opened the Beach Club in Palm Beach. To circumvent Florida law, which prohibited gambling, the casino operated as a private club and no citizen of the state could become a member. From the first, the Beach Club was known both for the excellence of its cuisine and for its high stakes.[9]

A typical day for the winter visitor to Palm Beach began with a visit to the beach; swimmers at The Breakers' casino, which served both hotels, could choose either ocean or pool. At noon guests returned to the hotels to dress for luncheon. In the afternoon the more active played golf, tennis, or croquet; the more leisurely minded sat on hotel verandas or went riding in "afromobiles" (large wicker tricycles pedaled from the rear by blacks). At five o'clock guests again changed clothes and assembled in the Royal Poinciana's Cocoanut Grove for the afternoon tea dance. Finally, after another change of clothes, they assembled for eight o'clock dinner. Whether at the hotel dining room or the Beach Club, evening dress was strictly enforced. At the hotel, dancing followed dinner.[10]

Very little had changed by 1918. Although a few vacationers rented cottages at The Breakers for the season, and a few, like Singer, had purchased their own, most visitors still registered at the hotels and conformed to the formality of the Palm Beach season. With Mizner's aid, Singer brought this era to a close when he built the Everglades Club.

After the transformation of the Chinese Villa the restless Mr. Singer looked for other projects to occupy his time. Having established three European hospitals, he naturally turned to the concept of founding a hospital in the United States. During World War I, as a result of battlefield experiences, servicemen suffered intense nervous strain usually called shellshock. Authorities believed that the shellshocked needed a period of rest and quiet to help them adjust to civilian life, and Singer decided to build a convalescent home and hospital for these soldiers in Palm Beach.[11]

Touchstone Magazine took the lead in educating American women to help victims of shellshock. Mary Fanton Roberts, *Touchstone*'s publisher, supported Singer's concept of a convalescent home. To help these soldiers the magazine sponsored a series of lectures in New York for "ladies wintering in Palm Beach" to qualify them as "useful companions and nurses"; Singer's hospital became the focus of *Touchstone*'s effort. In recognition of this support, Singer named his hospital the Touchstone Convalescents' Club.[12]

Before deciding to build a club, Singer asked Mizner his opinion on suitable architecture for Palm Beach. At one oceanfront site Mizner told Singer he pictured "a Moorish tower, like on the south coast of Spain, with an open loggia at one side facing the sea, and on this side a cool court with a dripping fountain in the shade of these beautiful palms." When shown the location Singer chose for the convalescent club on the shore of Lake Worth, Mizner also envisioned a Spanish building. He said the site's beauty made him think of something religious, "a nunnery, with a chapel built into the lake . . . a mixture built by a nun from Venice, added onto by one from Gerona, with a bit of new Spain of the tropics." Singer purchased the land, formed the Ocean and Lake Realty Company, and made Mizner its president. Singer decided to build the club near the end of February 1918. During the summer Mizner designed and supervised construction of the building and its convalescent facilities. Since Florida produced little fresh milk and vegetables at this time, Singer also purchased several hundred acres "in the Everglades" to start a truck farm and a dairy to supply the club.[13]

On a quick trip to New York in May, Mizner sold his Port Washington house and "picked up" two draftsmen. Returning to Florida in June he began work on the design. In early July Mizner convinced Singer to build a permanent structure for use as a private club after the war. On 10 or 12 July he staked out the main building and two days later started on the foundations. Then Mizner's problems began: none of his workers could read blueprints; he could not purchase necessary materials; and Florida carpenters only understood the construction of frame buildings. To train his workers Mizner opened a "trade-school," demonstrating how to lay brick and hollow tile and how to apply stucco. To supply the needed materials he bought a sawmill, built kilns for the roof tiles, and imported clay from Georgia; he took over a blacksmith shop to make lighting fixtures and ornamental iron grills, and to produce furniture, he purchased the Novelty Works, a small black-owned company.[14]

Just when his problems seemed solved, on 1 August the carpenters walked off the job, demanding $6 a day, fifty cents more than their current pay. On 2 August Mizner announced that Singer had threatened to move his hospital to California. The carpenters' strike led to the first demonstration of the area business leaders' commitment to the development of the Palm Beaches; prominent citizens organized to save "the most important development that Palm Beach has ever had." Stressing the patriotic nature of the hospital project, Judge E. B. Donnell and *Palm Beach Post* publisher Joe Earman convinced the carpenters' union to return to work. The civil leaders also emphasized the hundreds of thousands of dollars Singer planned to spend in the area if "unembarrassed" by labor troubles.[15]

Singer's motives in building the club may have been patriotic; however, by fall plans for its operation made it far different in scope than his European hospitals. The shellshocked had to undergo screening for membership in the Palm Beach hospital and only army and navy officers who could pay the costs of their room and board were eligible. Singer also opened membership in the club to other winter visitors.[16]

By November seven residential villas and a medical house had been completed on the north side of Worth Avenue across from the main club building (Fig. 16). Each two-story villa contained seven bedrooms and baths, a small kitchen, and a servant's room. The identical structures had stucco walls, red-tiled roofs, and porches and balconies. To furnish the medical center, which also contained

16. The Everglades Club and Villas, Palm Beach, 1918.

rooms for "resident assistants" and nurses, Singer purchased laboratory and surgical equipment and fittings for an operating room. For the villas Mizner chose "soft Mediterranean colors" of mauve, yellow, pink, blue, green, and white. The white villa, the first completed, became his office and drafting room; it also contained his architectural library, which he had moved from New York.[17]

With the armistice, Mizner worried about the future of the project. Singer reassured him: "If we start things off right, [the club] will make Palm Beach the winter capital of the world." Singer intended to start things off right. As early as September he changed the name "Touchstone Convalescent Club" to "Everglades Club." Singer had doubtless committed himself to the development of Palm Beach; his original purchase of land for the club stretched from the lake to the ocean. On the ocean side he laid out streets and began selling lots in what became known as Singer Addition. Mizner said that every time Singer visited Palm Beach he purchased more property, giving his architect additional problems to solve.[18]

Singer proved his commitment by shipping to Florida much of his private collection of antiques. Spanish pieces attracted him, as they did Mizner: rare carved paneling from old churches, Alpujara rugs, furniture from ancient houses, fine tapestries, and paintings. They arrived all summer for storage in a warehouse Singer bought on Gardenia Street in West Palm Beach. Interest in these items became so great that Mizner arranged an exhibition in a local pharmacy. Singer had also purchased many 2,000-year-old Tunisian tiles which Mizner incorporated in the decoration of the club. He told reporters that Tunis served as the Roman Empire's Palm Beach. Thus, "it was quite appropriate that relics of that splendor should be employed in adding distinction to the community building which is to lend new interest to Florida's resort." A Palm Beach legend claims that many years later a group of Islamic guests fell in prayer before the tiles.[19]

As work on the main club building proceeded, Mizner supervised every detail. In Mizner's case this meant much more than the architect's usual supervision, since he had to instruct the workmen in new and unfamiliar techniques. His early training in construction allowed him to demonstrate the methods involved. Mizner also planned the landscaping, dug the yacht basin and built the sea wall, and operated the dairy and truck farms to the west of town. In clearing the club grounds he left all palms and other valuable trees in place, and developed "a derrick on wheels" to move large plants. He also constructed five greenhouses "in the heart of the jungle" to grow crotons and other landscaping plants.[20]

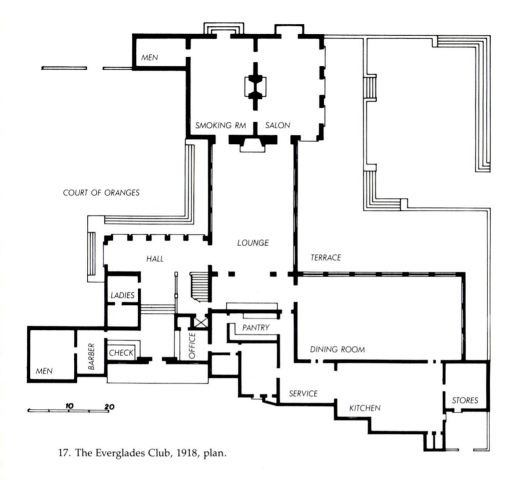

MEN

SMOKING RM   SALON

COURT OF ORANGES

LOUNGE

HALL   TERRACE

LADIES

PANTRY

MEN

BARBER

CHECK

OFFICE

DINING ROOM

SERVICE

STORES

KITCHEN

10   20

17. The Everglades Club, 1918, plan.

By early January 1919 Mizner had completed the club building. Then, with the opening scheduled only days away, the dredge
digging the yacht basin broke down before providing the fill for the
terrace. Mizner bribed a tugboat operator towing another dredge to
have engine problems in front of the club. "Before they could get it
fixed, they had 'poured' my terrace." Mizner moved all of his trees
in one night and planted grass seed that he had soaked for two days
in warm water. The grass sprouted as Mizner's men raked the seed
into the sand. He also helped nature along by hanging oranges on
his trees with hairpins.[21]

In the completed clubhouse, as in many of his later buildings,
the "nun's chapel" became a great dining hall. Its carved paneling,
taken from a Spanish church, pecky cypress ceiling, and setting on
the edge of the new yacht basin, made it the club's most dramatic
room. It could seat two hundred for dinner. A large living room, a
salon, and smoking room completed the major public spaces of the
first floor (Fig. 17). Mizner's unique staircases became a trademark
of his later houses. The principal stairs of the Everglades Club, which

18. The Everglades Club, main stairway.

seemed to float unsupported, began this tradition (Fig. 18). A mezzanine floor contained offices, a boardroom, and balconies that overlooked the dining and living rooms. On the second floor were nine
bedrooms and a sitting room. A tower, which soared above the club,
had apartments for Singer and Mizner. Singer's three-story apartment overlooked the western terrace and the lake. The first floor
contained a large living room, a dining room, and service areas. The
second floor had two bedroom suites separated by a sitting room. A
balconied stairway from the sitting room gave access to the third
floor master suite of bedroom, dressing rooms, efficiency kitchen,

and ornately tiled "Moorish" bathroom (Fig. 19). As befitted the artist-patron relationship, Mizner designed a much smaller apartment for himself.[22]

    Singer sent invitations to "eligible" army and navy officers to use the club; one source said as many as 300,000 were sent. However, by January 1919 the war had ended; Florida remained relatively unknown, and most returning veterans preferred to recuperate closer to their homes and families. Thus the Everglades Club never served its original purpose as a convalescing hospital. After less than a year, Singer donated all of his expensive medical equipment to the new Delphine Dodge Hospital under construction in West Palm Beach.[23]

    The Everglades Club opened on Saturday, 25 January 1919, with twenty-five charter members from the resort community. Before the end of the season Singer decided to limit membership to

19. The Everglades Club, Paris Singer's bathroom.

three hundred. From the first, the Everglades became the new center of Palm Beach resort life. Unlike the old hotels, a marked degree of informality characterized daytime life at the Everglades. Singer led the way by introducing Riviera-style clothing: striped shirts, colorful sweaters, baggy pants, and espadrilles. According to one source, Singer's fashions transformed male Palm Beach overnight, turning "stuffed shirts" into "gay little numbers." Singer, who summered in the south of France, brought to Palm Beach some of the relaxed qualities of European resorts. Nonetheless, evenings remained strictly formal. Dinner at the club became the occasion for "long trains and large jewels." When a society reporter entered the dining room after sundown in her daytime clothes to pick up a guest list, Singer happened to see her. Although she served as editor of her society newspaper, an infuriated Singer told her, "Don't ever come here again in the evening unless you are properly dressed." Singer relaxed the formality only on New Year's Eve, when the club issued paper hats and noisemakers, and at the annual costume party.[24]

Mizner moved into the Everglades tower for the 1919 season, while Singer and Joan Bates, his new wife, remained in the Chinese Villa on Peruvian Avenue. Mizner stayed in this apartment for only a short time. One of his earliest commissions after the club, a house for E. Clarence Jones, became cause for a celebrated feud between Mizner and Jones. As a rule, Mizner and his clients enjoyed good relations. He said that in forty years of practice he had had "only one real row." Unfortunately, E. Clarence Jones was that exception. Jones asked Mizner to design and furnish a $10,000 house for him on County Road. Labor costs and a rise in the price of materials forced Mizner to add $3,000 of his own money to complete the job. Jones wanted more furniture, which Mizner purchased in West Palm Beach. When Jones refused to pay, the furniture store owner hired a deputy sheriff to serve Mizner with a subpoena before a client. Mizner, never bashful, gave everyone his opinion of "Swillcan" Jones. As president and owner of the Everglades Club, Singer chose the other officers and board members. He named Jones vice-president, giving him an influential voice in the club's governance. At the first meeting of the board, it adopted a rule against dogs. Mizner owned two pet Chows. At the second meeting, a rule limiting ladies to the first floor passed. Since Mizner lived in a tower apartment, he decided to build his first "tiny" Palm Beach house.[25]

The club's architectural success equaled its social triumph. During construction, Mizner claimed, the "locals" criticized the style of the building, saying they preferred the architecture of the Royal

Poinciana or The Breakers. With the coming of the winter visitors, the criticism turned into an architect's favorite form of praise: new commissions. Over the next five years Mizner designed houses for dozens of clients. Nonetheless, Singer and the Everglades Club continued to occupy much of his attention. Almost every year saw additions, remodelings, and new buildings added to the club complex.

Before the end of the first season, Singer decided to enlarge the club and add to its facilities. Since he also planned to spend the summer in France, once more he placed Mizner in charge of the work in Palm Beach. First among the priorities came the construction of a nine-hole golf course to the south of the clubhouse. Although Singer engaged a golf course designer and a landscape architect, Mizner directed the clearing of the sixty acres of jungle land. He saved and moved every tree of value and many flowering shrubs found growing wild. Before Mizner's landscaping the preceding year, professional gardeners generally believed that tropical trees and plants could not be successfully transplanted. The architect developed a method that included root pruning, trimming, and careful preparation of the new planting bed. South Florida natives expressed disbelief when the fifteen-year-old orange trees he moved lived, and they were astonished when the trees bore fruit. Mizner also learned to trim his flowering shrubs to bloom at the height of the season. The golf course, which opened in February 1920, and the newly completed tennis courts gave the Everglades Club sports facilities unequaled by any resort in southeast Florida.[26]

After completion of the golf course, Singer extended Golfview Road to County Road and created a small subdivision within the grounds of the club. The lots, overlooking the fairways of the course, quickly sold to club members who wished to build their own houses while still enjoying the conveniences and privacy of the club. In the next two years Marion Sims Wyeth (1889–1982), a Princeton graduate and Beaux-Arts-trained architect who came to Palm Beach in 1919, designed Spanish and Italian style villas along the street for clients like E. F. Hutton, Clarence Geist, and Jay F. Carlisle.[27]

During the summer of 1919 Mizner remodeled the Everglades villas and converted the medical house into thirteen bedrooms and baths for bachelor members. He also supervised construction of a building east of the clubhouse along Worth Avenue with shops on the ground floor and apartments (called maisonettes) above. The club immediately rented all of the eleven apartments and most of the sixteen shops. Because of his increased work load, Mizner only completed facade drawings, hiring Martin L. Hampden, a Miami

architect, to design the interiors and supervise the details. Across
Worth Avenue Mizner also added a second story to the Everglades
garage, which provided twenty-four rooms for maids and valets.[28]

During this summer Mizner began remodeling and adding to
the main clubhouse, a process which continued for many years.
During the first season the club became a popular setting for private
dinner parties. Since this meant closing the dining room to other
guests, Singer decided to add a private room. Mizner reclaimed
more of Lake Worth and built the addition directly west of the old
dining room. At the same time he enlarged the kitchen and service
areas, added a children's dining room, and more rooms for servants
on the second floor. He also moved the Court of Oranges to the west
front, surrounding it with terraces overlooking the lake. Over the
years he also gradually extended the club on the east. A new motor
entrance with porte cochere, hall, and waiting room added to the
Worth Avenue facade (Fig. 20). Mizner surrounded the old Court of

20. The Everglades Club, Worth Avenue facade.

21. The Everglades Club, original Court of Oranges.

Oranges with this new entrance, a new ballroom, and a new wing with additional apartments, creating a magnificent patio enclosed by cloisters (Fig. 21). Finally, as luncheon parties followed by afternoon bridge became popular, Mizner enlarged the old salon, creating a new card room (Fig. 22).[29]

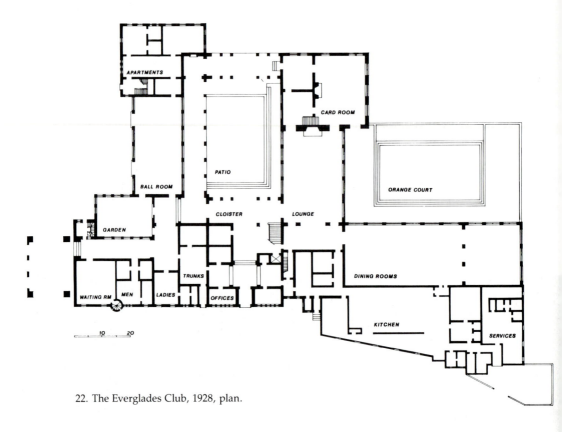

22. The Everglades Club, 1928, plan.

Mizner's last major commission for Singer at the Everglades came in the 1925 season when he completed a studio residence for the English portrait painter, Sir Oswald Birley. Singer brought Birley to the United States to paint his portrait and also one of Mizner. Birley completed the portrait of Singer that hangs in the club, but the architect never found time to sit for him. Mizner sited Birley's studio directly on the water at the southeast corner of the yacht basin (Fig. 23). A plain three-story structure, with an arcaded porch on the water, the first floor contained a dining room, kitchenette, and servants' rooms. Bedrooms made up the second floor, while the living room and high-ceilinged studio with views over the lake were on the third. The club later converted the building into apartments, calling it Lake House.[30]

When resorters arrived in December 1918 and found the nearly completed club, several asked Mizner to design Palm Beach houses. At first Singer seemed delighted; Mizner's commissions justified his decision to invest in the town's future. Later, when Singer realized the architect would no longer devote full time to his projects, he "got jealous" and decided to close down the pottery. Mizner needed the pottery's handmade tiles for his houses (he described commercial American roof tiles as looking like "painted tin" the color of "a slaughterhouse floor"). Nonetheless, he refused to argue, saying Singer often acted like a spoiled child. Finally, Singer asked Mizner about roof tiles for his new projects. When the architect replied that he might build his own kilns, Singer suggested that Mizner buy his plant. Mizner borrowed money from a bank and established Las Manos Potteries, the first division of Mizner Industries. He placed his nephew Horace B. Chase, Jr., who came to Palm Beach in the fall of 1919, in charge.[31]

23. House and studio of Sir Oswald Birley (right), and Everglades Club, with the Via Parigi and Villa Mizner in the background, c. 1940.

Las Manos began operation with Singer's three kilns. The largest held 10,000 tiles; the second largest, 3,000. The third kiln, intended for decorative pottery, could fire three hundred additional tiles when necessary. To achieve the subtle variations in shadings of the tiles, Mizner bought white and dark Georgia clay. Through mixing, drying, and firing, he obtained tiles that ranged in color from flesh pink to almost black-brown. Using a mule to propel the blades, a mill blended and worked the clay. Workmen then patted and thumped the refined clay into sanded wooden molds. When they were dry, a worker drilled a small hole in each end of the tiles and they were fired for four days and nights. Mizner developed this process by trial and error. The first batch came out of the kilns overbaked and broken. Experimentation in method and temperature produced both perfect tiles and the variations in colors the architect demanded. When Mizner purchased the plant he could fire 13,000 tiles every four days. As his building activity increased, and as other south Florida architects began to specify Las Manos tiles, he enlarged his capacity until ultimately Mizner Industries operated seven kilns.[32]

Shortly after acquiring Singer's plant, Mizner began making floor tiles. At first he produced only plain, unglazed, handmade square tiles. When treated and waxed the tiles achieved a rich shade of brown "which cannot be obtained by the use of paints, varnishes or other products." As demand increased Mizner produced floor tiles in different sizes and shapes and added glazed tiles. Later catalogues listed thirteen standard colors: Mizner blue (a distinctive turquoise), light blue, Valencia blue, light green, green, neutral green, Mizner yellow (another distinctive hue described as between mimosa and apricot), orange, red, brown, blue, blue-black, and black. Las Manos also made decorative pottery, either unglazed or in these same colors. The pots, hand-molded in standard shapes "made to follow as nearly as possible the original productions of old Spain," ranged from 3 or 4 inches high to a size that could hold a large orange tree. With the expansion of the potteries Mizner also opened a shop on South County Road to sell his various products.[33]

After the completion of the Everglades Club, Singer had ordered Mizner to sell the various enterprises organized in 1918 to make furniture, wrought-iron work, and lighting fixtures. When he acquired the potteries, Mizner also began reestablishing these workshops. Blacksmiths turned out wrought-iron grills, gates, lanterns, andirons, and hardware "for every use." A furniture factory, established in 1923, produced both "antique" pieces and furniture de-

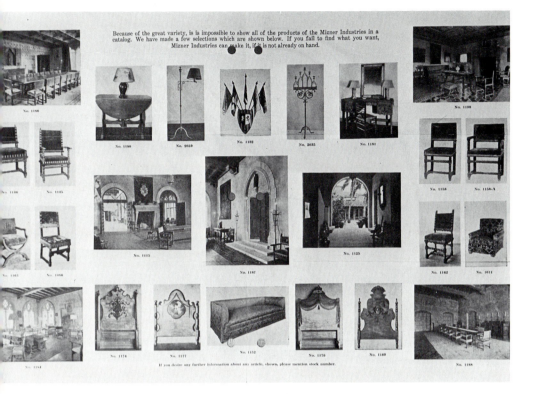

24. Mizner Industries furniture brochure.

signed by the architect (Fig. 24). The large overstuffed "Papa Mizner chair," while obviously designed to fit the architect's great bulk, also answered the plea of a client who, when confronted with a house full of antique Spanish furniture, demanded a comfortable chair. The deep, richly colored velvet and brocade upholstery was the only concession Mizner made to Spanish styling. He also sold a smaller version of the chair dubbed the "Mama Mizner." For his patios the architect designed a line of wicker furniture which included arm and side chairs, settees, and tables. These pieces, whose straight lines and simplicity made them quite modern in feeling, adapted well to the Florida climate.[34]

The fame of the furniture plant rested upon its antique reproductions. His factories specialized in "quality workmanship, not quantity"; he refused to turn out cheap copies of the original. Buyers purchased Mizner's furniture because of the scarcity of real antiques and because he produced copies that withstood the ravages of the south Florida climate. Using the finest aged woods, his workers

25. Workmen and products of Mizner Industries Cast Stone plant.

carefully handcut all joints, which they doweled and glued. To achieve
the proper look of antiquity the piece might be scraped with broken
bottles to remove rough edges, or beaten with chains to give the
surface a worn appearance. Although several sources tell of ice picks,
and even air rifles, used to produce worm holes, a former employee
said the architect liked his furniture in good repair; since worm holes
implied decay, he never added them to the finishing process. While
Mizner insisted on an antique appearance, contrary to later claims,
his catalogues clearly labeled his furniture as reproductions.[35]

Mizner Industries also developed a process to reproduce
wooden ceilings, doors, and panels out of "Woodite," a pulpy com-
posite of wood shavings, plaster of Paris, and fibrous material. The
Woodite was poured into a plaster-cast mold of the original. When
dry, it could be treated like wood and stained, painted, nailed, or

sawed. One writer saw the panels dropped from a height of 18 feet
and treated with great roughness to show their sturdy qualities. The
process exactly reproduced "knotholes, knots, grains, holes, worn
spots, even the partially rotted portion." Mizner Industries boasted
that a "layman absolutely cannot tell the difference" between real
wood and a Woodite panel.[36]

In Mizner's first buildings in Palm Beach his contractor made
cement molds for ornamental "stone" work on the job. In other
cases Mizner hired stone carvers to complete the work. As the architect's commissions increased, he needed great quantities of ornamental stone work. This led to the establishment of a plant for
making cast stone (Fig. 25). In the beginning Mizner produced his
ornamentation for window and door-surmounts, columns, capitals,
and balustrades by pouring plain cement into molds. From a dis-

26. Addison Mizner with Palm Beach mayor and Mizner client,
Barclay H. Warburton, at opening of Quarry Key Stone plant, 1929.

tance the product looked like carved stone; up close it looked newly cast. He constantly experimented, searching for a method to produce a more authentic appearance. Later he tried casting cracked limestone gravel and cement in crude molds. Workers then sculpted the roughness from the surface, giving the appearance of carved stone. Mizner also experimented with color and shadings, producing a substitute for travertine and marble.[37]

In 1929 Mizner added another industry when he began production of Quarry Key Stone (Fig. 26). He leased a quarry from the Florida East Coast Railway on Windley's Island near Islamorada in the Keys and began quarrying coquina rock. Brought to West Palm Beach in eight-ton blocks, a powerful saw cut the solid rock into building and paving stones. Mizner believed that the more attractive coquina would supplant "artificial" molded cement blocks as a building material. One Palm Beach architect immediately contracted to use the new material for two houses under construction on South Ocean Boulevard and for another in California.[38]

Mizner spent $40,000 on equipment to handle the stone in West Palm Beach, including a gigantic new saw powered by a fifty-horsepower engine. He also spent over $10,000 for equipment at the quarry. Unfortunately, this meant a refinancing of the company just before the Wall Street crash. Mizner Industries, Inc., had been organized in 1925 to acquire the various business interests developed over the years by the architect. These included Mizner's professional office, his workshops, plants, antiques business, and sales shops. A reorganization in 1928 transferred to Addison Mizner, Inc., all the capital stock of Mizner Industries, along with its assets, liabilities, and a large stock of antique furniture "purchased abroad some years ago." The company, under its various forms, earned an average of $39,000 a year throughout the twenties. When Mizner invested in the new Quarry Key Stone Works, the company had a net worth of over $250,000. The Wall Street crash greatly curtailed construction, ending the demand for quarry stone and the other products of the workshop. In 1931 Mizner Industries, now separated from the architect's professional office, went into receivership. After Mizner's death in 1933 a sheriff's auction sold the bankrupt company.[39]

At its height, the Bunker Road location of Mizner Industries encompassed a maze of kilns, drying yards, casting and furniture factories, drafting rooms, and storage sheds. Mizner artists and sculptors such as Percival Dietsch created designs for the draftsmen and woodmakers who completed the drawings and castings for production. Every architect and builder in the Palm Beaches, and many throughout south Florida, looked to Mizner Industries for the items needed to decorate their houses. Thus, Mizner tiles on the roof and on the floor, Mizner ironwork for grills, gates, screens, and lighting fixtures, Mizner cast stone for window- and door-surrounds, columns, and capitals, and even Mizner lead and stained glass windows, enclosed in Mizner bronze frames, can be found in practically every Palm Beach house built in the 1920s.

Mizner's design for the Everglades Club helped establish a new architectural style for Florida. He had been interested in Spanish architecture since his boyhood experiences in Guatemala. Even during his New York years, he designed several Spanish-style houses. That he chose this style for the Everglades Club seems only natural. As Mizner said of Palm Beach, "the history, the romance and the setting were all Spanish." Earlier architects also had seen these associations. When Flagler asked Carrère & Hastings to design the Ponce de Leon Hotel, Thomas Hastings said a study of the site led him to the conclusion that the "logical expression of the semi-tropical climate and historical background was in some form of Spanish Renaissance style." Florida, and Saint Augustine in particular, remained sensitive to its Spanish heritage. Nonetheless, with the exception of a few nondescript frontier houses, only the great fortress of San Marco (which Americans had renamed Fort Marion) continued as a monument of the Spanish era. When the Spanish departed Florida in 1821, after several centuries of rule, they left no architectural legacy. Carrère & Hastings drew on the Spanish romance for inspiration, not on an indigenous architectural tradition.[40]

Flagler approved of the style for Saint Augustine, calling upon the architects to build another Spanish hotel and two churches. When Flagler extended his railroad south, the hotels he built bore no trace of Spanish influence. Although Carrère & Hastings designed his Palm Beach mansion around a central courtyard and used red tiles on the roofs, the Doric columns of Whitehall's gigantic portico placed it closer to the southern plantation tradition than that of Spain.

Prior to the Everglades Club, the only other acknowledgment of Florida's climatic relationship to the lands of the Mediterranean came in Vizcaya, the Italian palace on the shores of Biscayne Bay designed by F. Burral Hoffman for James Deering in 1914. Deering dictated Vizcaya's style, for he had collected Italian architectural detailing—including ceilings, doorways, gates, and paneling—for over a quarter of a century. The vastness of the undertaking, the elaborate detailing, and the comparative isolation of the location kept

Vizcaya from setting a new style for Florida architecture.[41]

Mizner's architectural vision for the Everglades Club made it the first major building in south Florida in the Spanish style. Moreover, Mizner designed a practical adaptation of the style. By using hollow tile covered with stucco and cast-cement detailing, he made the gangs of skilled European stonecutters and artisans responsible for Vizcaya unnecessary; untrained Florida labor could learn the simple skills of construction. Unlike the isolation of Vizcaya, the Everglades Club stood at the heart of America's most fashionable winter resort. Paris Singer's name called attention to the club. His control assured a membership of Palm Beach's wealthiest and most socially prominent citizens. Finally, the architecture of the Everglades Club offered resorters a romantic alternative to the stark wooden hotels and drab shingled bungalows of the community. The club's soaring tower, projecting above the rambling tiled roofs, its elegant yet restrained decoration, its richly paneled and beamed rooms, and particularly its open plan, which brought each room into intimate relationship with its secluded patios and broad terraces, created a picturesque quality that harmonized completely with the tropical landscape and the lakeside location. Clients came to Mizner because they admired the Everglades Club and saw its Spanish architecture as both unique and appropriate for Palm Beach.

After he completed the Club, Mizner gave up plans to return to his New York practice. As he said, "I was in love with [Palm Beach] and Mr. Singer had fired me with a dream." With the club as a new and elegant center, resort life no longer depended upon the less exclusive hotels. Many visitors now decided to build winter homes. Just as the club encouraged a new style of resort life, so it served as a model for a new Palm Beach architectural style. Within a few weeks of its opening Mizner received four commissions for houses. With the critical success of the club gaining him additional clients, Mizner embarked on a career that would make him America's foremost society architect of his era.[42]

4

Creating the Palm Beach Style

Climate had originally brought visitors to Palm Beach. In the period after the war it continued as the great attraction. Participation in sports, either to pass time or to maintain health, came to symbolize resort life. While snow covered northern fairways, the Florida sun kept Palm Beach's green. Thus golf, tennis, swimming, and even high-goal polo became a part of the resorters' routine. Moreover, Florida's inlets and inland waterways appealed to both fisherman and sailor.

By the end of the war Palm Beach had direct telephone connections to the major cities of the north. The banker or stockbroker or factory owner could enjoy winter resort life and still keep in touch with developments in his office. When necessary, the railroad allowed him to be in New York or Philadelphia in a day.

In 1919 few vacationers owned houses in Palm Beach. Those who did most often built along the Lake Trail, on the Lake Worth side of the island. The formal dignity of Flagler's Whitehall and its neighbor to the south, the Corinthian-columned E. M. Brelsford house, contrasted sharply with the informal shingled cottages that lined the lakefront. In the center of the island a number of modest houses of "the suburban villa or Maine cottage variety" could be found in Colonel Edward Bradley's development north of Main Street, on the newly laid-out streets south of the Royal Poinciana golf course, and in Poinciana Park where nearly forty "dwellings of the bungalow type" in "a rather free use of the pure colonial" had been constructed by Oscar A. Jose, an Indianapolis developer. Only an occasional pioneer braved the oceanfront. Far to the south former Tammany

Hall boss Richard Croker had built the Wigwam, and Cleveland's Bingham family owned Figulus, a shingled "tropical" house sheltered by broad verandas. Although a few seaside cottages clustered near the grounds of The Breakers hotel, only the Robert Dun Douglass house, a large stucco villa with classical detailing designed by H. H. Mundy of Miami in 1917, and the houses for Michael Grace and his son-in-law Henry C. Phipps had been built on the oceanfront north of Wells Road. Whether on ocean or lake, the typical unpretentious and often builder-designed Palm Beach cottage gave way in 1919 to a new era of architectural magnificence.[1]

With the new wealth produced by the war allowing greater numbers the luxury of a winter vacation, the hotels began to lose their earlier social standing. Owning a villa and belonging to the Everglades Club with its carefully selected membership, permitted the very few to maintain an air of exclusiveness. Many of these same people regularly summered in Newport or Bar Harbor. To them Palm Beach became a stop on a continuing circuit of resort life. As they maintained large houses and staffs, and participated in an active social life in the other resorts, they naturally decided to establish the same type of household in Palm Beach. Their decision inaugurated the era of the Palm Beach mansion.

Northern architects designed several large villas in 1919, and their architectural style often reflected northern resort life. Of these early mansions, a reporter described F. Burral Hoffman's new oceanfront house for the Frederick E. Guests as "suggestive of the classic Greek type" and "especially majestic." The New York architectural firm of Hoppin & Koen created a formal Beaux-Arts mansion with classical details for the Theodore Frelinghuysens on Barton Avenue, and Horace Trumbauer of Philadelphia also designed a formal house for the Edward Stotesburys. Nonetheless, even in this early period, some northern architects shared Mizner's vision. Hoffman added a large Spanish music room to the lakeside house of Joseph Riter, and Abram Garfield, the Cleveland architect and son of the former president, designed a Spanish oceanfront villa for the Bolton family.[2]

When the war ended only Mizner and August Geiger maintained architectural offices in Palm Beach. Geiger, who established his Palm Beach office in 1915, designed the first Otto H. Kahn house at Sunrise Avenue and North Ocean Boulevard and the Fashion Beaux-Arts building, a shopping center on the lakefront at the foot of Seminole Avenue. While the shopping center had tiled roofs, neither building could be termed Spanish. In 1920 Geiger closed his Palm Beach office although he continued to practice in Miami where he designed many Spanish-style houses and public buildings during the period of the Florida land boom.[3]

Marion Sims Wyeth and Bruce Paxton Kitchell (1872–1942) both came to Palm Beach in 1919. Wyeth, the partner of Frederick Rhinelander King, who managed the New York office of the firm, quickly established a profitable practice. As highly social as Mizner, the two architects vied for the same society clients throughout the early twenties. Wyeth designed his largest house, Cielito Lindo, for James P. Donahue in 1927. He also served as Joseph Urban's associate during the construction of Marjorie Merriweather Post's Mar-a-Lago. In a career that spanned over fifty years, Wyeth designed houses for practically every street in Palm Beach.[4]

During the 1920s Kitchell, like Mizner and Wyeth, produced many Spanish-style buildings. In Palm Beach he designed the large towered villa at 120 Dunbar Road for Dr. and Mrs. W. Seward Webb, Otto H. Kahn's second oceanfront house on Sunrise Avenue, and a shop for Hatch Stores at Sunset Avenue and County Road. In West Palm Beach he designed both the Palace and Florida theaters, and during the Depression he served as chief architect on two New Deal housing projects, Southridge and Dunbar Village.[5]

Before the end of 1919, confirmation of the fashionableness of Mizner's Spanish style came when he received a commission for a great mansion from the leader of Palm Beach society. Late in the 1918/19 season Mizner saw Mrs. Edward T. Stotesbury measuring the Everglades Club terraces. When he offered to help, she said, "Oh, Mr. Mizner, you have made me so discontented with the plans I have had done for 'El Mirasol'; I don't think I will ever be content with them after seeing this." Within a few weeks the Stotesburys dismissed Horace Trumbauer and asked Mizner to design their Palm Beach house.[6]

By 1919 Eva Cromwell Stotesbury had become the recognized *grande dame* of Palm Beach society. The widow of a New York banker, she married Edward Townsend Stotesbury in 1912 after the death of his first wife. During his first marriage he had worked long and hard, but his family had lived frugally. Starting as a clerk he eventually became a senior partner in the Philadelphia banking firm of Drexel and Company, and after its association with J. P. Morgan and Company, he became a senior Morgan partner. Stotesbury's first wife died before she could enjoy his now immense fortune; he decided to deny Eva nothing. Although of an old Philadelphia family, Stotesbury was not "Old Philadelphia." When the Vanderbilts decided to assert their right to enter New York society, they commis-

27. El Mirasol, Edward T. Stotesbury house, Palm Beach, 1919, ocean facade.

sioned Richard Morris Hunt to design their great Fifth Avenue chateau. When the Stotesburys decided to enter Philadelphia society
they had Trumbauer design Whitemarsh Hall, a six-story 154-room
mansion in Chestnut Hill. Old Philadelphians called the house os-
tentatious and remained unimpressed.[7]

Nathaniel Burt, the historian of Philadelphia society, said that
when a Philadelphia parvenu felt snubbed, he appealed to a higher
court. Thus the Stotesburys came to Palm Beach, where for "lack of
competition" they became the social leaders. Yet many of those same
"old" families also came to Palm Beach. In fact, in the early years of
the twenties the town seemed to be a Philadelphia resort, with its
Biddles, Wanamakers, Warburtons, Munns, Thomases, Glenden-
nings, Wardens, and Carstairs. Other sources suggest that Mizner's
great palace gained the Stotesburys social success. More likely, Mrs.
Stotesbury's "charm, maturity, and grace" conquered Palm Beach
society. El Mirasol only confirmed her leadership.[8]

Mizner found Mrs. Stotesbury a difficult taskmaster. He made
seven changes in Mrs. Stotesbury's bathroom, even though "there
are only three pieces that must go in," before she approved. Then
she decided to move her sitting room to the bathroom location and
make the sitting room the bath. The architect later said he preferred

the client who signed a contract for a house at the end of the season and then departed for the north, giving him complete control over construction, landscaping, and furnishing. He envied the doctor's advantage over the architect, saying "[the doctor can] chloroform his patient and do as he likes." Even with its problems, El Mirasol established a pattern that the architect followed from season to season. After finally approving the design, a client signed contracts before going north in the spring. At the beginning of the next season a completed and furnished house awaited him in Palm Beach. The Stotesburys returned to Florida on Tuesday, 29 January 1920. A small army of workmen installed the furniture on Sunday and Monday, working through the nights to complete every detail.[9]

El Mirasol became the standard for judging later great Palm Beach mansions (Fig. 27). Mizner sited it on top of the beach ridge and used a general plan that he repeated in many other oceanfront houses. Entrance was from the north and on a floor below the principal rooms of the house. The lower level held the kitchen, service areas, and servants' rooms in its north and south wings (Fig. 28). A large entrance hall with marble fireplace faced a cloistered patio with fountain. Next to the entrance Mizner placed dressing rooms with showers. A wide staircase allowed the Stotesbury guests a grand entrance to the main floor which overlooked the ocean from the top

28. El Mirasol, western facade from service court.

29. El Mirasol, cloister.

of the ridge. At the head of the stairs a cloistered corridor gave access to the public rooms, the guest rooms in the south wing, and a series of tiled loggias surrounding the patio (Fig. 29). The living room, "capable of seating 175 people," had six large French doors, three opening onto the patio loggia, and three onto the ocean terrace. A dais on the north end of the room held a large open fireplace. Chandeliers from an old Spanish castle hung from the richly paneled ceiling. To the south the dining room "of stately proportions" had two large French doors facing the ocean with steps down to the terrace (Fig. 30). The library, the most intimate of the major rooms, opened off the living room to the north. The Stotesburys' rooms were on the top floor. One description mentioned the "grilled windows placed in the ceilings which guarantee absolutely complete ventilation."[10]

30. El Mirasol, dining room.

The Stotesburys' estate ran from ocean to lake, just north of Wells Road. Mizner planned the landscaping so that County Road, which cut through the property, disappeared completely from view. In addition to the house, Mizner also designed entrance gates and a small tea pavilion near the lake. The grounds included lavishly land-scaped gardens, an orange grove, an aviary, and a small zoo. On the practical side, Stotesbury insisted on a vegetable garden and a chicken house.[11]

El Mirasol did add force to Mrs. Stotesbury's position as Palm Beach's foremost hostess. Ablaze with jewels, she took her place at the top of the stairs to greet guests for her dinners and parties. Over the years leading artists played for her recitals and distinguished authorities delivered lectures at her invitation. The annual birthday party for Mr. Stotesbury on 26 February rivaled the Washington

Birthday Ball as the social event of the season. When Mrs. Stotesbury's daughter, Louise Cromwell, married General Douglas
MacArthur at El Mirasol on Valentine's Day in 1922 the guest list
read like an East Coast social register. In reporting the various events
the social columnists rarely failed to point out the beauty of their
setting. In fact, at one party a former ambassador to Spain exclaimed
that El Mirasol "far surpassed anything in Spain with the exception
of the Royal Castle of the King and Queen."[12]

The Stotesburys remodeled and added to El Mirasol practically every year. During this period Stotesbury announced achievement of his life goal: his fortune stood at $100 million. While he
could well afford his three large estates and his 70-foot yacht, the
Nedeva, he often complained of Mrs. Stotesbury's lavish spending.
Nonetheless, Mizner's "refinements" continued at El Mirasol until
he became almost completely involved in his land development
schemes. Mizner said that while Stotesbury attempted to cut his
commission from the usual ten percent to five, he still paid the
bills.[13]

31. Louwana, Gurnee Munn house, Palm Beach, 1919, southern and beach facade.

32. Louwana, entry, south facade.

Mizner also completed in January 1920 two houses for Gurnee and Charles Munn, who had purchased oceanfront land just north of the Henry C. Phipps estate. The architect sited Gurnee Munn's Louwana, like El Mirasol, on the beach ridge with entrance and service quarters on the ground floor and the principal living rooms on the floor above facing the ocean. Much less pretentious than El Mirasol, Louwana was designed as a family vacation house (Figs. 31, 32). A loggia connected the large living and dining rooms. Mizner placed the Munns' rooms over the living room and those for the children and nurses in the opposite wing. One early account called Charles Munn's Amado "attractively pretentious from without, modernly convenient from within." In Mizner's U-shaped design the patio faced the ocean with a loggia connecting the north and south wings (Fig. 33).[14]

33. Louwana, patio.

During the summer Mizner built El Solano, his own first Palm
Beach house (Fig. 34). The architect chose a jungle setting far removed in 1919 from the center of town, almost a mile south of Worth
Avenue at 720 South Ocean Boulevard. In this "tiny house" he hung
old red velvet and embroidery from Toledo in the living room and
used 300-year-old paneling and furniture in the dining room. A
second floor loggia, with an excellent view of the sea, separated
Mizner's rooms from a guest wing to the south (Fig. 35). In less than
a year he sold the house to Harold S. Vanderbilt, who immediately
asked him to plan additions, including a large new living room and

one of the first private swimming pools in Palm Beach.[15]

Mizner had two summer projects in 1920. He designed Costa Bella at the corner of Dunbar Road and North Ocean Boulevard for Mrs. Elizabeth H. G. Slater of Washington, D.C. A marble-floored and vaulted stone entrance loggia overlooked a patio sheltered from the street by a high wall. The extremely large and formally proportioned living and dining rooms faced the ocean. Mizner's detailing included "stalactite" lighting fixtures and Gothic tracery for the dining room ceiling and a massive carved stone staircase at the end of the entrance loggia. Although more formal than the architect's typical Palm Beach work, the extensive fenestration created an open and light vacation house.[16]

Willey Lyon Kingsley, a Rome, New York, banker, commissioned an oceanfront house on almost deserted beach far to the south of town. In order to capture every ocean breeze and view Mizner planned the facade as a series of recessed bays (Figs. 36, 37). The bays represented major rooms on the first floor. As the house enclosed a patio, this allowed each room to have windows on three

34. El Solano, Addison Mizner house, Palm Beach, 1919.

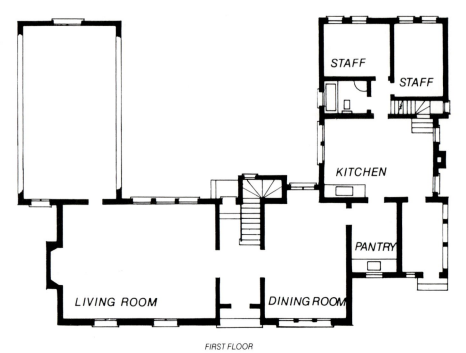

FIRST FLOOR

SECOND FLOOR

35. El Solano, plan.

36. La Bellucia, Willey Lyon Kingsley house, Palm Beach, 1920, ocean facade.

37. La Bellucia, entry.

38. La Bellucia, patio.

sides (Fig. 38). A great tiled loggia, open to both patio and ocean
terrace, connected the paneled living room and sunken dining room
(Figs. 39, 40). A covered walkway separated the three-story servants'
quarters and garage.[17]

    Cooper C. Lightbown, a young carpenter from Washington,
D.C., who came to Palm Beach in 1912, served as Mizner's contractor in building the Stotesbury house and several other Mizner commissions in 1919 and 1920. The two men developed a good working
relationship; Lightbown willingly followed the architect's directions
and soon learned his building techniques. Since Mizner trusted
Lightbown's ability and judgment, he decided to spend the summer
of 1921 in Europe replenishing his supply of Spanish antiques. After
completing the design work he sailed in early summer, returning in
September with "a half shipload" of furniture. This trip established
a pattern the architect followed for the next several years. The European visits allowed him to renew his inspiration, shop for furniture
and other decorative items for his clients, and purchase pieces for

39. La Bellucia, loggia from dining room.

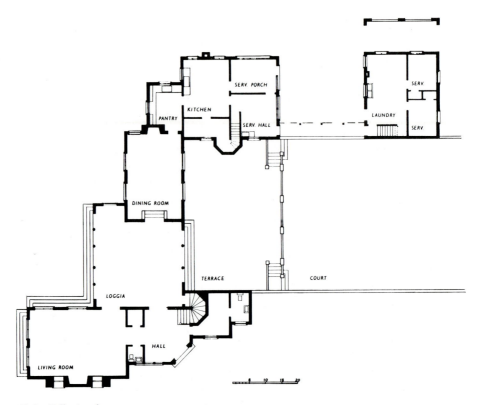

40. La Bellucia, plan.

reproduction in his workshops, or to sell in the antiques store he opened on South County Road. By returning in September he could supervise the finishing details of the houses built during the summer and oversee their furnishing.[18]

   The work in progress never suffered during Mizner's absences in Europe because he involved his designers and draftsmen, who were often young apprentices, in the complete design process. They then supervised the actual construction. Mizner, whose interest centered on design, established an office routine similar to that of many architects with adequate staffs. He prepared preliminary sketches of the elevations and the complete layout and sizes of the rooms. Often these included watercolor drawings of the facades. His fine line sketches suggested enough of the detail to allow his chief designer, always a well-trained architect, to begin plans. As the designer worked, Mizner marked and modified the drawings. The chief designer and draftsmen shared the same office and all joined in the ongoing process. Moreover, Mizner, perfectly secure in his own design concepts, often held client conferences in the drafting room, encouraging participation by the entire staff.[19]

When the design satisfied Mizner, he turned it over to the draftsmen who completed the final plans. Toward the young apprentices and architectural students who served as his draftsmen, Mizner adopted the fatherly air of a patient teacher, giving directions and instruction. One draftsman remembered that although Mizner often "gave hell to others and could cuss like a stevedore," when the work of the young men in the office failed to meet his standards he only suggested alternatives. Another associate recalled the architect as a patient and understanding teacher. Mizner once told him to design stone balusters and a handrail for a staircase. Mizner criticized the results, saying he had made the balusters too thin. Two days later Mizner showed him a wooden mock-up of the proposed design, allowing the associate to see his mistake.[20]

Mizner gave his assistants great latitude in working out their design details. Over the years he had built a large collection of architectural photographs and sketches which he consulted for inspiration. He also used the collection to show his draftsmen the effects he wished to attain. He rarely asked them to copy the exact details, suggesting instead modifications and simplifications of the original. In fact, a draftsman recalled Mizner's only definite instructions as: "never design a stairway you can't walk up with a hat on," and "don't design a fireplace that smokes." Mizner's continuing and fatherly interest in the work of his associates gave the office an atmosphere of intimacy, as one said, "a feeling you are with him. . . . It was a pleasure working for Mizner." Nonetheless, from beginning to end, Mizner's concepts shaped and molded the design.[21]

Alva Johnston and others tell of Mizner's "dress rehearsals" when he visited nearly completed buildings, ordering walls changed or torn down and other major alterations in the construction. In reality, the contractors followed the plans and specifications as drawn and written in the architect's office. Like other members of his profession, a clause in Mizner's standard contract stated that no changes or alterations could be made unless in writing and approved by both the architect and client "for sum stated." He also adhered to normal professional practice in billing, charging a set fee for new construction and an hourly rate for alterations.[22]

Mizner reserved morning hours for his studio and drafting room. "Up and doing" before six in the morning, he completed his own work before office hours, which always brought a "stream of people." He reserved afternoons for supervision and inspection of the various jobs under construction. In the late afternoons and evenings he attended to the second most important part of his professional duties, the social life which brought the firm commissions. The *Daily News*, Palm Beach's social newspaper, regularly published dinner and party lists during the season; Mizner's name constantly appeared in these columns. Mizner needed his social life in order to meet and influence new clients. Gregarious since childhood, the mature architect genuinely relished social life. After a hard day he sometimes dreaded his evening's engagement, "but when I would get to a party, I always enjoyed it." A *raconteur* and gossip of considerable talent, he understood the value of novelty—and a little notoriety—in advertising himself and his profession. Thus he often became the center of amusement in his own stories. Many of the legends of Mizner's architectural failures—the missing stairways, bathrooms, kitchens, and the claims that he never drew plans or elevations until he completed a building—probably stem from his own attempts to amuse and entertain. In effect, he became a Palm Beach institution, regaling the town with his stories and creating his own legend.[23]

In 1921 Mizner lived and worked on South County Road near Sunset Avenue. When the Everglades Club opened he moved his office from the White Villa to a building owned by E. W. Histed, the fashion photographer. After Harold Vanderbilt bought Mizner's first house, the architect remodeled a former "mule shed" on Histed's property: "I added a kitchen, pantry, and baths, and divided it up into a bedroom and huge living room. By boarding it up inside and hanging tapestries and velvets on the wall, with one end a library, I transformed it into quite an attractive and comfortable place." During the next four years Mizner built two more houses for himself. As in the case of the first, he sold them almost immediately, returning to live in the "mule shed" next to his office. The convenience of this arrangement later prompted him to build his last house next door to his office building on Worth Avenue.[24]

When Mizner went to Europe in 1921 he left G. Sherman Childs and Julius Jacobs, his two chief designers, in charge of the office. Their summer projects included supervising a house on Lake Worth for Leonard Thomas, one in the El Bravo Addition for the Honorable Charles Winn, another for Alfred Kay, a similar house for O. Frank Woodward, a great oceanfront mansion for John S. Phipps, further additions to the Everglades Club, and a new house for Mizner.[25]

The Leonard Thomas house saw Mizner turning to a new

41. Casa de Leoni, Leonard Thomas house, Palm Beach, 1921, from Lake Worth.

Mediterranean style for his design inspiration. Thomas, a former husband of Tessie Oelrichs's niece, had served as secretary of both the American legation in Madrid and the Embassy in Rome. The son and heir of one of Edward Stotesbury's partners in Drexel and Company, his long service in Europe placed a cosmopolitan stamp on his tastes. He purchased the first lot west of the Everglades Club, directly on Lake Worth. Mizner recognized that the setting called for a Venetian palazzo. Thomas agreed, making plans to import Italian furniture and a gondola, and to hire an Italian cook and servants (Fig. 41). Mizner arranged the house around the patio, which had steps down to the lake. From the lake side, the house seemed to rise out of the water. Its arched windows with elaborate trefoil surrounds, stone balconies, and gondola slip all confirmed the Venetian heritage. On the street facade, a carved St. Mark's lion over the door and Thomas's first name accounted for the house being called Casa

42. Casa de Leoni, entrance.

de Leoni (Fig. 42). Mizner's Venetian Gothic style became very popular with his later clients. Within a few years his pointed and trefoil
arched windows, the standard frames made by Mizner Industries,
appeared on houses across the island.[26]

One author termed Captain the Honorable Charles John Frederick Winn, a younger son of the English Lord St. Oswald, "Palm Beach's pioneer title." Although the resort had long entertained European nobility, Winn and his wife Olive, a member of the Whitney family, became the first to own property. Winn also served as an early town booster. When asked why he chose Florida over the Riviera for his winter residence, he replied, "I consider Palm Beach superior in every way—first as to climate; then as to society, sports and bathing."[27]

Mizner used the same basic plan for the Winn house on El Bravo Way; the Alfred Kay villa, Audita, on South Ocean Boulevard; and the O. Frank Woodward house on Seminole Avenue. In all three

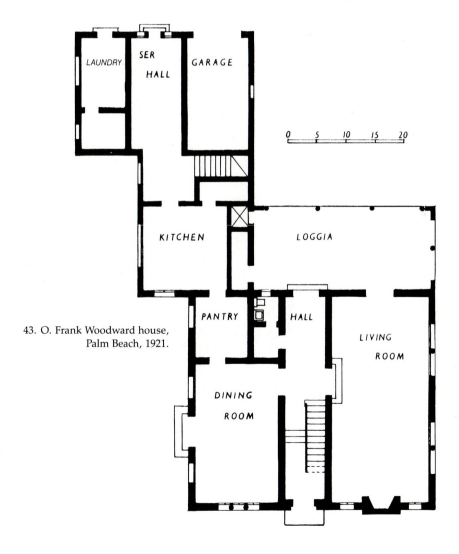

43. O. Frank Woodward house, Palm Beach, 1921.

small houses a center hall entrance with open stairway led to living
and dining rooms on either side. In each case a loggia opened off
the living room (Fig. 43). For the Winns Mizner designed his first
tower house. In order to ensure privacy for family and guests, the
architect used two stairways, the second giving access to a three-
story tower on the ocean side of the house (Fig. 44). On the second
floor Mizner separated the guest rooms from the family bedrooms
with an open deck and a sheltered exterior cloister. With the exception of a large wooden grill covering the southern windows of the
Winn tower, and a few trefoil window-surrounds similar to those of
Casa de Leoni for the Kay villa, Mizner designed plain and unadorned exteriors, making all three houses good examples of the

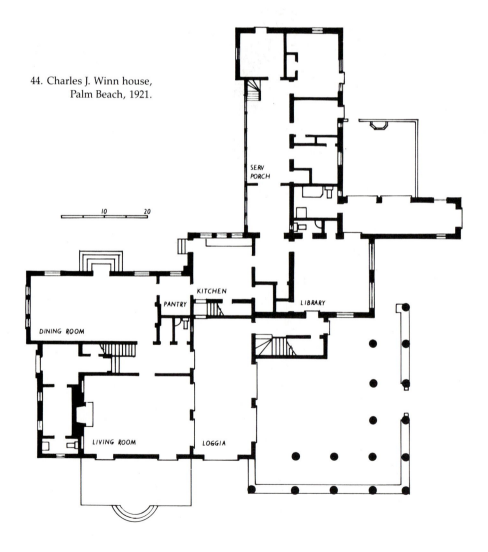

44. Charles J. Winn house,
    Palm Beach, 1921.

45. Casa Bendita, John S. Phipps house, Palm Beach, 1921, ocean facade.

architect's dictum: "If [the clients] have money, let them keep it inside."[28]

The major summer project of 1921 was Casa Bendita, a great oceanfront house for John S. Phipps. The Phipps family had been part of the Palm Beach scene since the Flagler era. John Phipps's father, Henry, an original partner of Andrew Carnegie, built a lakeshore house in West Palm Beach and invested in property all along the Florida east coast. Both John's sister, Mrs. Frederick E. Guest, and brother, Henry C. Phipps, built large houses on the ocean in Palm Beach; Casa Bendita bordered his brother's house, Heamaw. A long winding drive from County Road brought the visitor to the front door set into the base of a four-story octagonal tower. From the ground floor northern entrance a stairway led up to an open cloister on the patio. The principal rooms faced the ocean from the top of the beach ridge (Fig. 45). An open staircase rose from the cloister to the second floor. Later additions incorporated an elaborate colonnaded swimming pool into the southern wing of the house (Fig. 46). The architectural historian George Edgell called the house a "monumental work" in which "a perfect Spanish flavor is maintained." A major commission (newspaper articles referred to the house as "Phipps's castle"), Casa Bendita, unlike Mizner's usual projects, took two years to complete.[29]

Mizner built his own new house, which he called Concha Marina, at South Ocean and Jungle Road. He placed a two-story section along Jungle Road with a one-story wing facing the ocean. The open entrance framed a vista of the patio, formed by the ell-shaped house and terraced walls overlooking the still untamed jungle growth (Figs. 47, 48). Mizner occupied the house only one season, selling it to George and Isabel Dodge Sloane.[30]

With the sale of Concha Marina, Mizner immediately began a new house at 1800 South Ocean Boulevard, five miles south of town

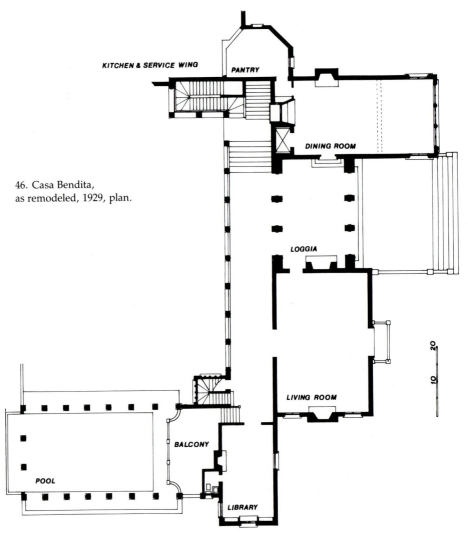

46. Casa Bendita,
as remodeled, 1929, plan.

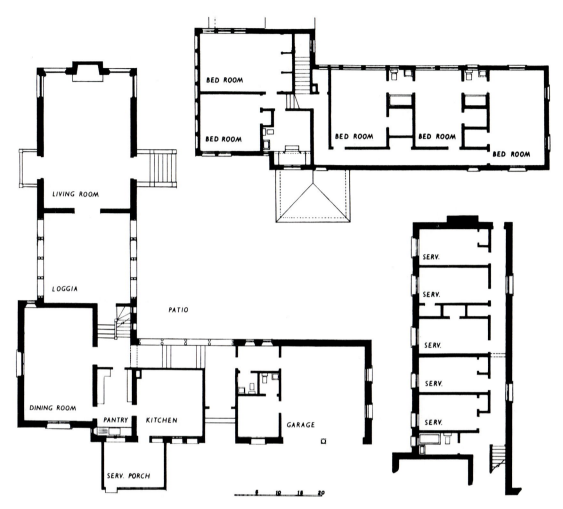

47. Concha Marina, Addison Mizner house, Palm Beach, 1921, plan.

(Fig. 49). He allowed the topography of the site to determine the plan for this small house (Fig. 50). From a ground floor entrance, stone stairs with wrought-iron rails led to the dining room, loggia, and living room that formed the ocean facade of the house. A separate two-story building housed eight servants' rooms and the laundry. Mizner said he moved so far from the center of town to keep anyone from buying his house. In less than two years, however, he sold it to Edward S. Moore, who immediately engaged the architect to add bedrooms over the loggia and living room, a new bedroom wing north of the dining room, and garages and caretaker's quarters near the old servants' house.[31]

48. Concha Marina, Jungle Road entrance.

49. Sin Cuidado, Addison Mizner house, Palm Beach, 1922,
living room with loggia and stairway beyond.

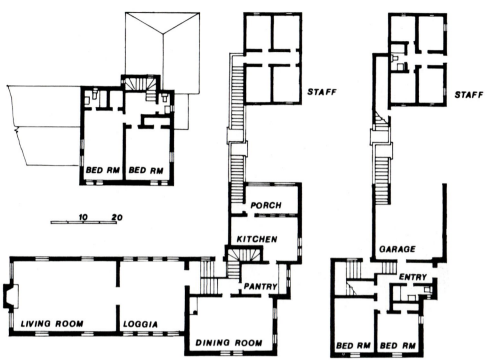

50. Sin Cuidado, plan.

51. Casa Maria Marrone, Barclay H. Warburton house,
Palm Beach, as remodeled, c. 1926, plan.

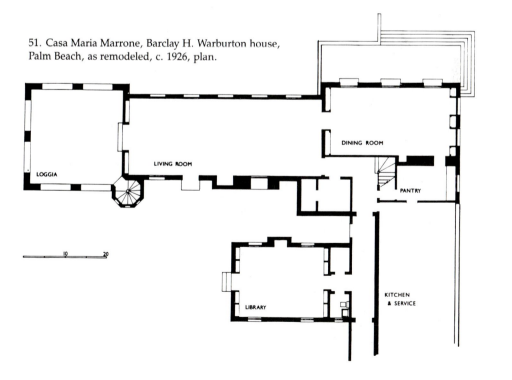

52. Walter G. Mitchell house, Palm Beach, 1922, from South Ocean Boulevard.

By 1922 the recession of the early months of the Harding administration had ended and Palm Beach embarked on a period of great prosperity. The next three years marked Mizner's most productive period as he designed almost thirty villas, including his largest mansion, and completed his own new studio and house, numerous shops and offices, and another private club. Mizner had at least seven commissions in 1922. With the exception of the house at 150 South Ocean Boulevard for Madame Jeannette Gais, who owned several Palm Beach apartment houses and managed a fashionable clothing store, all came from substantial members of the resort community, the social clients who made Mizner's professional reputation. These included the Grace Trail residence of Joseph M. Cudahy, president of the Sinclair Oil Refining Company; the lakefront house for Major Barclay H. Warburton, son of the founder of the *Philadelphia Evening Telegraph* and son-in-law of John Wanamaker (Fig. 51); and a towered villa at 182 South Ocean Boulevard for Walter G. Mitchell, an Atlanta lumberman (Fig. 52).[32]

The Mizner files also contain 1922 plans for a small house for Alice De Lamar. The house, built on the lake, had a boat slip, garage, and service rooms on the ground floor and a loggia and bedrooms on the second. A *Palm Beach Post* photograph of July 1922 showed

the house completely framed and roofed. The caption named Mizner as the designer and said Miss De Lamar was in Florence buying
tiles, cornices, mirrors, and windows for her Italian-style house.
Actually Miss De Lamar, a close friend of the architect's nephew
Horace Chase, designed the house with the help of Mizner's office
staff. On returning from Europe she found the small house inadequate for her needs and stopped construction. As her property extended from lake to ocean, she started over on the ocean side. She
later sold the lakefront land and the new owner razed the partially
completed house.[33]

William Gray Warden of Philadelphia commissioned Mizner's
major 1922 house. Warden's father, who founded the Atlantic Refining Company, joined the Standard Oil Trust as early as 1874. He
became a key man in the larger company, setting policy for Eastern
Pennsylvania and Philadelphia. Although the younger Warden remained associated with Standard Oil, he also served as chairman of
the Pittsburgh Coal Company. Mrs. Warden asked Mizner to design
a large villa. Warden, though certainly unworried about costs, told
the architect he wanted a small unostentatious house. Mizner said
he sketched the Warden house in half scale to the two houses on

53. William Gray Warden house, Palm Beach, 1922, Seminole Avenue facade.

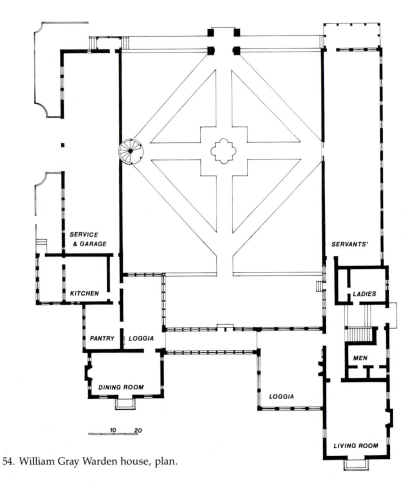

54. William Gray Warden house, plan.

either side. This satisfied both Warden, to whom it looked "truly insignificant," and Mrs. Warden, whom the architect told of his trick. According to Mizner, Warden arrived in Palm Beach on an inspection trip in October. He seemed pleased with the house, and particularly the large patio. As he boarded the train to return north, Warden asked for a set of elevations. Afraid of betraying his secret, Mizner claimed that he answered, "Elevations! Why, Bill, you look intelligent at times; how could I send you elevations when the house isn't finished yet." Although a typical Mizner story, in reality both Wardens inspected the house together in late June. At the time the *Palm Beach Post* quoted them as "very much pleased with the re-sults," and surprised at the excellent summer weather in Florida. Nonetheless, Mizner delighted in telling how the humble architect bested the great oil man. His repeating of the tale helped establish the myth that he never drew floor plans or elevations until he completed a house.[34]

The Warden villa occupied the entire oceanfront block between Root Trail and Seminole Avenue (Fig. 53). The thirty-two-room house, "excluding bathrooms and several large closets almost as large as a room," followed Mizner's usual U-shape, enclosing a very large 100-by-85-foot patio on the west (Fig. 54). On either side of the formal entrance on Seminole Avenue Mizner placed dressing rooms with shower baths for the convenience of beach users. From the large double doors a flight of stone steps led up to the main hall and the living room and loggia facing the ocean. Mizner often pictured the living room with its cypress ceilings, black-tiled floors, and large French door in advertising brochures for his industries. The loggia's three walls of plate glass in sliding bronze frames afforded views of both ocean and patio. A 33-foot-long cloister joined the loggia to the south wing of the house. In this wing a long dining room overlooked the sea and a breakfast and luncheon loggia faced the patio (Fig. 55). The rest of the wing contained butler's pantry, kitchen, garage, and other service rooms.

55. William Gray Warden house, loggia.

A stone staircase in the entrance hall led to the second story in the main section of the house (Fig. 56). Mizner used Las Manos tiles for the floors throughout, supporting the weight on this floor with steel beams. The architect placed the owners' rooms, which included a sleeping porch, over the living room. Five guest suites made up the rest of the north wing's second floor. An outside staircase rose from the patio to the bachelor guest rooms on the second floor of the south wing. In this commission Mizner achieved an open and informal plan particularly suited to a vacation villa. Moreover, his subtle massing of the various elements, the gradual changes in level, and the creation of interior and exterior vistas, produced a visual excitement rarely found in his previous houses.[35]

Each year since its opening, membership in the Everglades Club had grown. Some members believed this compromised the club's exclusive character; others, wishing golfing vacations, complained of the crowds on the Everglades course. In response, a group led by Warden and including Singer, Stotesbury, Edward Shearson, and John Harris purchased land just north of Delray Beach for the Gulfstream Golf Club. The new club limited membership to two

56. William Gray Warden house, stairway.

57. Gulfstream Golf Club,
Gulfstream, 1923,
stairway and western facade.

hundred and imposed a $2,500 membership fee. According to Miz-
ner, the organizers of the club completed their work late in the
season and wished to approve plans for the clubhouse before returning north. In just six hours Mizner drew the plans and sketches of
the building. A quick meeting of 17 March 1923 saw his plans accepted, Donald Ross hired as the golf course architect, and Cooper
Lightbown given the contract to construct the building.[36]

Even though Mizner said his drawings for the Gulfstream
Club took only six hours, Matlack Price, in an *Architectural Forum*
article on Mediterranean architecture in Florida, declared the building the most attractive "Spanish-Italian adaptation" in the United
States. Mizner's clubhouse sat on a narrow strip of ground between
the sea and the ocean road. He gave the facade of the small structure

58. Angier Duke house,
Palm Beach, 1923, plan.

59. Arthur D. Claflin house,
Palm Beach, 1923, plan.

60. Arthur D. Claflin house from Lake Worth.

added importance by designing an arcaded loggia and a double flight of curving stairs (Fig. 57). A living room, dining room, and oceanfront terrace led off from the loggia. Mizner placed locker rooms on the ground floor, including a fireplace in the section of the men's locker room facing the ocean. The club opened in early January 1924 with Warden as president and the other founders as officers and members of the board of governors. Later in the season, John S. Phipps purchased land north of the golf course for polo fields and stables. Within a few years Gulfstream became the winter polo capital. Phipps and many other club members also built small houses in Gulfstream (which they incorporated as a town in 1925) to use for entertaining during polo season.[37]

 Before 1923 Mizner had only a few commissions each year for major houses. With the exceptions of the Stotesburys, Wardens, and several members of the Phipps family, most Palm Beach cottagers seemed content to build moderately sized vacation villas for the two or three months they spent in Florida. In 1923 the character of Palm Beach building changed. Although Mizner still had some commissions for smaller houses, most of his clients now demanded large, lavish mansions. Of his twelve known commissions of that year, the only small house, that for Angier Duke at 160 Barton Avenue, included a 45-foot-long living room (Fig. 58). Six others were among Palm Beach's largest houses.[38]

The heavy work load of the summer failed to stop Mizner's annual buying trip to Europe. Alex Waugh, in an unpublished memoir of the early twenties in Florida, told of this trip. Waugh, a young English interior decorator, had met Mizner in Palm Beach during the preceding season. Returning to Europe to search for employment, he ran into Mizner in Paris. When the architect heard Waugh needed a job, he hired him to act as general factotum on the buying trip. On board the train to Spain, Mizner dictated from memory detailed lists of the items needed for his various commissions. In Spain they traveled from city to city, with Mizner buying from antiques dealers, impoverished nobility, church officials, and anyone else who had anything that interested him. The items ranged from place mats to hundreds of antique tiles to an entire large staircase. Waugh expressed surprise at the architect's ability to coordinate the numerous items with his various commissions, and even to visualize their lo-

61. Daniel H. Carstairs house, Palm Beach, 1923, facade from North Ocean Boulevard.

62. Daniel H. Carstairs house, entrance hall.

cations in his still unfinished houses. Mizner also bought for his own collection and for his Palm Beach antiques store.[39]

During Mizner's European trip his office staff supervised construction of the 1923 projects. In addition to the six large mansions and the small Duke house, these included La Guerida for Rodman Wanamaker II at 1113 North Ocean Boulevard; Casa Joseto for Joseph Speidel of Charleston, West Virginia at 942 South Ocean

Boulevard; a "Spanish farmhouse" for Daniel H. Carstairs just north of Dunbar on North Ocean Boulevard; the Villa Tranquilla for Dr. DeGrimm Renfro at El Brillo and South Ocean Boulevard; and a larger version of the Casa de Leoni for Arthur B. Claflin on the lakefront at 800 South County Road (Figs. 59, 60).[40]

63. Daniel H. Carstairs house, stairs in hall.

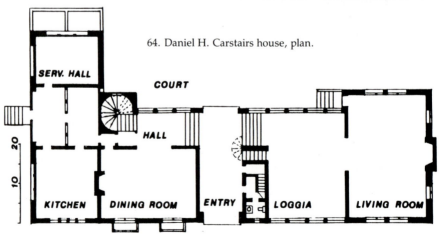

64. Daniel H. Carstairs house, plan.

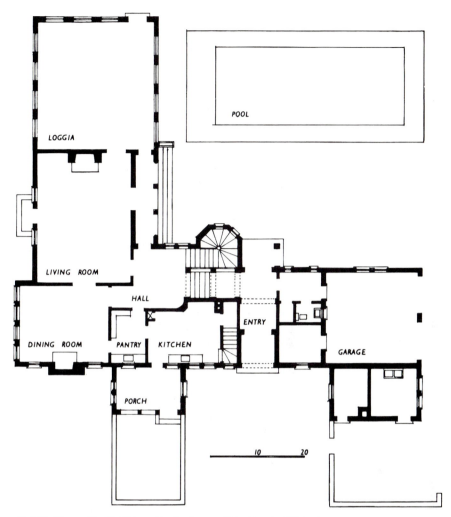

LOGGIA

POOL

LIVING ROOM

HALL

ENTRY

DINING ROOM   PANTRY   KITCHEN

GARAGE

PORCH

10   20

65. Villa Tranquilla, DeGrimm Renfro house, Palm Beach, 1923, plan.

Mizner said he designed a "farmhouse of the Ferdinand and Isabella period" for Carstairs, though only the extra-large doors and entrance hall indicated its inspiration (Fig. 61). The large entry allowed "farm carts to drive into the inner courtyard." He terraced this court, placing a pool at the first level and a wall fountain at the highest. With both hallway doors open, the vista extended over garden and pool, centering on the distant fountain (Fig. 62). A circular staircase, which provided a private entrance to the master suite from the loggia, appeared high above the hall in a wrought-iron cage (Fig. 63). To the right of the entry a short flight of tiled steps rose to the loggia and the living room beyond (Fig. 64).[41]

Dr. Renfro's Villa Tranquilla resembled Concha Marina in plan (Fig. 65). From the entrance on El Brillo a vaulted stone hall led to

66. Villa Tranquilla, entrance from El Brillo Way.

the dining and living rooms and a loggia on the ocean side of the house (Fig. 66). The kitchen, service rooms, and garage extended westward along El Brillo. In 1931 Mizner remodeled the entrance facade and added several staff rooms.[42]

The six great mansions of 1923 confirmed Mizner's position as Palm Beach's leading society architect. These six houses also mark the change to greater grandeur in Palm Beach architecture. After their construction the owners of older villas began to remodel. Small living rooms became large drawing rooms, dining rooms became banquet-sized, and new wings of guest rooms appeared throughout the town.

Mizner followed the general plan of the Warden house in designing the Villa Flora for Edward Shearson, the New York stockbroker, at the corner of Dunbar and North Ocean Boulevard. The important rooms faced the sea with guest and service wings enclosing the patio (Fig. 67). A formal entrance from Dunbar Road led to a cloistered stone hall that extended through the house (Fig. 68). An arcade opened the living room to the hall. The long living room had a raised dais on the fireplace end. A door opposite the fireplace led to the dining room through a small hall with paneled walls. The dining room formed a separate wing on the southeast corner of the house. The low enclosed passageway helped emphasize the grandeur of the dining room with its many windows and high, beamed

67. Villa Flora, Edward Shearson house, Palm Beach, 1923, North Ocean Boulevard facade.

68. Villa Flora, cloister.

69. Casa Florencia, Preston Pope Satterwhite house, Palm Beach, 1923, living room.

70. Casa Florencia,
dining room.

ceiling. Mizner used pointed arches for window and door-surrounds, completing the Venetian effect with murals "of the rich colors found in the ruins of Pompeii . . . over the doorway and the arches."[43]

At this time, Mizner also designed a larger and more elegant version of the Villa Flora for the corner of South Ocean Boulevard and Clarendon Avenue. His client, Dr. Preston Pope Satterwhite of New York, had married Florence Brokaw Martin, the widow of James E. Martin, who left her a Standard Oil fortune on his death in an automobile accident in 1905. The then "Widow Martin" had also been one of the party on Mizner's first visit to Palm Beach in 1906.[44]

The general plan of the Satterwhites' Casa Florencia conformed to that of the Villa Flora. Mizner placed the entrance and stair hall to the north on Clarendon. From the entrance a two-story guest wing opened to the right and the library and living room to the left. The living room also had a raised dais with a marble railing from the "de Medici Monastery Chapel in Florence, Italy" (Fig. 69). Although Mizner also placed the dining room in a separate wing, at the Casa Florencia he connected it to the main section of the house by a cloister in a style similar to the Warden house. While the dining room of the Villa Flora merely hinted of a churchly origin, the stone

71. Casa Florencia, main stairway.

72. The Towers, William M. Wood house, Palm Beach, 1923, North Ocean Boulevard facade.

walls, vaulted ceiling and ribbed groins, raised apse, stained glass
windows, and iron-grilled altar screen proclaimed the source of the
Casa Florencia's dining room (Fig. 70). The Satterwhites' guests
complained that the "cathedral-like atmosphere" made the room a
place of beauty, "but not altogether cheerful as a place to dine." A
stone stairway, arching over the entrance hall, led to the master
bedrooms on the second floor of the main section of the house (Fig.
71). A large loggia gave access to a roof garden over the cloister.
Statuary mounted in the Italian manner adorned the balustrades of
the roof garden.

Dr. Satterwhite, a noted collector of fifteenth-, sixteenth-, and
seventeenth-century paintings and furniture, proved a demanding
client. Mizner met the challenge and produced one of his most elegant houses. In fact, the Satterwhites' pleasure with Mizner's work
prompted them to commission Percival Dietsch to sculpt a portrait
of the architect in bas-relief to adorn the facade of their villa.[45]

Mizner designed The Towers, another oceanfront project, for
William M. Wood of Boston, the president of the American Woolen
Company. Two towers, one five stories high, gave this house its
name (Fig. 72). On the first floor the towers were joined by a large
loggia with French windows opening on both an interior patio and

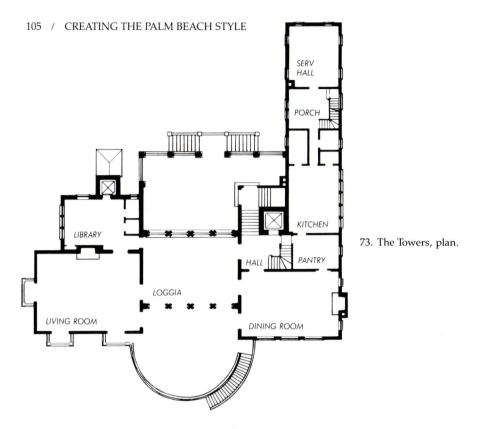

73. The Towers, plan.

74. El Sarimento, Anthony J. Drexel Biddle house, Palm Beach, 1923, original South Ocean Boulevard facade.

75. El Sarimento,
stairway.

an ocean terrace. In the south tower Mizner placed a large open
living room and a small secluded library (Fig. 73). In the north wing
the dining room faced the ocean with the kitchen and service rooms
to the west. A colonnade joined the two towers on the second floor.
Each of the towers had its own elevator. Wood, whose brother-in-
law served as American consul in Madrid, traveled to Spain to purchase the furniture, tapestries, and paintings used to decorate the
first floor. He furnished all the other floors in "art craft style" supplied by workers from the model village he established for his employees in Andover, Massachusetts.[46]

Anthony J. Drexel Biddle purchased Mme. Jeannette Gais's
house shortly after its completion. He then asked Mizner to design
a much larger villa next door (Fig. 74). In 1923 a service road to the
west provided entry to the new house. A heavy iron and cypress

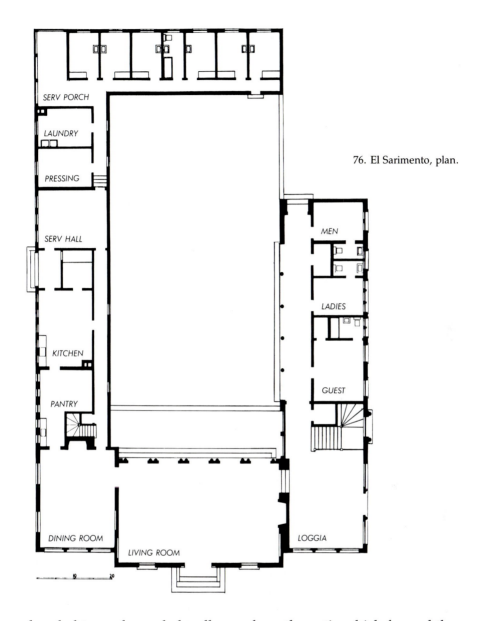

SERV PORCH

LAUNDRY

PRESSING

SERV HALL

KITCHEN

PANTRY

DINING ROOM

LIVING ROOM

MEN

LADIES

GUEST

LOGGIA

76. El Sarimento, plan.

door led to a colonnaded walkway along the patio which formed the approach to the stair hall and loggia (Fig. 75). Along the oceanfront Mizner placed a loggia, massive living room, and dining room (Fig. 76). A kitchen wing on the south and a servants' wing on the west completely enclosed the patio. Joseph Urban remodeled the house in 1927. He moved the entry to the ocean side, making the old dining room the entrance hall, and added a new dining room of ballroom proportions to the south. He also removed the old kitchen wing, forming a far greater patio. To add a new kitchen and service rooms he razed Mme. Jeannette's house.[47]

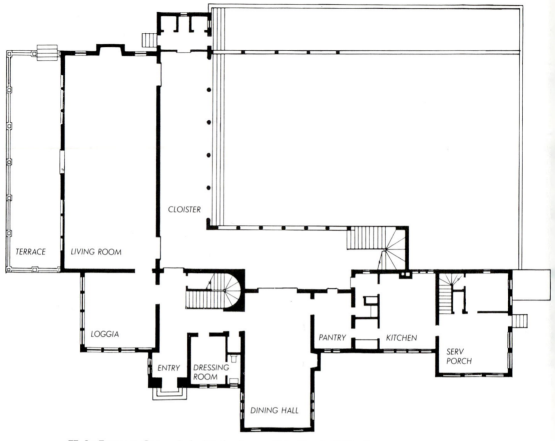

77. La Fontana, George Luke Mesker house, Palm Beach, 1923, plan.

78. Playa Riente, Joshua Cosden house, Palm Beach, 1923, western facade.

79. Playa Riente, entrance showing tunnel to beach.

80. Playa Riente, the great hall.

Mizner described the house for George Luke Mesker, owner of an Evansville, Indiana, steel firm, at 270 South Ocean Boulevard, as in the style of the sixteenth-century Italian Renaissance. A marble patio fountain with life-sized cherubs playing with a fish established the name La Fontana for the house. Mrs. Mesker collected Italian paintings and furnishings and asked Mizner to design the house around her collection. The first floor contained a reception hall, a 63-by-20-foot living room with linen-fold paneling and an ornate ceiling from Italy, a "dining hall," and kitchen and service areas (Fig. 77). The library, bedrooms, and servants' rooms were on the second floor. A tower, which Mizner added later, held an additional bedroom for Mr. Mesker.[48]

On the ocean just north of the Palm Beach Country Club, Mizner designed Playa Riente, his largest house, for the Joshua Cosdens (Fig. 78). Once more, Mizner placed the house directly on the beach ridge, allowing for a lower-floor entry from a western patio. A tunnel through the ridge gave a vista of the beach and ocean from the great double entry doors (Fig. 79). The stone entrance hall, over

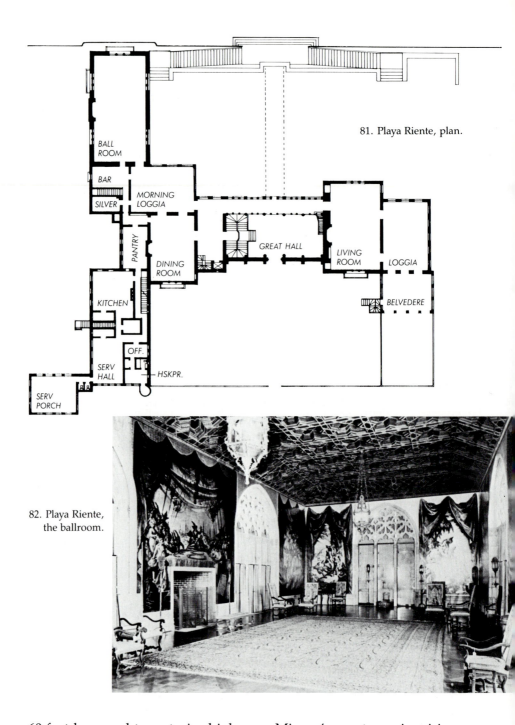

81. Playa Riente, plan.

BALL ROOM

BAR

MORNING LOGGIA

SILVER

PANTRY

DINING ROOM

GREAT HALL

LIVING ROOM

LOGGIA

KITCHEN

BELVEDERE

OFF.

SERV HALL

HSKPR.

SERV PORCH

82. Playa Riente, the ballroom.

60 feet long and two stories high, was Mizner's most awe-inspiring Palm Beach room. He used a rib-vaulted ceiling supported by twisted columns to emphasize the sense of height and space. Filling the north end of the hall, a double stone staircase rose to the main level of the house (Fig. 80). An arcaded mezzanine connected the rest of

the house to the living room and loggia wing. Rising from the mezzanine at the south end, and floating over the hall below, a stairway
encased in a wrought-iron cage led to the master bedrooms. At the
top of the main stairs a lobby gave access to the dining room and
morning loggia (Fig. 81). This loggia also formed the entrance to the
ballroom and the barroom beyond. Later Mizner designed an immense cloister to the north of the ballroom. The kitchen and service
areas, to the northwest, enclosed the western patio.

If the Stotesburys built El Mirasol to assure their social leadership in Palm Beach, the Cosdens built Playa Riente to gain social
recognition. Newspaper reports always stressed the villa's size, often comparing it to the smaller El Mirasol. Starting life as a Baltimore
streetcar conductor, Cosden made a $50 million fortune in Okla-
homa oil. Like other newly wealthy Americans with social ambitions, the Cosdens saw the advantage of the season in Palm Beach.
Their personally vivacious and charming ways, combined with the
largest house in town, gained them early acceptance in Palm Beach
society.[49]

In 1926 the Cosdens sold Playa Riente to Mrs. Horace Dodge,
the widow of the auto maker. Mrs. Cosden said they sold because
Mrs. Dodge offered a million-dollar profit on their investment. Actually Cosden had lost his company and fortune. They sold their
Sands Point and Newport houses at the same time. With the money
raised from these sales Cosden began again and made another fortune, only to lose this one in the Wall Street crash of 1929. He died
in 1940 while working on his third.[50]

Mizner said the Cosden site inspired a vision of "an old Gothic
palace built out into the sea." After receiving the commission he
worked all night on the sketches and never changed them. He was
also proud of the engineering. "The great September storms beat
against foundations and the waves dashed forty feet up its sides,
and they have never had five cents worth of damage." Mrs. Cosden
took a particular interest in the decoration of Playa Riente and traveled to Europe with Mizner to help choose furniture. Mizner said
she became an excellent judge, able to spot the slightest restoration
in an old piece. While in Europe she engaged painters to do frescoes
for the dining room and loggia similar to those in the Davanzati
Palace in Florence and purchased "an ensemble of decorative panels" from José Maria Sert, the Spanish painter. These panels, one of
several sets, depicted the adventures of Sinbad the Sailor. Wilden-
stein Galleries in New York showed the panels before Sert installed
them in the Cosden ballroom (Fig. 82).[51]

The summer of 1923 also saw Mizner constructing a new building to house his design studios and the headquarters for Mizner Industries. As his practice and his various enterprises had produced good profits for several years, the architect believed he could afford a more fashionable office than Histed's remodeled "mule sheds." Until this time, with the exception of the Club and its stores, Worth Avenue had remained largely residential. Palm Beach shopped on Main Street (Royal Poinciana Way) and at the Beaux-Arts Center to the north, along the lake. During this summer Mizner completed a three-story office building on Worth Avenue opposite the Club. The first floor, with a street-front arcade, contained display space for Mizner's pottery and antiques businesses. Mizner's private office and studio, and offices for his business staff, were on the second floor, while a large studio for the architects and draftsmen, and a small apartment, made up the third floor. Mizner's staff moved into the new office before he returned from Europe. This building, the first in the Via Mizner complex, signaled the changing character of Worth Avenue. Within a few years the street became one of the most fashionable shopping thoroughfares in the world.[52]

83. Via Mizner, Palm Beach, 1924.

84. Via Parigi, Palm Beach, 1925, under construction, Via Mizner to the right.

Before he left for Europe on 1 June, Mizner completed design work for these commissions and for remodeling projects for Harold Vanderbilt, the Everglades Club, and J. Leonard Replogle, who had purchased Otto H. Kahn's former house on North Ocean Boulevard. The extent of his summer projects caused the *Palm Beach Post* to exclaim that "those who departed for their northern homes in April will return to find such magical transformation that it would seem nothing short of Aladdin and his lamp could have wrought such miracles."[53]

As Mizner had sold his house on South Ocean Boulevard to Edward Small Moore, he needed a new house once more. During the summer of 1924 he began the Via Mizner shopping complex and Villa Mizner just to the west of his newly completed office building on Worth Avenue. In explaining his concept for the new building, he told a reporter that Spanish castles contained numerous small cellar rooms to house the household army:

With the advent of more civilized times the armies were dismissed and commercially minded people converted the cellar-like rooms into small shops. They usually faced on small winding streets and were entirely open to the people who traversed the narrow pathways.[54]

From its Worth Avenue entrance between the new villa and the office building, an irregular pedestrian street wound its way to Pe-

85. The Plaza Building, Phipps
Plaza, Palm Beach, 1924.

ruvian Avenue, creating the Via Mizner. A covered walkway on the
second floor connected Mizner's house and office and formed the
entrance to the shops (Fig. 83). The small scale of the via with its
many twists and turns allowed the visitor to feel transported to a
small Spanish village.

The five-story villa contained shops on the first floor, living
room, dining room, and kitchen on the second, a mirador studio-
library on the top floor, and bedrooms on the floors in between. The
large living room, furnished with his antiques and the products of
his workshops, was often pictured in Mizner Industries brochures.
He installed paneling from the University of Salamanca in the dining
room. The mirador, reached by elevator, allowed the architect to
survey the entire island. Mizner's only regret in building the villa
was his loss of a garden, a regret shared by his animal menagerie of
Chows, cats, birds, and monkeys. To compensate, Mizner designed
terraces opening off the rooms on the second floor.[55]

Once in his new house, Mizner began a ritual of regular after-
noons-at-home. Sometimes a visiting artist, or even a string quartet,
entertained his guests; more usually, they came to hear Mizner tell
of his adventures in and out of society. At these afternoon parties
Mizner's butler served rum cocktails in antique silver mugs collected

by the architect. Mizner, who disliked drunkenness and the excesses often associated with the Prohibition era, never encouraged his guests to have a second drink.[56]

With the success of the Via Mizner, the architect erected a similar shopping arcade immediately to the west the next summer. In recognition of Singer's financial involvement in these projects, he named it the Via Parigi. The construction of the two vias hurried the process of converting Worth Avenue into a shopping street (Fig. 84). In the next few years various businesses built new stores and converted existing houses to commercial purposes. The eastern end of Worth Avenue retained its residential character for several more years. During the summer of 1923 Mizner had built a small two-family house for his brother Wilson on this part of the street.[57]

Mizner completed several other commercial projects during the summer of 1924. These included a series of shops and apartments for the Phipps family on North County Road (Fig. 85). The Plaza Building formed the anchor of Phipps Plaza and housed the Palm Beach stores of Brooks Brothers and Bonwit Teller. In another commercial project of the summer, Mizner designed a West Palm Beach station for the Seaboard Railroad. The Seaboard, probably

86. Collado Hueco, Paul Moore house, Palm Beach, 1924.

87. Collado Hueco,
loggia.

88. Collado Hueco, dining room.

feeling his plan lacked sufficient grandeur, turned down Mizner's design. The West Palm Beach firm of Harvey & Clarke then received the commission for a more elaborate Spanish Renaissance structure. Although often attributed to Mizner, perhaps because his industries furnished much of the detailing, the overelaboration and ornamentation of the facade lacked the subtlety found in Mizner's work.[58]

The summer of 1924 was the last to have numerous Mizner projects under construction in Palm Beach. While adding to his former house on South Ocean Boulevard for Edward Small Moore, he also built one next door for Moore's brother Paul. This house departed from Mizner's usual construction, since he used coquina rock for the first floor with half-timbering above. As in the design for the Edward Moore house, Mizner took full advantage of the ocean-to-lake site. He placed the loggia and living room in a north wing, giving both rooms vistas of the sea and also allowing them to open upon an enclosed patio on the west side of the house. The dining room in the south wing overlooked the lake (Figs. 86–88).[59]

Mizner also designed a large mansion for John Magee far south of town at this time. The grounds of Lagomar on South Ocean Boulevard stretched from ocean to lake. An arched portico

89. Lagomar, John Magee house, Palm Beach, 1924, dining room with Woodite reproductions of the Salamanca panels.

gave entrance to the imposing hall with tiled floor and wrought-iron
railed staircase. Mizner designed an octagonal room off the hall to
house a carved ceiling imported from Spain. Although he followed
the general plan of living room and dining room separated by a
loggia, in this case he placed the dining room in a separate wing
facing the patio and lake. He used Woodite reproductions of the
Salamanca paneling in this room (Fig. 89). The 50-by-34-foot living
room had a high carved and coffered ceiling and views of both ocean
and lake. The second floor contained a large master suite with sitting
room, and five other bedrooms and baths. Mizner placed the kitchen
and service rooms in a ground-level basement under the dining
room, and the servants' rooms and laundry in a separate building
connected to the main house by an open covered walkway. From the
entrance court this bridge framed a lake view similar to that of the
Claflin house. Shortly after its completion, Magee sold the house to
the Henry Reas. Mrs. Rea, who became a close friend of the architect, commissioned several additions.[60]

Also in the summer of 1924 Mizner made his first trip to
California in twenty years. While there, he purchased a lot on Seventeen-Mile Drive in Pebble Beach and designed a house for his
niece Ysabel Chase. He claimed that he drew the plans on wrapping
paper using only a ruler. The contractor complained of receiving a
roll of wrapping paper and lists of specifications with orders to put
them together. "If I was a bum architect, he was a good contractor,
for it all fitted together." Mizner enjoyed this type of self-deprecating
story, and probably told it many times.[61]

The architect's involvement in land boom development schemes
in 1925 virtually ended his work in Palm Beach. Early in the year he
designed a two-family house on Peruvian Avenue for H. Halpine
Smith, the son-in-law of the supplier of the Georgian clay for Las
Manos potteries, who came to Palm Beach as business manager of
Mizner Industries, and his only known West Palm Beach house for
Karl Riddle, his engineer. He also designed a large three-story building for Singer on Royal Palm Way. The first floor, with elaborate
exterior Gothic detailing, contained offices. The second and third
floors held small apartments arranged around a tiled second story
patio.[62]

Many different versions of a Palm Beach house for Mrs. William K. Vanderbilt, Jr., also date from this year. Birdie Vanderbilt,
Tessie Oelrichs's sister, befriended the architect in his early years in
New York. The various plans for the large house all show a completely enclosed patio with a living room, loggia, and library over-

90. Casa Nana, George Rasmussen house, Palm Beach, 1926, western facade and stair tower.

91. Casa Nana, ocean facade.

looking the ocean. Mrs. Vanderbilt proved a difficult client, demanding many changes and revisions in the plans. Mizner, involved in
the Boca Raton project, became disgusted with a further request for
changes and told her to "pee or get off the pot." According to Alex
Waugh, the architect's insulting language led her to drop the project.
As a friend of twenty years, Mrs. Vanderbilt could not have been
surprised by Mizner's language; nonetheless, she never built the
house.[63]

In the spring of 1926 Mizner designed a large villa for George
S. Rasmussen, a Danish immigrant who founded the National Tea
Company, a chain of grocery stores based in the Midwest. The house,
named Casa Nana for Mrs. Rasmussen, at 780 South Ocean Boulevard, was entered from the west off County Road. A round stair
tower with an open stepped arcade following the rise of the stairs
dominated the western facade (Fig. 90). Mizner placed the entrance
at the base of the tower. A short flight of stairs rose to a rectangular
foyer and the dining room directly beyond. To the right a large
loggia, open to terraces on both the ocean and patio sides of the
house, led to the living room which occupied the entire southern
wing (Fig. 91). On the second floor Mizner repeated the loggia, thus
separating the principal bedrooms. The kitchen and service rooms
occupied a 65-foot-long wing on the north side of the house.[64]

92. La Puertas, Nate Spingold house, Palm Beach, 1929, loggia.

93. Casa Bendita, John S. Phipps house, patio.

The Rasmussen house is responsible for the most persistent of the Mizner myths, that he originally forgot the staircase and added the exterior stair tower to keep from spoiling the plan. Without the stair tower the western facade had no focus. The tower also functioned to shield the loggia and western patio from the entrance court. In fact, Lester Geisler, a Mizner associate, said the architect's design started with the stair tower. Mizner placed open exterior staircases on many houses, including those of John Phipps, William Warden, George Mesker, and Gurnee Munn. Given the Florida climate during the few months their owners occupied these houses, he saw no reason for enclosing the stairs.[65]

Casa Nana proved to be Mizner's last large Palm Beach mansion. Nonetheless, his work of just a few short years left an indelible mark on town architecture. His design philosophy adhered to simple rules: "to fit house to setting and to make people comfortable in it; and then to make it as attractive as possible without showing too much effort." Most of his Florida clients sought a carefree vacation life devoted to parties, house guests, and sport. While they might "dress for dinner," the daytime called for hours on the beach, the tennis court, and golf course. The houses Mizner designed for them uniquely expressed these multiple functions.

Daytime life in a Mizner house centered on the loggia. Perhaps inspired by the Hawaiian lanai and a legacy of the architect's island experiences, the loggia became a trademark of his design. Large houses, like the Warden villa, El Mirasol, and Playa Riente, often had two: one for breakfast and lunch, a second serving as an informal living room. While he specified subdued unglazed or black

94. Daniel H. Carstairs
house, patio.

floor tiles in more formal rooms, loggias became almost Moorish
with their colorful patterns of tile (Fig. 92). A common treatment
combined Las Manos glazed tiles, often including Mizner blue, on
the floor and polychrome imported tiles for wall fountains and niches.
Mizner's loggias had a close relationship to the out-of-doors. These
daytime rooms opened with walls of glass that in pleasant weather
could slide back to admit the sun and breeze. He broke the great
expanses of glass with doubled cast columns which provided both
exterior and interior decoration. These rooms also had easy access
to terraces and patios. Mizner recognized that the weather drew
people to Florida and his houses allowed them to take full advantage
of its benefits.

Every Mizner house had a patio. In large oceanfront villas like
those of the Stotesburys, Satterwhites, Wardens, and Phipps these
faced west and were enclosed by the house on three sides (Fig. 93).
In the case of smaller ell-shaped houses, such as the Winns, Renfros,
and Mizner's own Concha Marina, walls marked the patio's bound-
aries. Sheltered by house and walls, the patio provided a private

area for outdoor activities. Usually the major rooms, and particularly the loggia, opened onto a paved terrace. In the grandest houses, like El Mirasol, Casa Florencia, La Fontana, and Villa Flora, an arcaded cloister provided access to the patio. Wicker furniture from Mizner Industries made the terrace an informal outdoor room. At the center of the patio Mizner placed a tiled fountain or pool with paved walks radiating outward to entrances to the house, outside staircases, and wall fountains. Often, as in the Kingsley and Carstairs houses, he designed the patios on several levels with shallow steps and low retaining walls separating the different planes. On the second floor, arcaded galleries, bedroom balconies, and open decks provided views of the patio below (Fig. 94).

A contemporary critic said Florida architects made a "mistake" in the Spanish house by designing a court, a large walled garden, rather than a patio. He argued that a Spanish patio, as an outdoor room, needed room dimensions; that it should be no greater than 30 by 30 feet in even the largest house. Moreover, he also insisted it should be completely paved and furnished with potted plants. In 1922 Mizner designed a house for Willis Sharpe Kilmer, the multimillionaire owner of Swamproot, a well-known patent

95. La Bellucia, entry hall.

medicine, with a completely enclosed tiled central patio. Although Kilmer never built the house, the plans show Mizner's ability to use a "true" Spanish patio and yet adapt it to Palm Beach conditions. On the east-west axis of the Kilmer patio Mizner placed the loggia and dining room. Both rooms had floor-to-ceiling windows, allowing the eye to expand the size of the patio and at the same time providing the natural ventilation the south Florida climate demanded.[66]

96. Villa Flora, Edward Shearson house, stairway.

In reality, Mizner's clients asked for courts rather than "true" patios. Although Marion Sims Wyeth designed several houses with small centered patios, they never became popular in Palm Beach. The large court allowed a garden, even on the oceanfront, since the house protected delicate plants from the harsh seaspray. Moreover, these courts, lavishly landscaped with orange and mimosa trees that bloomed during the season, banyans and palms, colorfully leafed crotons and other exotic shrubs, served as the setting for Palm Beach's

97. The Plaza Building, stairway.

largest entertainments. Not even El Mirasol or Casa Florencia could hold the hundreds of guests who came to Edward Stotesbury's birthday party or Florence Satterwhite's opera recitals.[67]

Just as Mizner created an atmosphere for carefree daytime life, his designs also allowed the house to become the setting for the more formal activities of the evening. Mizner's clients entertained at home and wished to impress their guests. Even in his smallest houses, Mizner provided formal entranceways. Some opened to the out-of-doors and patio with only wrought-iron gates serving as protection from the street. From these open foyers, patio cloisters gave access to the main rooms of the house. In other villas heavy wooden doors decorated with bands of wrought iron or large ornamental hinges and nails opened into halls with walls and ceilings of vaulted stone, or incised plaster to give the appearance of stone, which imparted the impression of strength and permanence to structures completed in only a few months (Fig. 95). In the daytime these halls created a visually "cool" transition from the bright outdoor sunshine to the living areas of the house. At night they served as a foil to the more richly decorated party rooms.

The stairway became the usual focus of Mizner's entrance halls. He preferred stone risers with either stone or wrought-iron balustrades. As a characteristic mark of his work he often left the undersides of the seemingly unsupported heavy stone risers exposed, which, through the mystery, injected tension into the design (Figs. 96, 97). As few of Mizner's houses originally included swimming pools, his clients and their guests swam in the ocean. Mizner placed changing and shower rooms convenient to the entrance. He usually designed separate facilities for men and women that could also serve as party dressing rooms. In the Carstairs house he even fitted one on top of the other on a mezzanine level.

Mizner's living rooms and dining rooms showed his talents as a decorator. Even in small houses, Mizner designed large living rooms with high beamed, paneled, or coffered ceilings of pecky cypress. Mizner claimed credit for "discovering" the local pecky cypress, which he used for woodwork, doors, and especially ceilings. He found the "imperfections," which had caused the lumber trade to judge the wood nearly worthless, perfect for imparting a sense of antiquity to his rooms. All Mizner living rooms and most dining rooms included wide fireplaces with often elaborate stone mantels cast by Mizner Industries or, as in the case of the Rasmussen house, purchased by the architect on his trips to Europe. While he occasionally used paneling, more usually he painted walls in light

98. Villa Mizner, dining room with Salamanca panels.

colors to contrast with the ceiling and carved wooden doors. He
opened his living rooms with many windows and French doors,
often centering three each on ocean and patio sides of the room. On
oceanfront windows and doors he sometimes added patterned
wrought-iron gates for both security and decoration.

Dining rooms, reserved almost exclusively for evening entertainment, also had pecky cypress ceilings and often reproductions
of Mizner's Salamanca paneling (Fig. 98). While usually less detailed
than his living rooms, those in the Satterwhite, Shearson, and Cosden houses were among his most elaborate Palm Beach rooms. In
furnishing living rooms Mizner often combined Spanish or Italian

antiques and reproductions with contemporary furniture. In dining rooms he used long refectory tables surrounded by wood and leather chairs, again, either antique or made by Mizner Industries. He favored tapestries and works of religious art, particularly triptychs, for wall decoration and he hung plain velvet curtains at windows.

Mizner produced the splendor his clients required, though he never forgot that these formal rooms served primarily as settings for people. Even in the largest room, his scale rarely became overwhelming, and with his favorite lighting of cathedral candles in tall standards it could be intimate. With particularly long rooms, as in the case of the Shearson, Satterwhite, and Stotesbury living rooms, he raised the level at one end, visually dividing and shortening the space. Finally, he arranged furniture into conversational groupings, furthering the illusion of intimacy even in the largest room (Fig. 99).

Mizner designed his houses to provide a natural flow from room to room, allowing the circulation necessary for a large party.

99. Villa Flora, living room.

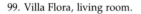

100. Casa Nana, George Rasmussen house, double loggias.

He also coupled the ease of movement with visual drama: a tiled wall fountain or a statuary niche seen as a distant vista down a long corridor, or a glimpse of ocean or patio pool framed by a carefully placed arch. The normal progression of a party took on theatrical qualities in a Mizner house. After assembling in the living room, guests at the Satterwhites' moved through the long cloister to the dining room with its high vaulted ceiling which opened like a cathedral before them. At the Shearson and Warden villas guests followed a similar path, and at Playa Riente the scale became even more grand as they moved along the second level cloister above the great entrance hall. In Mizner's smaller houses hallways or loggias separating living and dining rooms served the same dramatic purpose. Thus Mizner's houses could be informal and comfortable settings of convenience and relaxation, and elegant theatrical backdrops for the most formal entertainment. The architect, who understood his clients, gave them houses that met both their needs and their demands for pageantry.

The owner of a Palm Beach villa expected house guests. Mizner, often a house guest himself, understood the desire of both host and guest for privacy. In even his smaller houses he secluded family bedrooms from those of the visitors. In the Winn and Wood villas separate towers housed guests. Often Mizner's plans placed guests in isolated wings with private entrances, or used second floor loggias, as in the Vanderbilt and Rasmussen houses, to divide family and visitors' rooms (Fig. 100). His guest rooms provided private or adjoining baths, spacious closet space, and in some large houses, lockboxes for valuables. As life in the Palm Beach house centered on the downstairs public rooms, on the whole, Mizner designed plain, unadorned bedrooms, although owners' suites usually included fireplaces and often separate bathrooms for mistress and master.

Mizner also designed for the south Florida climate. During the months of the winter season daytime temperatures could reach the upper eighties, and even higher. To cool his houses in an era without air-conditioning he took advantage of the prevailing south and east winds siting his houses so that major rooms had eastern and southern exposures. In certain designs, such as the Kingsley house, by stepping the bays of each room he gained both exposures. He usually planned his houses around patios, making them one room deep and permitting through ventilation. Rooms open to two exposures were usual, three exposures common. Western cloisters shaded the major rooms during the hottest part of the day. Where possible he placed kitchens in separate wings to the north and west of his houses, allowing the natural breeze from the southeast to remove cooking odors. In oceanfront villas he included interior shutters and tinted and stained glass windows to protect against sea glare. High ceilings added to the natural ventilation. In some houses, as in the owners' rooms at El Mirasol, ventilators allowed the warm air to escape from the ceiling. Tile floors and the sparing use of rugs and curtains also contributed to the cooling effect as did small pools and fountains.

Alva Johnston called Mizner's adaptation of Spanish architecture "Bastard-Spanish-Moorish-Romanesque-Gothic-Renaissance-Bull-Market-Damn-the-Expense Style." Numerous writers have copied this phrase to explain the Palm Beach style of the twenties. Mizner might have approved; in fact, he might have said the same thing. Unlike the archaeologically correct Spanish Colonial work of Califor-

nia architects who had been influenced by the Bertram Goodhue
buildings of the 1915 San Diego Exposition, Mizner never claimed
to faithfully reproduce an exact copy of a Spanish period or particular building. He planned his houses for the climate and for modern
convenience:

. . . technically the old Spanish house was a castle. The windows were high above
the ground and usually barred. There was one heavy plank entrance door, some
six inches thick. This construction was necessary in view of the poor policing of the
times. Behind these heavy exterior walls the house was designed around a patio—
the open court in the center of the building. Of course in Florida there is no need
of designing a house in that way. There was nothing to do but to turn the old
Spanish house inside out, so to speak; put plenty of openings on the outside walls
to let the sunshine and air into the house, and, in other ways make people feel that
they were living out-of-doors. The patio was retained so that people did not lose
the openness inside the Spanish plan. . . . The important rooms of the living portion of the house are related to the patio, generally in such a way that they face both
ways, with a view outdoors as well as a view into the patio.[68]

101. Villa Flora, roof lines.

Mizner retained what he saw as the essential features of the Spanish parti, and especially the patio, while adapting the general plan for the south Florida problems of terrain and climate. As Spain served as a melting pot for so many architectural styles, he could choose elements from all and still claim he adhered to Spanish tradition.

In his Palm Beach buildings Mizner used flat facades with textured stucco walls painted in pastel colors to soften the glare from sun and sea, clay tiles for his roofs, which he found "lovely among the cocoanut trees," and masses of windows "to let in the sunshine and air"; he limited his applied exterior decoration and detailing to an occasional ornate cast-stone window or door-surmount, a series of columns separating bands of windows, or a balcony projecting from a stairway window. Finding Florida "flat as a pancake," he employed towers to project lift, varied roofline levels on even the smallest structures, and added chimney caps, often with several designs on the same house, to achieve the "strong skylines" that gave his buildings their picturesque quality (Fig. 101). Moreover, he believed his best inspiration sprang from envisioning a long and colorful history for his buildings. Although he gained inspiration from trips to Spain and Italy and from collections of architectural photographs, he never copied specific historical structures or attempted to adhere to a strict style. His painterly approach to design meant that he visualized a complete building with each of the elements a part of the whole. Combining simplified and modified components from various regions and periods, Mizner's synthesis produced a unique architectural style all his own.[69]

As to the "Bull-Market-Damn-the-Expense" aspect of Johnston's description, Mizner might have disagreed. The architect claimed his clients almost always asked for inexpensive houses, arguing that they occupied them only a few months each year. While Mizner rarely designed inexpensive houses, their costs have often been exaggerated. Builder Cooper Lightbown secured a $300,000 permit for Playa Riente, the largest and most expensive. Later newspaper stories claimed the final cost exceeded a half-million dollars. While this excluded land and furnishings, the total figure remained far less than the artisan-crafted mansions of Flagler and Deering. Moreover, Mizner originally designed only a few very grand Palm Beach mansions. His houses became large as he and other architects constantly remodeled and added to them over the years. Mizner planned additions for at least twelve of his earlier houses; other architects enlarged at least eighteen of them. Permits filed with the Palm Beach buildings department and articles from the *Palm Beach Post* record original estimated costs for many Mizner houses. Of these, the town issued permits for Satterwhite at $175,000, Mesker and Wood, $100,000, Warden and Shearson, $80,000, Carstairs, $70,000, and Claflin and Speidel, $60,000. The Gais, Woodward, Thomas, Cudahy, Mitchell, and Wanamaker houses had permits for under $50,000, while the recorded cost of the frame and stucco villa of Angier Duke was only $20,000. Although final costs always exceeded the permit figures, even in terms of 1920 dollars most were hardly extravagant houses.[70]

The actual number of houses and other buildings that Mizner designed for Palm Beach between 1919 and 1926 will probably never be known. His office inventory list included names that no longer can be matched to specific houses. To add to the problem, in some cases the inventory also omitted known projects. Mizner's influence on Palm Beach architecture is not dependent on the number of buildings he completed. Mizner set a style. His wealthy and socially prominent clients dictated fashion in the resort. Conservative in their tastes and outlook, they wished to live and play in established settings mellowed by time. They pointed with pride to the staircase like the one in the Burgos Cathedral, or the ceiling similar to the Davanzati Palace. As many also possessed new fortunes, the antiquity Mizner built into their houses substituted for the impressive family histories they lacked. Moreover, Mizner designed attractive buildings. A master of proportion, his architecture seemed perfectly suited to locale and climate. Thus the style itself became fashionable.

In 1919 Palm Beachers lived in Cape Cod cottages, Swiss chalets, shingled bungalows, and Beaux-Arts mansions. By 1925 Mizner's influence could be seen in almost every structure built in the town. Even owners of earlier houses remodeled to conform to the new style. Whether designed by Mizner or other architects, stucco walls, red-tile roofs, and Mediterranean architectural ornamentation had become the rule for Palm Beach.

5

Boca Raton

By the time of the Florida land boom of the mid-twenties, Addison Mizner had become one of America's leading society architects. His Palm Beach success provided him financial security and fame. Now in the most productive period of his life, he continued to design mansions for Palm Beach, received the commission for his first church, planned a hotel for Paris Singer's Palm Beach Ocean venture, and opened his own gigantic development at Boca Raton. The Boca Raton resort, projected as the capstone of Mizner's career, gave him an opportunity to design an entire city in his own unique interpretation of Spanish-style architecture. He was able to complete only a few of the projected buildings before the boom ended, however. The collapse also saw the waning of the popularity of Mizner's architecture in Palm Beach.

The area from Miami to West Palm Beach had developed rapidly during the time Mizner was laboring to fashion a new Palm Beach for America's elite. Following Henry Flagler's railroad, which opened southeast Florida to settlement, Carl Fisher's Dixie Highway and Henry Ford's flivver made it available to the large American middle class. Coolidge prosperity gave many the ability to enjoy a holiday in Florida's mild winter climate and to consider owning their own vacation houses. The prosperity convinced others that their fortunes lay in Florida land. The success stories of early arrivals fed these hopes. With increasing use of the automobile and Florida's easy accessibility to the populous cities of the Northeast and Midwest, an ever-enlarging stream of tourists found its way south. Some, revolting against life in northern cities and longing to enjoy their

134

leisure in Florida's sunshine, or lured by promises of freedom from state income and inheritance taxes, came to stay.[1]

All these factors accounted for the growing interest in Florida. Various state business and real estate boosters promoted this interest to produce the great land boom. Carl G. Fisher, founder of the Indianapolis Speedway, realized the possibilities for Florida real estate in the period before World War I. Having recently sold his Prest-O-Lite Company to Union Carbide, he decided to invest his profits in Miami Beach. After helping to complete the first bridge from the mainland, he began large-scale dredging operations that filled in acres of mangrove swamp with bottom sand from Biscayne Bay. As an early motoring enthusiast he organized the effort to build the national coast-to-coast Lincoln Highway. He now turned his attention to the construction of the north-south road system that became Dixie Highway, the artery that brought millions of people to Florida and to her land bargains.[2]

Many of the sales techniques originated by Fisher on Miami Beach became standard with later real estate promotions. He built a hotel to house prospective purchasers of his lots. Later developments almost always began with the announcement of plans for a large hotel. He produced large-scale plat maps showing individual lots for buyers to choose from in his offices. This practice, always followed by later promoters, could lead to abuses. The maps never showed the several feet of water that might cover the lots much of the year. Fisher realized that numbers of Americans had become increasingly interested in sports, both as spectators and participants. He therefore built golf courses, polo fields, and a course for motorboat racing. Plans for sports facilities, and especially golf courses, became a necessity for later developments. Finally, Fisher launched a national publicity campaign. He invented the Miami Beach bathing beauty who appeared on billboards in snowy northern cities over the caption, "It's Always June in Miami Beach." He placed full-page advertisements in newspapers across the country, and he did everything possible to keep Miami Beach stories on the front page. In one case Fisher persuaded President-elect Harding to play golf on a Miami Beach course using Rosie, a pet elephant, as caddy. Every later developer understood the need for publicity, and the bizarre and ballyhoo promotions that followed came to characterize the era.[3]

Fisher's plans for Miami Beach included extensive tropical landscaping, but no architectural guidelines. There resulted an eclectic mixture of styles, so characteristic of later Miami Beach. Although George E. Merrick followed many of the practices originated by Fisher, he saw his Coral Gables development as a new town, providing recreational, cultural, and educational facilities, all unified by a Spanish architectural style. Merrick, who said he wished to "build castles in Spain," planned to make Coral Gables Miami's finest and most elegant suburb.

Like Fisher, Merrick understood the uses of publicity. He even hired the former Democratic presidential candidate William Jennings Bryan as a lecturer and salesman to promote his enterprise. Both Miami Beach and Coral Gables drew national attention. Other developers announced plans for new subdivisions and cities. Soon the boosters talked of a seventy-mile-long city of millions that would include the entire southeast coast in its borders.[4]

Moreover, Floridians decided to promote their state. Their objectives included bringing tourists to Florida and then selling them land. They set out to accomplish these goals in two ways. First, they inaugurated campaigns to take the Florida "message" to as many northerners as possible. These campaigns, sponsored by the chambers of commerce of various cities and local real estate organizations, aimed at attracting tourists. One plan called for local residents to mail 100,000 postcards before the start of the 1924/25 winter season bearing "pictures and messages calculated to draw friends and relatives" to Florida. The West Palm Beach Chamber of Commerce published 50,000 publicity booklets featuring the "best-appearing young men and women" in the area to show the "allurements of this section." Finally, businessmen formed the All-Florida Development Conference to raise $200,000 to advertise the state "throughout the world."[5]

The second part of the campaign aimed at convincing investors of the soundness of real estate values in Florida. To accomplish this, a continuing flow of stories in local newspapers told of the opening of new projects, developments, and subdivisions; of the profits made from land and real estate sales; of constantly rising values in building activities and bank clearings; of famous individuals who purchased land in the area; and of projected plans for new streets, parks, and water and sewerage systems. Promoters designed these stories to show the dynamic growth of southeast Florida and boost the confidence of prospective buyers that property could only increase in value.

Since a boom is based on confidence, the local newspapers particularly emphasized the profits to be made by investors. A common story told of property reselling several times in a few weeks, doubling in price with each resale. The tales seemed endless. A lot increased in value $750 an hour when a buyer paid $11,000 for a 100-foot lot at three in the afternoon and resold it at five for $12,500. In Palm Beach a thirty-two acre tract purchased in 1916 for $76,000 sold in 1924 for a million. Nine months later the same tract, subdivided into building lots, sold at auction for $1,757,647.[6]

The campaigns worked. By the 1924/25 season millions of Americans had caught the "boom bacillus." They poured into the state, choking the 18-foot-wide Dixie Highway with a constant stream of dense traffic; the railroads and steamship lines proved inadequate to the demands made upon them. The newcomers bought at least $300 million in real estate during the season.[7]

Palm Beach attempted to remain aloof from the land rush; the typical seasonal visitor had no interest in speculating in 35-foot lots. Like his friends and clients, Mizner also seemed unaffected by the growing boom. His office remained busy. In just seven years he completed the Everglades and Gulfstream Clubs, over thirty large houses, and several commercial and office buildings. Nonetheless, as the 1924/25 season approached, even staid Palm Beach no longer remained immune to the "Florida Frenzy." James H. R. Cromwell, Mrs. Stotesbury's son, gathered a group of investors (which included his mother) and founded the American-British Investment Corporation to build Floranada, a gigantic development on the ocean just north of Fort Lauderdale; Paris Singer planned the new island resort of Palm Beach Ocean, across the inlet north of Palm Beach; and Mizner announced his great development at Boca Raton.

It is not surprising that Mizner, too, succumbed. His entire life had prepared him for the land boom. He had always been interested in the main chance, the possibility of an easy dollar. Moreover, he had always associated with people of great wealth: as an architect, and often as a friend, but never as an equal. Thus, Boca Raton became his chance for fortune and equality. By the fall of 1924, although financially secure, his responsibilities had also become heavy. He felt a continuing obligation to his brother Wilson. His sister Min and her husband had lost Stag's Leap, their California estate, and their children, Ysabel and Horace, became a part of Addison's extended household. Finally, the Rev. Henry Mizner's health had suffered and he retired to Florida with his family. The possibilities of fortune from land development would solve the family's problems and help cement Addison's position as its head. Finally, as an architect and an artist, Mizner saw the possibility of designing his masterpiece. Although his work had transformed Palm Beach, it had been done within the framework of the existing town, and side by side with the work of many other architects and builders. The development of Boca Raton gave Mizner his opportunity to create an entire city, an opportunity to design a harmonious community in his unique interpretation of Spanish architecture which would capture the picturesque and romantic appeal of Old Spain.

Mizner became actively involved in development schemes in the summer of 1924. He first planned a community at "Mizner Mile," a strip of oceanfront land at Boynton Beach, ten miles south of Palm Beach. The project included a 2,000-room hotel modeled along the "lines of a Spanish monastery," a polo field, and several large Mizner-designed houses. Unfortunately, Ocean Drive at this point ran along the beach. To provide privacy and direct ocean access for his development, Mizner built a new road to the west. Landowners in the area protested the loss of the public beach. Before the protesters could take legal action, Mizner attempted to destroy the old road in the middle of the night. Local landowners stopped the bulldozers, which Wilson directed in white tie. The unfavorable publicity, the growing cost of land in the Boynton Beach area, and the lack of local cooperation all convinced the architect to end development of the Mizner Mile.[8]

The first hint that Mizner had transferred his major interest to the small, newly incorporated town of Boca Raton came on 17 March 1925 when the *Palm Beach Post* reported that Rodman Wanamaker had purchased three-quarters of a mile of beachfront property for $1 million. In the next few weeks Mizner and a group of associates quietly purchased additional parcels of land. By mid-April the Mizner organization had acquired two miles of beachfront at the Boca Raton Inlet and a total of 1,600 acres of "ideally situated high land directly back of this ocean frontage—probably the finest piece of property anywhere in the south of Florida."

With the necessary property acquired, Mizner announced his plans for Boca Raton on 15 April 1925. To spearhead Palm Beach County's largest development, the architect unveiled sketches of "Castillo del Rey," the world's "most complete and artistic hostelry." The $6 million, 1,000-room hotel centered on a projecting pavilion with an ornate Gothic entry surrounded by tracery (Fig. 102). Severe six- and seven-story wings connected by arcaded and balconied sections of three stories, soaring bell towers, walled gardens, and acres of red barrel tiles completed the design.[9]

Mizner planned Boca Raton as "the world's most architecturally beautiful playground." Immediate construction of the hotel, two golf courses designed by Donald Ross, a polo field, a casino, and a

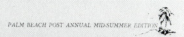

102. Mizner Development
Corporation advertisement
showing sketch of
oceanfront hotel
for Boca Raton, 1925.

million dollars in other improvements projected for the first year
placed the development in the forefront of Florida real estate ventures.

The syndicate which formed the new Mizner Development
Corporation included such "noted personages" as Lytle Hull, Harold Vanderbilt, J. Leonard Replogle, the Duchess of Sutherland, Paris
Singer, Jesse L. Livermore, Irving Berlin, W. K. Vanderbilt II, Madame Frances Alda, Wilson Mizner, W. C. Robinson, H. H. Rodgers,

D. H. Conkling, A. T. Herd, Porte Quinn, Elizabeth Arden, Clarence H. Geist, T. Coleman du Pont, and Rodman Wanamaker. Although all had Palm Beach connections, and several had been Mizner clients, they were also well-known leaders of America's social, financial, business, and entertainment worlds. In spite of this, Mizner insisted that the "average Floridian" be allowed to participate in the venture and made $500,000 of the corporation's $5 million capital stock available to the public. In less than a week, all of the stock had been subscribed.[10]

As Mizner feared, once the plans for Boca Raton became public the remaining tracts of land in the town doubled and tripled in value with investors bidding higher and higher to purchase any available acreage. Nonetheless, the Mizner Corporation continued to add to its holdings, buying a 255-acre tract in May and purchasing an additional area for $4 million in June.[11]

Within a week of the announcement, George Fryhofer, a prominent West Palm Beach real estate dealer and auctioneer, was appointed sales manager, and advertisements for Boca Raton began to appear in both local and northern newspapers. These advertisements combined a curious mixture of snob appeal and greed appeal:

The owners and controllers of the Mizner Development Corporation are a group of very rich men—men of unlimited means, who propose to build from the creative genius of Addison Mizner, what will probably be the most wonderful resort city in the world . . . the combined wealth of the stockholders . . . probably represents considerably over one-third of the entire wealth of the United States. . . . It is reasonable to suppose that every lot buyer . . . should make quick and large profits.[12]

From the beginning, company advertisements also prominently displayed the names of Mizner's backers. The first land sales in Miami and West Palm Beach caused automobile-jammed streets and "pandemonium" in the offices. Purchasers paid $2 million for lots, an opening day record.[13]

East Flagler Street in Miami quickly became the center for South Florida real estate speculation. All major developers and real estate companies felt compelled to have offices on the street. The Mizner Development Corporation paid $275,000 to take over a ninety-nine year lease on "Ye Wayside Inn" at 133 East Flagler. The company then spent many more thousands to convert the restaurant into a Spanish showplace with a "magnificent cathedral-like interior," a small sample of the new Boca Raton.[14]

Just before the first lots went on the market, Mizner reported that the Ritz-Carlton Investment Corporation had contracted to build a Ritz-Carlton hotel in place of his Castillo del Rey. Since the Ritz management involved personal service to a limited number of guests, the new plans called for a reduction in the size of the hotel. Warren & Wetmore, the New York architectural firm that designed the Grand Central Terminal and the New York Central Building, received the commission for the interior plans and layout of rooms. Still, Mizner remained the principal architect, with responsibilities for the hotel's exterior appearance. Ritz-Carlton participation added to the interest that Mizner's project had aroused around the country.[15]

Although obviously pleased by the Ritz-Carlton connection, Mizner feared that Warren & Wetmore's participation could delay construction. Since he believed a hotel necessary for the promotion of the development, on 23 May he announced plans to build the 100-room Boca Raton Inn on the west shore of Lake Boca Raton. In his haste to start construction of the hotel, Mizner ordered the site staked out immediately. This forced his engineer to advise him that he first needed dimensions and floor plans. Mizner hastily complied, but continued to rush completion of the small inn, scheduling the opening for January 1926.[16]

Throughout the summer and into the fall of 1925 the Mizner organization's publicity, now under the direction of Harry Reichenbach, a professional press agent, seemed calculated to maintain the concept of constant growth and activity in Boca Raton. When Reichenbach had no news of lot sales or company plans to release, his advertisements hinted at the untold thousands of people interested in Boca Raton. "English, French, Spanish, Austrian, and Italian people like the zest and snap of American life." With T. Coleman du Pont, W. K. Vanderbilt, J. L. Replogle, and others supplying the money to build hotels, shops, restaurants, and theaters to attract them, European tourists would buy real estate in Boca Raton. The climate acted as the "magnet" that brought Americans and their "surplus wealth." In fact, one advertisement avowed that the Gulf Stream "bends westward at Boca Raton until it almost touches the land." Readers could draw only one conclusion: Mizner's resort represented America's greatest investment opportunity.[17]

Interest in Boca Raton remained high. With the second offering of lots the company again sold over $2 million worth in Miami and West Palm Beach. The organization claimed sales of over $1 million in the first twenty minutes, with baskets of sales slips remaining uncounted. Moreover, additional offices opened in New York City, Philadelphia, Pittsburgh, Chicago, and Boston.

As the Mizner company continued its sales pitch, other developers, anxious to be part of the great Florida venture, also planned Boca Raton projects. In early June, George W. Harvey, a West Palm Beach and Boston real estate man, opened "Villa Rica at Boca Raton." Harvey proposed to build a complete 1,400-acre Spanish-style city within the Boca Raton city limits. He announced plans to spend $2 million immediately on a Florida East Coast railway station and a 100-room hotel. Other early south-county developments included Del-Raton, Boca del Faro, and Del Boca. As activity picked up in the fall, W. A. Mathes, a West Palm Beach promoter, purchased a tract for $3 million to develop an "American Venice," and G. Frank Croissant, a Fort Lauderdale and Chicago developer, announced "Croissantania," a 2,360-acre tract north of the Mizner land and west of the Dixie Highway at prices "available to working men who could aid in the upbuilding of the entire community." Boca Raton Heights; Boca Vista, on the "highlands of Boca Raton," 30 feet above sea level and "overlooking the entire city"; and Boca Centrale, "in the heart of the city," all quickly joined the first list of projects.[18]

Some of these developers purchased land from Mizner and conformed to his standards. Others competed with the Mizner Development Corporation and hoped to profit from its publicity. The company attempted to protect its interests whenever possible. It ordered competitors' signs removed from Boca Raton property and protested Villa Rica's passenger station advertisement to the Florida East Coast Railway.[19]

In late May Mizner received appointment as city planner for Boca Raton. The company announced that the mayor, city officials, and residents wished the entire area of incorporation to be uniformly platted. Although there is no evidence that Mizner had a particular interest in city planning, as an architect he had formed concepts of what he found appropriate and interesting in urban design. Moreover, he could call upon Karl Riddle, his engineer, to undertake the technical side of the platting.

Mizner's scheme for the new resort city combined the artist's appreciation for picturesque and unified design, and the developer's need to divide the acreage into as many saleable lots as possible. Mizner took responsibility for the layout of the city and its most important buildings. Moreover, he retained artistic and architectural approval of all major construction. One company advertisement avowed, "Under the hand of Addison Mizner every public building shall take its form and no building shall take form, color or substance until his approval shall indicate that his vision shall be carried forward to completion by such a structural contribution." On the

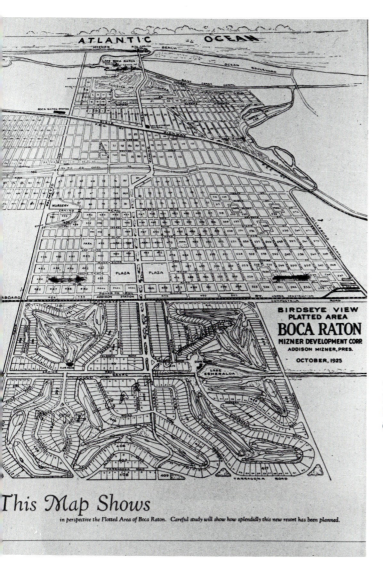

103. Plat plan for
Boca Raton, Mizner
Development
Corporation, 1925.

other hand, the actual platting, in the hands of Riddle's engineering firm, conformed to the common South Florida scheme of uniform, squared blocks with 25- and 35-foot lots. The exception to this pattern, Ritz-Carlton Park, a subdivision at the extreme western end of the city, had Olmstedesque meandering streets and spacious lots overlooking the fairways and lakes of the Ritz-Carlton golf courses (Fig. 103). In the usual development, land far from the ocean could not command premium prices. Mizner solved this problem with his golf course community.[20]

Mizner designed the 160-foot-wide Camino Real as the principal east-west street and as the focus of his city. In his plans, this new road began at the Ritz-Carlton hotel on the beach, crossing the Intracoastal Waterway on a Venetian bridge that Mizner also designed. The bridge scheme included a tower with an apartment for the keeper. After passing through the hotel golf course, Camino Real became the major shopping and business street of the city. Here Mizner sited the Administration Buildings—headquarters for the development company—several other projected office buildings, and shopping arcades similar to those he had constructed in Palm Beach. Mizner modeled this section of the street, with its central canal, on the Botofago of Rio de Janeiro. The company even imported electrically powered gondolas from Italy to ply the canal. As the street continued westward it passed first through platted residential areas and then opened upon a great Plaza at the Seaboard Railway tracks. Small parks connected the Plaza to the Seaboard's proposed "Addison Station." Camino Real ended two-and-a-half miles from the ocean in the middle of Ritz-Carlton Park.

Camino Real's plan allowed Mizner to completely overshadow the former main east-west street, Palmetto Park Road. The old town and its buildings did not conform to the plans for the new city. Notwithstanding, to the west of the town, Mizner planned to take advantage of an existing drainage ditch to provide a median canal for Palmetto Park Road. He wished eventually to transform the old section of the town. He projected a new station for the East Coast Railway, a new city hall, and a waterworks with a storage tower in the form of an ancient lighthouse.[21]

Mizner envisioned a complete city. While company advertisements emphasized resort facilities and exclusive residential areas, the scheme for Boca Raton also included sections for workers and an industrial district. Mizner intended to place branches of his factories in the city and encouraged other companies also to establish plants. Usually these companies supplied construction materials for the development. He also platted a black subdivision and began construction of twelve houses.[22]

In a *Palm Beach Post* interview, Mizner said that he planned a city as perfect "as study and ideals can make it." His goals included "homes that are livable, . . . streets that are suitable for traffic, . . . shops that are inviting and parks that are beautiful." All of this in Spanish-style architecture because it "is the most direct and simple . . . lending itself perfectly to climate and country." He avowed that the millions of dollars in lot and acreage sold by the company proved the acceptance of his vision for the city.[23]

By June the Mizner organization owned two-thirds of Boca

Raton property. A new list of planned improvements included an air terminal equipped for the largest passenger-carrying planes and hydroplanes, a deepened inlet with an inland sea and yacht basin, a Venetian lake with gondolas, a Spanish village "large enough to hold much of the color and old world charm of those Spanish cities with which Mr. Mizner is familiar," and Irving Berlin's Cabaret, which promised the best theatrical talent of America and Europe.

Throughout May and June a force of 350 workmen cleared land for the Ritz-Carlton golf course to the west of the city. As sales climbed to $6 million, Mizner signed contracts to build the small hotel, now renamed the Cloister Inn, and to pave streets. At the peak of construction during the summer, over 3,000 men worked on the various projects. Committed to making Boca Raton one of the world's most beautiful cities, Mizner demanded that his workmen save trees of every size. He also took over an existing local nursery and reserved forty additional acres to grow landscaping plants. At this time the company also purchased two "pullman buses" to carry prospective purchasers to the development from Miami and Palm Beach. Emphasizing the Spanish nature of the development, the battleship-gray buses had vivid yellow stripes with the words "Boca Raton" painted in deep red.[24]

On 6 August a board-of-directors meeting elected Anderson T. Herd vice-president and general manager of the company. The directors included T. Coleman du Pont, newly elected Senator from Delaware, as chairman, Jesse L. Livermore, the Wall Street operator, as head of the finance committee, L. A. Bean, vice-president of the Dwight P. Robinson Company, the New York firm building the Cloister Inn, Congressman George S. Graham, Herd, H. S. Meeds, a Delaware banker, Addison and Wilson Mizner, A. A. Thompson, William A. White, and Ward H. Wickwire. Du Pont took this opportunity to thank Mizner and the company officers for their management, adding that it met "with our unqualified approval."[25]

As fall approached, the Robinson Company received a contract to build the Ritz-Carlton hotel and the Venetian bridge. Mizner also released sketches for his own house, a castle on an island in Lake Boca Raton (Figs. 104, 105). For the design he envisioned "a Spanish fortress of the twelfth century captured from its owner by a stronger enemy, who, after taking it, adds on one wing and another—and then loses it in turn to another who builds to suit his taste." Mizner planned a working drawbridge which led to a large entrance hall on a level between the servants' floor and the principal rooms of the house. These included a 36-by-52-foot living room, a

104. Castle Mizner, proposed Addison Mizner
house, Boca Raton, 1925, entrance and patio.

105. Castle Mizner, southern elevation.

loggia, and a dining room with his famous Salamanca panels. A
tower contained his own rooms on the third floor and a fourth floor
mirador—in all, a more elaborate version of the Villa Mizner. The
architect planned to spend a million dollars for the castle, which he

promised to will to Boca Raton "for Posterity as a museum." A Palm Beach reporter wrote that Boca Raton's designer planned no city of air castles. Americans would one day thank Mizner for his gift, she declared, adding that Boca Raton stood as "a cornerstone to American architectural prestige" and "a monument to American money."[26]

Unfortunately, at this time the money flow began to slow. To be realized, Mizner's plans plainly demanded great sums. Although lots continued to sell, they did not sell in the necessary volume. To stimulate sales, the company added a line to its newspaper publicity: "Attach this advertisement to your contract for deed. It becomes a part thereof." With this pledge the company hoped to counteract growing northern newspaper claims of fraud in Florida real estate sales. One reporter concluded that the problem lay with the difference between promoters and developers. Promoters sold real estate, taking their profits without building their developments. Developers, on the other hand, sold real estate so that they could fulfill their promises. Mizner must be accepted as a developer who believed in Boca Raton. Although this pledge later proved an embarrassment, at the time he intended to fulfill his promises. Other promoters might never start improvements; Mizner sincerely wished to fashion his city of red-tiled roofs.[27]

Thus Mizner hurried completion of all the Boca Raton improvements that promoted sales. At the end of October work started on radio station WFLA, a proposed 1,000-watt clear channel station to broadcast the Boca Raton message to Florida and most of the eastern United States. The *Palm Beach Post* and the *New York Times* agreed to share a news hour every day between five and six o'clock. When not broadcasting news, or the "facts of Florida," the station planned to feature modern adaptations of Seminole Indian music.[28]

Mizner also rushed completion of the Administration Buildings at Camino Real and Dixie Highway to provide a center for sales activities in the city (Figs. 106, 107). By the end of October the company could report that it now employed two thousand workers to grub and clear land and level and grade streets. The same report said that Wilson Mizner had purchased ships and barges in Baltimore for the "Pirate Ship Cabaret" to be anchored in Lake Boca Raton near the Cloister Inn. Plans for the ship, which seated four hundred, included two chefs—French for dinner and Spanish for after-theater supper.[29]

In October the company also announced construction of two hundred houses. Building had started on many of these, including twenty-nine in the Old Floresta section of the city. Mizner projected

106. Mizner Development Corporation, Administration
Buildings, Boca Raton, 1925, porch.

107. Mizner Development
Corporation,
Administration Buildings,
Camino Real entrance.

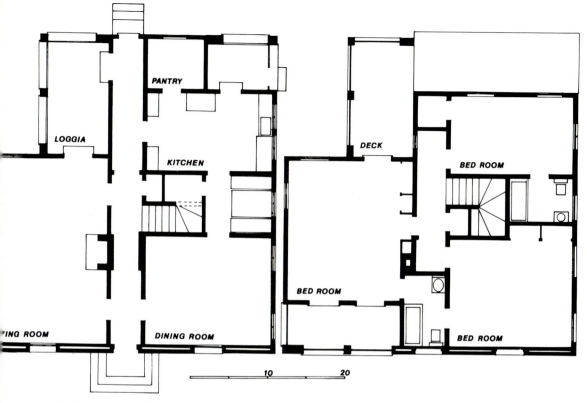

PANTRY

LOGGIA

KITCHEN

DECK

BED ROOM

BED ROOM

ING ROOM

DINING ROOM

BED ROOM

10   20

108. House "E," Old Floresta, Boca Raton, 1925, plan.

these houses for the executives and directors of his company and for
his brother Henry. The twenty-nine houses represented only a small
segment of those planned for the subdivision. Mizner designed ten
houses which he labeled "A" through "J." He sited these houses,
and their mirror images, so that no street had more than one house
of the same plan. The models ranged in size from one bedroom and
bath to three bedrooms and two baths. Henry Mizner's house also
included a study.

In Old Floresta Mizner followed the same basic principles as
in his larger houses (Figs. 108, 109). Where possible, he placed kitchens to the north and west and living rooms to the east and south.
He designed four exposures into many living rooms, with full-length
casement windows to take complete advantage of the natural breezes.
All of the exceptionally large living rooms contained fireplaces, with
cast stone mantels. The bedrooms took advantage of cross ventilation, and plans for the larger two-story houses included sleeping
porches and sun decks on the second floor. He placed arcaded porches
on all of the houses and designed several around patios (Fig. 110).
As in his Palm Beach work, he used pecky cypress for doors, ceilings, and exterior trim, Florida hard pine and Las Manos tiles for

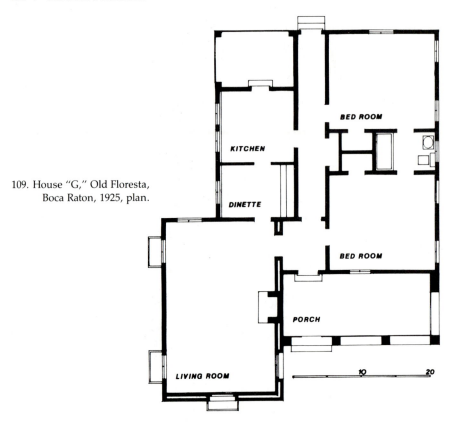

109. House "G," Old Floresta,
Boca Raton, 1925, plan.

floors, and wrought-iron lighting fixtures and ornamental work made by Mizner Industries.

An article in *Ladies' Home Journal* explained the design philosophy Mizner employed in the Old Floresta houses. In this article Mizner published three small houses commissioned by Dr. Maurice Druker for a Boca Raton subdivision. Although smaller and more compact than most of the Old Floresta houses, those for Druker relate in many details. Like the Old Floresta models they had plain facades ("simplicity being always dominant in the best of Spanish architecture") of rough-finished stucco with numerous windows and doors that frequently opened onto balconies of ornamental ironwork (Fig. 111). The roofs, covered by barrel tile, were uneven with low-pitched, hipped lines alternating with flat parapets. Also in many of the Old Floresta houses the dining room, "fast becoming an unnecessary appendage in a very small house," made way for the dining alcove.[30]

In December the Administration Buildings opened for alfresco lunch and tea service on the patio, which Mizner modeled

110. House "G," Old Floresta.

111. House "E," Old Floresta.

112. Mizner Development Corporation, Administration Buildings, patio.

after El Greco's home in Toledo, Spain (Fig. 112). At the same time, the first Boca Raton houses designed by Mizner were nearing completion. Harry Vought and Company built these small bungalows in a section later called "Spanish Village." Vought planned to build one hundred houses, though he completed less than twenty. The modest two-bedroom houses contained 13-by-21-foot living rooms with "lofty beamed ceilings of the peak type, finished in attractive antique effect." They sold for $7,000.[31]

By the time the first Boca Raton houses went on the market, the south Florida land boom had ended. For Mizner, the first sign of the collapse came as early as 24 October 1925. On that date T. Coleman du Pont and Jesse Livermore arrived in Palm Beach to attend a meeting of the Mizner Development Corporation's board of directors. Both men expressed grave concern about the management of the company's publicity. They objected to the use of their names in advertisements, and expressed particular concern about the implications that they personally guaranteed the millions of dollars in construction planned for the city. They also protested against allowing promotional advertisements for the company to be attached to deeds. Some of these advertisements had been very explicit, promising the construction of the Ritz-Carlton hotel, the Cloister Inn, three golf courses, polo fields, and miles of paved palm-lined streets.

Before coming to the board meeting, du Pont had been a member of a delegation of Florida businessmen and investors, headed by Governor John W. Martin, that visited New York to counteract the unfavorable Florida publicity found in many northern newspapers. For this "Truth about Florida" seminar, held at du Pont's Waldorf-Astoria hotel, the sponsors invited representatives from the country's leading newspapers and magazines. Various speakers stated that the real estate activity in Florida did not constitute a boom: the great increase in values only represented real worth. Although several speakers admitted that some "fraudulent misrepresentation" had taken place, they said Florida planned to curb this activity. The New York Times drew the conclusion that the meeting proved Florida businessmen had become uneasy about the boom. Certainly, several directors now questioned their association with the Mizner Development Corporation. Within a month, du Pont, Livermore, Bean, and Meeds had severed their connections with the board.[32]

In a statement to the New York Times on 24 November 1925, du Pont said he had resigned because of differences between himself and the officers of the company as to proper business methods. Nonetheless, he added, under proper management Boca Raton still offered "wonderful possibilities." The same article also quoted Mizner as saying that du Pont had resigned because of differences over membership in the board, implying that du Pont had proposed to elect his friends as directors and had resigned when he failed. Mizner also stated that he and his associates now controlled the company, and that they planned to continue the building and developing program without interruption.

Four days later the New York Times published a letter from du

Pont and the other newly resigned board members. The men said that as they held little financial interest in the company they objected to the use of their names in advertisements. They had left the board because the company officers met their attempt to eliminate exaggerated publicity with "criticism rather than cooperation." The letter marked the end for the Mizner Development Corporation, and probably for the entire south Florida land boom as well.

Although du Pont might claim little financial interest in the company, as chairman he actively participated in development affairs, receiving reports on purchases, approving expenditures, and conferring on zoning matters. He also planned to build an oceanfront house north of the Ritz-Carlton site. As late as August he had lent his name to the board's statement praising the work of the company officers. After the New York meeting he obviously concluded that the boom was over. Moreover, he feared that remaining associated with the Mizner company might make him personally responsible for its obligations.[33]

Du Pont's great fortune made him the financial name behind the Mizner organization. His interest in Boca Raton assured investors of stability. His decision to disassociate himself from the development warned prospective buyers of possible financial problems. According to Alva Johnston, du Pont's attack on the corporation's officers "put a wet blanket on the entire boom." Sales of Boca Raton real estate, which totaled over $25 million in its first six months, practically ended after du Pont's resignation from the board. The high point for sales and building permits in all of south Florida was October 1925. Although the end of the boom was not abrupt, activity began to slacken after that month.[34]

Problems for Florida's development surfaced even before du Pont's resignation from the Mizner board. One of the most serious difficulties resulted from the breakdown in transportation services. The area depended upon outside supplies to continue the massive building programs. On 17 August 1925, the Florida East Coast Railway announced that freight car congestion on the southeast coast forced an embargo of all but perishable goods. Railroad officials said that while one hundred cars a day came into the area, only eighty were unloaded. This left hundreds of loaded cars in south Florida rail yards.

Protests, the formation of committees, and the publication of lists of uncollected freight did little to solve the problem. High wages paid to unskilled labor by contractors made it impossible to hire workers to unload the cars. Moreover, the embargo soon spread to other railroads. In West Palm Beach a Citizens Committee on Freight Congestion organized a "volunteer army" which emptied four hundred cars in one day. Unfortunately, the work of the merchants, real estate men, Boy Scouts, and women's club members failed to convince the railroads to lift the embargo.

A housing shortage also hit south Florida in the summer of 1925. Although summer was usually the off-season, thousands of Americans decided to drive to the state "when it was quiet." Since hotels often closed for the summer, many visitors were forced to sleep in their automobiles or in hastily pitched tents. Fresh vegetables were almost unobtainable, overtaxed electrical power resulted in stoppages lasting for as long as twelve hours, water supplies gave out, and in August an ice shortage added to the general discomfort.[35]

Finally, the campaign waged by northern newspapers warning of shady and fraudulent Florida real estate promotions began to take hold. If booms feed on strong assurances, small doubts erode them. By November 1925, the freight embargo and the ensuing construction problems, the inconveniences of the housing shortages, and the growing doubts about the boom produced by northern newspapers, promoted an uncomfortable atmosphere for speculation.

Of all the great boom developments, Boca Raton had appeared the soundest investment. Although the very magnitude of the concept attracted many, and others saw Addison Mizner's leadership as assurance that fashionable America approved, speculators actually bought because of the association of prominent financiers like T. Coleman du Pont. Any serious shock to confidence can collapse a speculative boom. The many problems plaguing the state paved the way; the du Pont letter to the *New York Times* produced the shock. To the speculator the message seemed clear. If you could not place your trust in Boca Raton, could any Florida venture be safe?

With the boom collapsing all around him, Mizner still believed that he could save Boca Raton. He began a campaign calculated to show that the development remained financially secure and that men of substance remained interested in its future. To counteract the effect of du Pont's resignation, the company announced the election of W. E. Shappercotter, "a powerful figure in Northern financial circles . . . associated with the rise of the Lehigh Valley Railroad," as chairman of the board of directors. Later it claimed that Otto H. Kahn, "internationally known banker and financier," had purchased both stock in the company and property in Boca Raton— proof, according to the publicity release, of the continued prosperity

of the company. When Charles M. Schwab, an organizer of both the
United States Steel and Bethlehem Steel companies, lunched with
Mizner, the publicity department made the occasion evidence of the
capitalist's endorsement of the project, quoting him as saying that
he had never seen anything "so artistically beautiful" as the city.[36]

Mizner publicity also emphasized that "reorganization" of the
company had changed none of the plans for the development of
Boca Raton. News releases and advertisements stressed the continuing nature of the project. In early November the company told of
building permits for September and October totaling $918,066. This
led to the assertion that "they are buying to live in Boca Raton." On
the day that du Pont's resignation became public, the company claimed
21 percent of all Palm Beach County's October land transfers for its
property.

In order to continue construction on the various projects the
company needed money. In January, therefore, Mizner opened sales
in the *Distrito de Boca Raton*, whose plat plan included fifty-eight
oceanfront lots and a beach club. The *Distrito*, which lay between
the ocean and the Intracoastal Waterway, south of the inlet, contained the city's most expensive waterfront land. Moreover, Mizner
thought of the subdivision as the development's most exclusive area.
The Mizner Development Company consequently limited the privi-
lege of purchase to those who "enjoyed recognized social positions."
Mizner also retained the right to approve all exterior designs, which
had to include roofs of "hand-made Spanish style, cover tile." For
houses on the ocean and other waterfronts, the company set a min-
imum of $40,000; no house in the subdivision could cost less than
$20,000. In order to protect the tropical beauty of the site, Mizner
specified underground conduits for electrical wires, an idea far ahead
of its time for south Florida. Mizner built no houses in the *Distrito*,
though he completed designs for at least eight luxury residences.[37]

January also saw the release of Mizner's sketch for Boca Raton's new city hall. His original design called for a two-story building of magnificent proportions (Fig. 113). Unfortunately, the town
counted upon revenue from real estate taxes to finance the building.
By the time Mizner finished the plans, town officials realized the
boom had ended, forcing a decision to reduce expenditures. Although Mizner published the original sketch as late as June 1926, he
had already revised the plans by eliminating the second story and
the south wing. Before the completion of the hall, William Alsmeyer,
a Delray Beach architect, added a small second story under the pitched
roof of the building's main section and a garage for the town fire

113. Mizner's sketch for proposed Boca Raton City Hall, 1926.

truck in place of the original south wing. However, Mizner continued as supervising architect until the fall of 1926. His design and decoration, which included pecky cypress ceilings and doors and unglazed floor tiles, and his external elevations for the first story, remained part of the completed building. In addition, the stonework, ornamental grills, electrical fixtures, and other architectural details came from Mizner Industries.[38]

The construction of the Cloister Inn proceeded at great haste (Fig. 114). Even before its completion, Mizner entertained some of his former Palm Beach clients at a Christmas Eve dinner in the "Salamanca Room." At this time Mizner announced that the Ritz-Carlton organization had assumed management of the new inn. The formal opening came with another dinner on 6 February with the architect as host. The guest list "rivaled the social registers of two continents," according to Mizner's publicity men. Red-coated and gold-braided footmen served a "Lucullan repast" to five hundred guests which included Stotesburys, Warburtons, Astors, Wanamakers, Charles Norris, the novelist, and Mrs. Stanford White, widow of the architect. After the guests heard Grant Clarke's new song, "In Boca Raton," Mizner announced his plan to build a "remarkable" cathedral as a memorial to his mother. A later advertisement quoted Mrs. White's reaction to the Cloister Inn: "Addison Mizner is the foremost genius of the age. Since Stanford White, there has been no one with such exquisite sense of artistry. This building is superb."[39]

Almost all critics agreed with Mrs. White. Ida Tarbell wrote:

The Cloister was simple to severity in its whole yet rich in delights. Red tiled roofs rambled up and down, spreading comfortably in every direction. . . . There was a square tower for height; there was a great court and arcades with round arches and capitals alive with animals and grotesque figures.[40]

In an article on the hotel for *Arts and Decoration* Giles Edgerton asked, "What is in a man's spirit that could make a building he has designed an architectural personality, that could make forms of wood, or stone, or stucco so beautiful that they trouble the imagination?" Calling the building a "Spanish gem," Edgerton praised Mizner for his ability to adapt Spanish architecture to Florida's landscape and climate.[41]

The small Cloister Inn did not lack elegance. Entrance to the two-story lobby was gained through a Romanesque stone arch of "gigantic proportions." Heavy cypress-beamed ceilings capped the lounge, the card room, and loggia. Mizner modeled the 40-by-84-

114. The Cloister Inn, Boca Raton, 1925, entrance.

foot dining hall after the fifteenth-century hospital at Vich, Catalonia. With 40-foot-high peaked ceilings, plaster arches, and softly stained green, yellow, and rose glass windows, it was the hotel's most dramatic room (Figs. 115, 116). The "cloister" connected the public rooms with the bedroom wings, filling in the lake side of the hotel and forming an enclosed courtyard (Figs. 117, 118). Mizner

115. The Cloister Inn, dining room.

116. The Cloister Inn, dining room ceiling, 1977.

Industries supplied all fixtures, architectural details, floor tiles, and furniture with the exception of tapestries and antique furniture for the public rooms, which came from the architect's own collections. Although the Cloister's opening received national publicity, land sales continued to decline. Nonetheless, later in the month Mizner announced a construction schedule for the oceanfront Ritz-Carlton and gave tenants of a dance hall located on the property their eviction notice.[42]

In an effort to bolster sales, announcements in April described extensive summer projects. Maurice Druker started construction of ten Mizner-designed houses, the development company told of plans to build a $100,000 Camino Real shopping arcade modeled on the Via Mizner in Palm Beach, and Mrs. Joshua B. Cosden, who had sold Playa Riente to Mrs. Horace S. Dodge for $2.8 million,

117. The Cloister Inn, patio.

118. The Cloister Inn, cloister detail.

asked Mizner to design a new mansion in the *Distrito* to "rival in splendor" her Palm Beach house. Most of these projects never left the drafting boards. In fact, the only new commission completed this summer was an apartment house overlooking the Cloister Inn golf course for W. H. Dunagan. The modest two-story building contained six small apartments.[43]

By spring, even Mizner recognized that he could never fulfill his Boca Raton dreams. New sales of land had ended. This in turn stopped the flow of money needed to continue the building projects. Moreover, the purchasers of lots sold in the early spring of 1925 now found their second installment due. Many of these had bought for speculation alone, planning to sell at a profit before the date of the second payment. After December these speculators found they could not make a profit on their lots; in fact, they often could not resell them at any price. Many did not have the second payment. Others, seeing the declining prices of Boca Raton real estate, simply decided to take their losses. They, too, did not make the second installment. Almost every developer in Florida faced the same situation. Some, like Mizner, had committed themselves to huge expenditures for improvements, confident of a continuous income from new sales and yearly payments on previous sales. When the money stopped and they could not meet their commitments, many projects ended in bankruptcy.[44]

Although the Mizner Development Corporation survived into the summer, serious problems arose in April. The company had difficulty making payments on the promissory notes signed to purchase Boca Raton land. In May, various contractors, unable to collect on their contracts, began to file liens against the corporation. Then, in June, Guy C. Reed, a New York carpet manufacturer and minor stockholder in the Mizner concern, filed a petition in federal court asking that Boca Raton be placed in receivership. Reed's petition stated that the company could neither meet past obligations nor fulfill the promises made to purchasers. He also claimed that the officers of the company had sanctioned advertisements "so worded and pictured as to mislead the public." Although a federal judge dismissed the suit, deciding that Reed had no case for his mismanagement charges, Mizner's backers now forced a reorganization. Consequently, in July Mizner yielded his management to the Chicago-based Central Equities Corporation of United States Vice-President Charles Dawes and his brother. The Dawes brothers, recognizing the importance of the Mizner name to the project, allowed him to retain control of architectural development. In addition, the Chicago firm pledged to continue construction of the many projects. Then, just as Mizner again hoped that his vision for Boca Raton might still be fulfilled, a devastating hurricane struck the southeast Florida coast. Boca Raton suffered little damage, but the storm convinced the Dawes brothers that the project had no future. Ultimately, Clarence Geist, one of Mizner's original backers, took over the remaining assets of the company and reopened the Cloister Inn as the private Boca Raton Club.[45]

Monumental in scale and magnificent in concept, the vastness of the Boca Raton enterprise doomed it to failure from the beginning. Even as Mizner purchased land for the development, the boom was approaching its peak. Nonetheless, in little over a year, Mizner accomplished far more than most boomtime promoters. While other developers made promises, Mizner strove to build his dream city of red-tiled roofs. The Cloister Inn, Administration Buildings, city hall, the houses of Old Floresta and Spanish Village all remain as a testimony to the dream. Indeed, Boca Raton today stands as a tribute to his vision, since his plans for the city have largely been carried out. Camino Real begins at an oceanfront hotel on the site of Mizner's first grand design for his resort, the Castillo del Rey, and ends in a golf course community on the site of his projected Ritz-Carlton Park. The polo field, the airport, the golf courses, the yacht basins, and the Spanish-style shopping centers all have been built. Of more importance, the sense of uniqueness that today sets Boca Raton apart from other Gold Coast cities can be attributed to the heritage of Addison Mizner.

6

After the Bust

The collapse of the Florida land boom profoundly affected Mizner's career—financially, first of all, since, without question, the architect had put his personal fortune at risk in the Boca Raton venture. His practice also suffered. Although Spanish-style houses still found favor among Palm Beach resorters, the prevalence of the style in south Florida during the boom, and the ugliness of so many of these houses, certainly made it less fashionable. Moreover, while Mizner was absorbed in the various boom time projects, new architects established practices in Palm Beach. In the early twenties, Mizner and Marion Sims Wyeth had virtually monopolized the Palm Beach market for large villas. Competition increased in the latter half of the decade. In 1925 Maurice Fatio (1897–1943) opened the Florida office of Treanor & Fatio. Educated at the University of Zurich, he had come to the United States in 1920, establishing the partnership with William A. Treanor (1878–1946) the next year. Young, personable, and highly social, Fatio soon found his clientele among the rich and prominent vacationers who a few years earlier would have gone to Mizner. In fact, one of Fatio's largest commissions, an Italian mansion for Joseph E. Widener on South Ocean Boulevard, came after Mizner had prepared sketches for the house. During the late twenties Fatio designed a series of distinctive Mediterranean-style houses using Mizner Industries' coral key stone set off with courses of red brick. These included Casa Della Porta on Via Del Mar for William J. McAneeny and two South Ocean Boulevard houses for Mortimer L. Schiff and himself. In 1931 he designed a great ocean-front Italian villa in Manalapan for Mizner's former client, Harold S.

165

Vanderbilt. As in the case of Mizner's Palm Beach houses, Fatio designed large reception rooms for entertaining and oriented his plans around private patios.[1]

John L. Volk (b. 1901) arrived in Florida at the peak of the land boom in 1926. He had attended Columbia University and worked with several New York architects before coming to Palm Beach where he formed a partnership with Gustav A. Maass (1893–1964), a graduate of the University of Pennsylvania. The firm's first major commission was a large Spanish mansion on El Bravo Way for Charles M. Hayes. Volk and Maass continued to design Spanish houses into the early thirties.[2]

Howard Major (1883–1974) received his training at the Pratt Institute, and the atelier of Henry Hornbostel of the Society of Beaux-Arts Architects. After practicing in New York City, he came to Palm Beach in 1925. Although he, too, designed Spanish houses such as those for Nelson Odman and Richard Cowell in Palm Beach and Howard Whitney in Gulfstream, Major became the earliest critic of the style. In newspaper interviews, an article in *Architectural Forum,* and a book on Greek Revival architecture, Major condemned Spanish architecture as inappropriate for Florida because of climate (he pointed out that Florida's latitude was the same as Egypt's, while the climate of Spain and Washington, D.C., were similar), and because it failed to express American "national character." Although Major believed the Greek Revival, "our independent creation in architecture," fulfilled "every requisite of climate, convenience, and *nationalism*," he accepted British colonial, or West Indian, style architecture as also appropriate for Florida.[3]

All of these new architects willingly designed Spanish houses; all also encouraged clients to experiment with new styles. Before the end of the twenties Fatio designed a Norman half-timbered house for his mother-in-law, Mrs. Charles Curry Chase, on Via Del Mar, and Major built Major Alley, a complex of small houses in British colonial style. The new architects and Wyeth and Kitchell also soon had commissions for both frame and brick Georgian houses. Thus, when Mizner again turned his attention to Palm Beach, he found that he no longer held sway as before. He also found that prospective clients no longer demanded only his form of Spanish architecture.

During 1925/26 Mizner accepted few new Palm Beach clients, directing his energies to the development projects. He did accept commissions from Singer, his long-time patron, completing in 1925 the Via Parigi and the studio house on the Everglades Club grounds for Sir Oswald Birley. Mizner also became associated with Singer's plans to build Palm Beach Ocean, a new resort across the inlet north of Palm Beach. West Palm Beach envisioned itself in the future as a great seaport and refused to allow a bridge across the inlet. Mizner and Singer proposed to connect the project to Palm Beach by an aerial ferry. First reports said that Singer, Mizner, and Harry Kelsey, a former New England restaurant owner who began developing Kelsey City in 1919, planned to spend a million dollars on the enterprise. A few weeks later Singer organized the Florida Gulf Atlantic Company with E. F. Hutton, Anthony J. Drexel Biddle, Gurnee and Charles Munn, John Magee, George Sloane, and John S. Pillsbury as backers.[4]

Mizner contributed the design for the massive Blue Heron Hotel. Singer originally planned to build two hotels: the Blue Heron on the northern end of the island, and a small luxury inn to be known as the Paris Singer, near the inlet. Unable to secure clear title to the northern land, he decided to build the Blue Heron on the southern site. Singer believed the hotel necessary to house his prospective land purchasers and asked Mizner to rush the job. Actual construction started before completion of the plans. Mizner placed his associate, A.E.R. Betschick, in charge of the project, and the two worked out the details as the building progressed. Singer's decision to begin without plans forced him to contract with the builder on a cost-plus basis. He budgeted $2 million for the hotel, planning, as did Mizner in Boca Raton, to pay construction costs from the sales of lots in the development. A small army of workmen began building in April 1925. By the fall of 1926 Singer had spent $2 million on the still uncompleted hotel. Palm Beach Ocean land sales, like those in Boca Raton, dropped sharply at this time. With his budget reached and sales slow, Singer suspended construction. When the boom ended, no one wanted a partially completed hotel on an isolated island connected to the mainland only by a narrow single-lane county bridge. "Singer's Folly," Mizner's largest structure, stood unfinished and empty until the summer of 1940 when a local company began razing it for the salvageable steel.

The Blue Heron hotel centered on an eight-story main section with step-down wings forming a large open U that faced the ocean (Fig. 119). On either side of the center section Mizner placed angled six-story wings which in turn led to four-story wings. A six-story service building made a Y of the northern section. Mizner added no architectural detail before Singer suspended construction.[5]

Singer fared far worse than Mizner in the controversies sur-

119. The Blue Heron Hotel, Singer Island, 1926.

rounding the land bust. On leaving Florida at the end of the 1927 season, he was arrested by state authorities and charged with fraud in making false statements in the advertisements offering Palm Beach Ocean for sale. Three weeks later, in a trial with legal staffs and sales directors of the leading real estate companies of the state represented, the judge dismissed the charges, ruling that under Florida law the facts were "insufficient to constitute a criminal offense." After this Singer retired to his house in the south of France, returning only occasionally to Palm Beach.[6]

Mizner retained his interest in Boynton throughout the boom period, holding property with assessed value of over $125,000. Wilson also owned Boynton land in his own name and in joint holdings with Halpine Smith. During the summer of 1925 Mizner designed a city hall with an attached fire station and jail for the city. The land boom ended before the town fathers could find the financing, and so they dropped the project. At the same time, Mizner also designed a new building for the city's Woman's Club. Founded in 1909, the club supplied Boynton with meeting rooms and operated the town's only library. When the heirs of Major Nathan S. Boynton, the town's founder, decided to give $35,000 for a new clubhouse as a memorial to the Major, members asked Mizner to donate his architectural services to the project. In the aftermath of the many problems Mizner had experienced with the city, he agreed as a gesture of good will.

Mizner planned the building around the large 63-by-54-foot auditorium on the second floor. To support the red-tile roof and form the ceiling of the auditorium he used tie rods masked as great cypress rafters (Fig. 120). Stairs placed in four dissimilar towers at each corner of the building gave access to the auditorium and provided the decorative interest on the massive structure's exterior. On the long facades, Mizner connected the towers with an arcaded porch on the first floor and an open deck above. On the southern entrance facade, he surmounted a series of three fanlighted French doors with five smaller windows and doors that gave access to a small wrought-iron balcony. The first floor contained a foyer, library, lounge, and kitchen. The great size of the auditorium roof precluded Mizner's usual subtle massing of elements; still, with the towers and porches he maintained an intimate scale.[7]

In 1926 members of Riverside Baptist Church in Jacksonville asked Mizner to design a new building for their congregation. He refused, pleading overwork and ill health. When the pastor wrote that he offered prayers at every service for the architect's speedy recovery, Mizner decided to accept the commission. Mizner, reared as an Episcopalian, knew little about the Baptist religion. The build-

120. The Boynton Woman's Club, Boynton Beach, 1925, auditorium.

121. Riverside Baptist Church, Jacksonville, 1926.

ing he designed suited high-church ritualism better than the ser-mon-oriented service of the Baptists (Figs. 121, 122). His octagonal nave focused on the wrought-iron screened altar rather than on the pulpit. In fact, the narrow, cramped baptismal pool, fitted behind an arcaded screen to the right of the altar, appeared almost to be an afterthought. Although Mizner took his inspiration from the early Romanesque, he created a great open space filled with light (Fig. 123).[8]

While completing the church Mizner also designed additions to a house on Riverside Avenue for H. Marshall Taylor, a prominent

122. Riverside Baptist Church, western facade.

123. Riverside Baptist Church.

Jacksonville physician. Dr. Taylor's house, a small two-story bunga-low, sat on a long narrow lot. Mizner's plans added a new nursery, entrance loggia, and guest suite to the front of the house, and a drawing room and dining loggia at the rear. These two rooms com-pletely encircled the study and may account for Taylor's rejection of the proposal. The next year he asked Fatio to design more imposing additions.[9]

During the summer of 1926 Mizner's office also received a commission from Mrs. Bessie Gardner du Pont for a house in Green-ville, Delaware. Pierre S. du Pont handled the details of design and construction for her. His brother-in-law and attorney, H. Rodney Sharp, was a friend of Albert Ely Ives, an architect in Mizner's office, who directed the project. At first Ives proposed an eighteenth-cen-tury Dutch house as appropriate for Wilmington. Mrs. du Pont then asked him to reproduce the facade of Bois des Fossés, Pierre Samuel du Pont's small French chateau near Chevannes in France. Ives agreed, saying, "It is such a relief to get away from Spanish things for a while." The plan remained unfinished in March 1927 when Ives realized the land boom had ended. He decided to leave Mizner's office and establish a practice in Wilmington, using the commission on the du Pont house to finance his move. He disliked Palm Beach and Mizner's office: "You will never know what a rotten place this is. Not only to work in but to exsist [sic] in. Nothing but backbiting and jealousy all of the time." In his correspondence with the du

124. Casa Serena, John R. Bradley house, Colorado Springs, 1927.

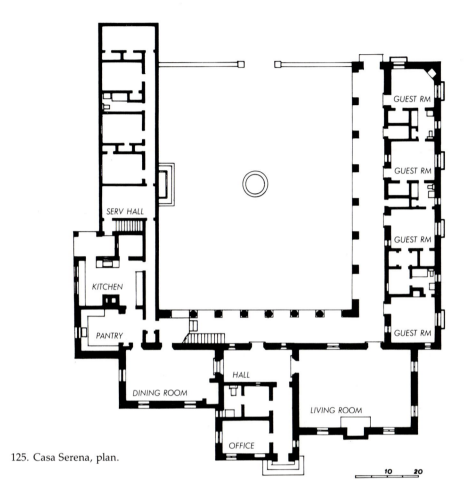

125. Casa Serena, plan.

Ponts, Ives used Mizner's stationery and signed his letters "Addison Mizner, Inc." Moreover, Mizner's name appeared on all the office tracings. The commission obviously belonged to the firm. Nonetheless, Ives moved to Delaware where he completed the house. Mizner, noted for his kindness to young associates, probably released the commission to allow Ives to establish a new practice.[10]

After the frenzy of work produced by Mizner in 1925 and 1926, the following year saw only two major commissions. Mizner's largest project, the Worth Avenue renovations and additions for Mrs. Glen Hodges, completed his work on that street. He also planned a ranch house in Colorado Springs for John R. Bradley, Colonel Edward R. Bradley's brother and his partner in the operation of the Beach Club in Palm Beach. In the barren valley setting Mizner designed a stark building that approached the Pueblo style of the

southwest (Fig. 124). The U-shaped house enclosed a patio surrounded by open porches. A tower for a water storage tank over the
flat-roofed central section dominated the design. Entry hall, an office, and living and dining rooms made up the main section, while
wings roofed in Las Manos tiles contained guest rooms, kitchen,
and service areas (Fig. 125). Mizner placed the master bedroom on
the second floor with an exterior staircase leading to an open fourth-
story deck over the water tower.[11]

In 1927 a group of Mizner's friends and associates put together a book illustrating his Florida work. *The Florida Architecture of
Addison Mizner* contained a foreword by Singer, an "Appreciation of
a Layman" written by Ida M. Tarbell, and 185 rich brown rotogravure
photographs of Mizner's buildings by F. E. Geisler. Alice De Lamar,
a close friend of Mizner's nephew Horace Chase, built a platform on
the back of an old Ford truck and drove the photographer around
the town. Miss De Lamar edited and subsidized the book, which
William Helburn, Inc., published in 1928. The architect autographed
one hundred special leather-bound presentation copies. Mizner's
friends wished both to document his work and to promote his practice. Curtis Patterson, reviewing *Florida Architecture* in the *International Studio,* a magazine associated with the *Connoisseur,* called both
the book and Mizner's work "monumental."[12]

The book did seem to promote Mizner's career, since during 1928 he received commissions for houses, offices, a dormitory,
and even a small hotel. In this year he undertook three projects for
John F. Harris, the New York stockbroker and Florida Republican
Committeeman. The architect remodeled and added a large four-
story tower with massive battlements to Harris's house on El Bravo
Way. The house sat on the second lot from the ocean. The new tower
allowed vistas of the sea over the oceanfront house next door. Harris
also had Mizner design a brokerage office for Harris, Winthrop and
Company in Miami Beach (Fig. 126). The building, on an oceanfront
lot at 2629 Collins Avenue, had an impressive 48-by-32-foot brokerage room with 15-foot ceilings and a large working fireplace. A
center hall separated the brokerage room from two ornate offices
and a secretary's room. On the second floor Mizner designed a *pied-
à-terre* for Harris of two master bedrooms, a servant's room, and a
small kitchen.[13]

Mizner's final Harris project in 1928 was a nurses' lodge for
Good Samaritan Hospital in West Palm Beach. Harris, a member of
the hospital board, donated the dormitory, which until 1960 was
known as Harris Hall. Mizner's plain, unadorned wing served as a

126. Harris Brokerage Building, Miami Beach, 1928.

127. Harris Hall, Good Samaritan Hospital, West Palm Beach, 1928.

128. Jerome D. Gedney house, Manalapan, 1928, oceanfront facade.

129. Jerome D. Gedney house, plan.

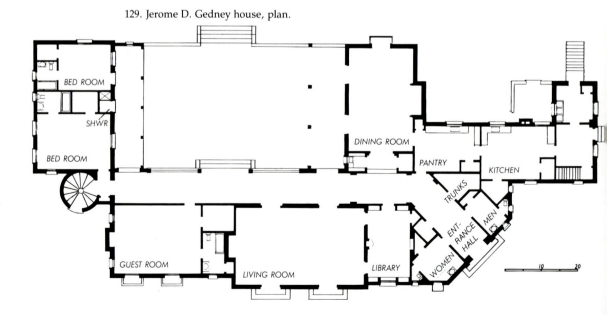

foil to Wyeth's earlier main building with its graceful Palladian arches (Fig. 127). The two-story structure contained ten bedrooms and six baths on each floor; a colonnaded passageway connected it to the hospital.[14]

In this same year, Mizner designed a house in Manalapan for Jerome D. Gedney, an attorney who represented the Florida interests of Clarence Geist. The Gedney lot stretched from ocean to lake north of the Boynton inlet. Mizner's rambling house of one and two stories, with varying roof levels, hanging wooden balconies, and angled entry, bore a closer relation to the Spanish colonial style of the American southwest than to his usual Palm Beach buildings (Fig. 128). Although the house surrounded a west-facing patio, its plan was generally freer than his usual work (Fig. 129). The angled and vaulted entrance hall led to twin dressing rooms, the kitchen and service wing, a small library, and the dining room which formed the northern side of the patio (Figs. 130–132). The 35-foot-long living room opened off a cloister on the east side of the patio; French doors facing the ocean gave the room through ventilation. A guest suite

130. Jerome D. Gedney house, patio.

131. Jerome D. Gedney house, dining room.

132. Jerome D. Gedney
house, entrance hall.

133. La Ronda, Percival E. Foerderer house,
Bryn Mawr, Pennsylvania, 1928, entrance court.

next to the living room completed the main section of the house, while two additional bedrooms enclosed the patio on the south. A staircase tower set in the angle formed by the south wing led to a master bedroom suite over the main guest room and two additional bedrooms over the south wing. A second story over the service wing provided space for servants' rooms. The massing of the various elements that created the house showed Mizner at his best.[15]

Mizner also designed his last great mansion in 1928 for Percival E. Foerderer in Bryn Mawr, Pennsylvania. Foerderer, who regularly wintered in Palm Beach throughout the twenties, inherited a large leather tanning operation from his father. Mizner designed La

134. La Ronda, great hall.

Ronda for Foerderer's 249-acre estate on Mount Pleasant Road. From
the street a drive led past gatehouse, garages, and servants' quarters
to a walled entrance court on the north side of the house (Fig. 133).
A small entry vestibule opened onto a great hall very similar in scale
and decoration to that of Playa Riente. Large windows surmounted
by cinquefoil Gothic tracery overlooked the patio on the south. On

135. La Ronda, upper-floor cloister.

the east side of the hall a stone staircase, set within a large arched alcove, led to a mezzanine-level cloister located above the entrance vestibule and double dressing rooms. From the mezzanine a hanging staircase, caged in wrought iron, gave access to the bedrooms in the west wing (Figs. 134, 135). As in the Cosden house, Mizner used stone for the walls, vaulted ceiling, and floor; nonetheless, the large

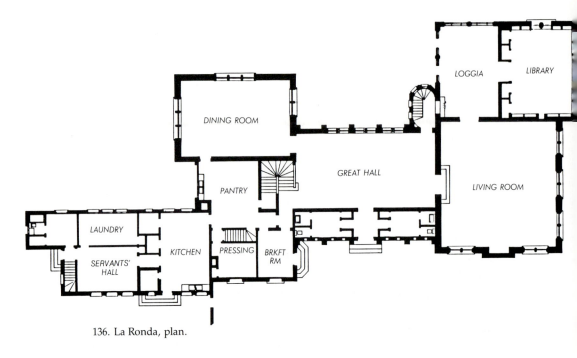

136. La Ronda, plan.

137. La Ronda, patio and gardens.

windows on the south wall and the glazing on the mezzanine produced a light-filled room. Mizner placed the 28-by-36-foot sunken living room, library, and loggia in the west wing (Fig. 136). A breakfast room and dining room, which enclosed the patio on the east, completed the public rooms on the first floor. A two-story wing containing the kitchen, service rooms, and servants' rooms extended to the east. On the second floor the west wing had two bedrooms and baths, and a master suite of bedroom, sitting room, sleeping porch, baths, and small secretary's office. An exterior stair tower provided a private entrance to the master suite and to a third floor mirador in a battlement-capped tower. The second floor of the eastern wing held children's and nurses' rooms. A second mirador acted as the children's playroom and sleeping porch (Fig. 137).[16]

Mizner Industries furnished practically every decorative detail used in the house and most of the furniture as well. Florida coral key stone for the great hall came from the quarry in the Keys; the cast-stone fireplaces, door- and window-surrounds, and stairway balustrades Mizner fabricated in West Palm Beach. Black Las Manos tiles bordered oak floors in the living room and library, while unglazed tiles floored the dining room, mezzanine cloister, and the loggia. As in the Cosden house, Mizner patterned the deeply coffered ceiling of the dining room after the Davanzati Palace in Florence. The dining room table, a seventeenth-century antique made from a solid plank, could comfortably seat twenty. A smaller "family" table, when joined with the larger one, lengthened the table to 23 feet. Twenty-four Mizner chairs upholstered in crimson velvet surrounded the enlarged table. For the great hall Mizner used largely fourteenth-century ecclesiastical antiques such as choir stalls and bishops' thrones for furnishings. In the living room he combined antiques and products of his own making. Since the windows in both the great hall and the living room had elaborate tracery and softly stained glass, he used no curtains in either room. Finally, richly colored Hispano-Mooresque rugs covered the floors, while tapestries and altarpieces hung on the walls. Mizner found inspiration for the Foerderer house from the Gothic castles of the plains of Castile, relating the harsh climate of Pennsylvania winters to that of northern Spain. Certainly the random, informal massing of square and rounded towers produced a picturesque and romantic house in an unlikely setting.[17]

Howard E. Coffin, an automotive engineer and organizer of the Hudson Motorcar Company, visited Georgia in 1911 for the Vanderbilt Cup auto races. He fell in love with the coastal islands and

began buying property on St. Simons. Later he discovered little Sea
Island, just to the east of St. Simons, with its five miles of ocean
beach and semitropical growth of ancient trees. In 1926 he purchased the island and asked the New York architectural firm of
Schultze & Weaver to design a large Spanish-style beachfront hotel.
The firm proposed an eight-story building for the middle of the
island surrounded by a cottage colony. Before construction started
Coffin had second thoughts: could Sea Island support a large hotel?
With land and hotel development at its peak in Florida, Coffin sent
his young cousin, Alfred W. Jones, and several others from his organization, on an investigative trip to the state. They returned with
the recommendation that the Sea Island Company build a small inn
for prospective purchasers visiting the island. On the trip through
Florida the men visited the Ritz-Carlton Cloister in Boca Raton. They
believed a similar hotel to be the solution for Sea Island and recom-
mended Mizner as the architect.

Coffin accepted the recommendation and sent Jones to per-
suade Mizner to design the hotel. Jones later said he felt the task
hopeless, expecting that Mizner's reputation and his great development in Boca Raton would make him uninterested in the small Sea
Island project. When Jones arrived he found Mizner completely at-
tentive, wooing and entertaining him "as if he were seeking a favor."
Unknown to Jones, the Mizner Development Corporation had col-

138. The Cloister, Sea Island, Georgia, 1928.

139. The Cloister, patio.

lapsed and the architect was eagerly seeking new commissions. Thus he readily agreed to design the Sea Island hotel.

After one trip to Georgia, Mizner began work on the plans. Coffin again sent his cousin to Florida to represent his interests. Jones remembered his ten-day stay as a period of parties every night, and little progress on the hotel. When he questioned Mizner about the design, the architect replied that "there was nothing to the architectural business but proportions." Mizner completed plans for the three-story hotel in April and construction began immediately. The L-shaped building contained a series of public rooms opening onto a patio on the first floor, and guest rooms on the second and third (Figs. 138, 139). From the entranceway, with its round stair tower, a hall led to a large lounge with a card loggia beyond. On the other side of the entrance Mizner placed another lounge and an enormous dining room.[18]

Although Lester Geisler supervised construction of the hotel, Mizner made two more trips to Georgia. On one of these Jones mentioned his plans to marry and asked Mizner to design an island house. Mizner planned a small, native-tabby-walled house with a typically large living room and a seven-sided loggia facing the sea. During construction Jones remembered his new wife asking Mizner to describe the fireplace mantel. The architect replied that he planned no mantel, "as some son-of-a-bitch will just put a clock on it." The small house blended with its island neighbors, yet showed the distinctive stamp of its architect.[19]

When Coffin sponsored a local competition to name the hotel, none of the suggestions seemed appropriate. Clarence Geist, who now owned the Boca Raton inn, no longer used Mizner's original name so Coffin decided to call his hotel the Cloister. Its immediate success prompted constant additions. Francis Louis Abreu (1896–1969), a Fort Lauderdale architect, moved to Georgia and designed many of the later Sea Island cottages and additions to the hotel building.[20]

As in previous years, Mizner also received commissions for additions to earlier houses. Mrs. Horace Dodge had purchased Playa Riente in 1925 from the Cosdens. After her marriage to Hugh Dillman, the Broadway actor and producer, the couple decided to enlarge the villa, asking Mizner to add a cloister and patio. The architect modeled the huge addition on the Claustro de Casa de San Juan de los Reyes at Toledo. The nearly square cloister, with outside measurements of 120 feet, lay to the north of the older house, its east side rising above the sea wall. At a cost of $175,000, it assured Playa Riente's title as Palm Beach's largest villa.[21]

For the John S. Phippses the architect designed a new outdoor swimming pool (he had earlier added a pool to the southwest wing of Casa Bendita). A continuous flow of water for the 85-foot-long pool came from a 20-foot-high replica of Charles V's Alhambra horse trough. Owners of Palm Beach villas never seemed satisfied; over the years remodeling and adding rooms became a way of life. Practically every house Mizner designed was altered, either by himself or by other architects. In the case of Concha Marina, his own early house on Jungle Road, at least four other architects made additions to the original building.[22]

Mizner's last commission of 1928 came from his former client, Alfred E. Dieterich, who had sold the family estate in Dutchess County, New York, and moved to Montecito, a suburb of Santa Barbara, in California. Mizner personally supervised construction of the large house on Park Lane which he planned around an east-facing patio, surrounded by an arcaded cloister. As in the Foerderer house, the architect shipped the products of his industries to the building site to produce the elaborate detailing of the decoration. Mizner spent much of the fall in California, staying with the Dieterichs and his niece, Ysabel Chase, at her Pebble Beach house.[23]

After abandoning practically all aspects of his practice in 1925/ 26 except those connected with Boca Raton, Mizner's ability to attract new clients suffered. While the many commissions of 1928 seemed to indicate a revival of interest in his firm, this proved untrue. The hurricane of September 1928 may explain why Mizner received so little Palm Beach work in 1929. The storm destroyed none of the houses he designed in the town, but it washed out Ocean Boulevard in several sections, caused extensive loss to buildings, and persuaded many prospective cottagers to postpone their plans. The storm also prompted the town of Palm Beach to establish an "art jury" to safeguard property owners against "unartistic building erections." The jury's membership included Mizner, Wyeth, Fa-

140. The Embassy Club (now The Society of the Four Arts), Palm Beach, 1929.

141. Memorial Fountain Plaza, Palm Beach, 1929.

tio, and H. Halpine Smith. This group reviewed all plans for new construction, calling "insubstantial" buildings to the attention of the town inspection department. The jury also acted to insure the "harmony" of new construction with surrounding buildings.[24]

In April, Lester Geisler announced that Mizner's firm had completed plans of the Florida Embassy Club for Royal Palm Way and South Lake Trail. The club, commissioned by Colonel Edward R. Bradley, opened at the beginning of the 1930 season. Operated along the lines of the London and New York Embassy Clubs, it provided dinner, late-night supper, and early-morning breakfast. A curved drive from Royal Palm Way led to the eighteenth-century Spanish colonial building (Fig. 140). Mizner placed a lounge and dining room on the right of the main hallway and the secretary's office and a loggia, which formed the entrance to the patio, on the left. An open loggia surrounded the patio. Colored lights hidden under the loggia flooded the dance area in the center of the patio, producing the effect of an illuminated glass floor. The club served breakfast in the "typically Spanish" grille room with its bare oak tables and plain wood chairs and tiled floor. Although private, and catering to a "select membership," like Colonel Bradley's Beach Club, dues were minimal. Bradley's friend Mae E. Andrews ran the club, and Mizner served on its executive committee.[25]

Mizner donated his architectural services to another Palm Beach project in 1929. Oscar G. Davies, a town councilman and publisher of the *Palm Beach Daily News,* raised a subscription from among resorters to build a memorial fountain dedicated to Palm Beach pioneers. A committee headed by Harold S. Vanderbilt collected $26,000 and persuaded the town to donate land for a park just north of the town hall. Mizner and the landscape architect gave their services, while the contractor provided his for cost. Mizner placed the fountain at the south end of the plaza with a long, narrow pool extending north (Fig. 141). Water from the fountainhead, resting on the backs of four chargers rising from the sea, fell gently into the pool.[26]

Nate Spingold, an art collector and motion picture executive, asked Mizner to plan additions and completely remodel his small Wells Road house in this year. Mizner designed a new wing which included a 54-foot-long loggia, a grille room with bar, and two servants' rooms on the first floor, and new master bedrooms and baths on the second. He combined the old living room and loggia making a large new living room, and added a fireplace and Woodite copies of the Salamanca paneling to the old dining room.[27]

Mizner also completed a series of stores and apartments on South County Road as his final commission of 1929. The complex, just north of Phipps Plaza between Seaview and Seaspray, housed McCutcheon's, a New York linen store, and Burdine's Palm Beach Shops on the first floor, and several small apartments on the second. A rounded flying staircase on Seaview gave access to the apartments.[28]

In 1929 Mizner also teamed with Alder & Harlow & Jones, a firm of Pennsylvania architects, to design new facilities for the Fox Chapel Country Club in suburban Pittsburgh. Although Mizner's partners in the project had designed the original clubhouse, the club membership refused to accept the elaborate Spanish structure proposed by Mizner and turned to Brandon Smith, a Pittsburgh architect, for their new building.[29]

From his arrival in Florida until 1925 Mizner built nothing outside the Palm Beach area. After 1925 he completed most of his

142. E. F. Hutton Brokerage, Palm Beach, 1930.

major work in other states. With hurricane damage curtailing many new projects in 1929, and the collapse of the stock market making large-scale building activity unlikely in 1930, Mizner considered moving his practice to California. Perhaps the Dieterich house gave hope of additional commissions in his native state. Moreover, by 1930 no member of his family remained in Florida. Henry Mizner and his family had moved to Paris after the land bust, Horace Chase had died in an airplane crash, and Ysabel, now married, lived in California. To escape the legal difficulties arising from the Boca Raton venture, Wilson had moved to Hollywood where he became a movie script writer. Boca Raton problems also continued to plague Mizner. In the spring of 1929 a group of investors charged the officers of Mizner Development Corporation with conspiracy to inflate the value of Boca Raton land. Their suit asked for the recovery of $1.45 million. The scarcity of Palm Beach commissions, the wish to be near the remaining members of his family, and the desire for freedom from the continuing lawsuits, all encouraged Mizner to move to California.[30]

In 1918 Mizner had applied for Florida State professional registration under the 1915 law which gave exemption from examination to an architect "long established . . . in his community who has to his credit a number of buildings recognized as being of good design and construction." He received Certificate #109, dated 29 January 1919, and practiced as a licensed architect throughout this period. California refused to grant exemption from examination to architects licensed out-of-state who had never passed a qualifying exam. As California demanded a particularly difficult examination, Mizner applied to the Florida Board to let him take a "Senior Examination." This exam, designed specifically for those who had practiced in the state for at least ten years, called for the applicant to submit examples of work, photographs of completed buildings, recommendations from clients, and solutions to specifically posed architectural problems. A board committee conducted an hour-long oral examination, basing questions on the work submitted. Mizner received a grade of ninety-four on the exam and the board voted unanimously to change his status from "Registered by Exemption" to "Registered by Senior Examination."[31]

Early in 1918, during his first months in Florida, Mizner had suffered a heart attack. Although he recovered much of his old vitality, by the end of the twenties his lack of exercise, his great weight, and the emotional shock of the failure of the Boca Raton development all took their toll. As early as 1928 Singer hinted at Mizner's

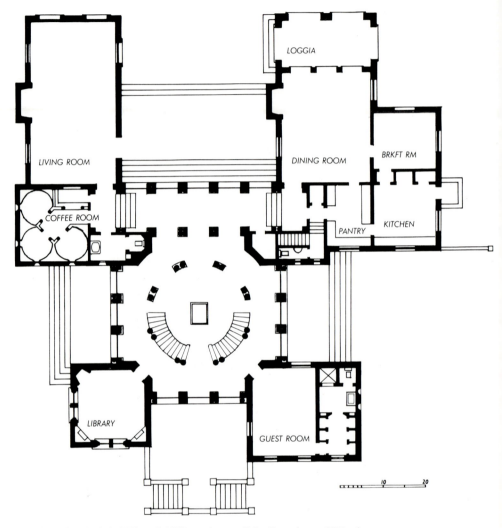

143. Casa Coe da Sol, William J. Williams house, Saint Petersburg, 1931, plan.

declining health in his foreword to *Florida Architecture:* "From his tall, imposing presence one would never think that his health is far from robust." Realizing he could never establish and manage a large practice again, the architect gave up his California plans.[32]

The last three years of Mizner's life saw many projects, though he completed only a few additional commissions. In 1930 he designed a brokerage office for E. F. Hutton on County Road just south of the Plaza Building (Fig. 142). The two buildings form the entrance to Phipps Plaza. Mizner used quarry key stone for the exterior walls and placed the entrance at an angle on the corner. Two massive

144. Casa Coe da Sol, rotunda.

rusticated piers topped by round finials framed the door. The architect designed a more utilitarian office space than in the earlier Harris brokerage, with a smaller brokerage room.[33]

Mizner spent much time in 1930 on two projects that were never accepted. The first, a Dallas, Texas, house for Alexander Camp, went through at least three revisions. Beginning with completely realized plans for a large Pueblo-style mansion, similar in detail to the Bradley ranch house, Mizner pared down both the number of rooms and their size in later proposals. After all Mizner's work, Camp then asked Maurice Fatio to design the Dallas house. The second project was an elaborate Spanish mansion for the Hugh Dillmans in Grosse Pointe, Michigan. The Dillmans had enlarged the estate of Mrs. Dillman's late husband, Horace Dodge, purchasing additional land and the original buildings of the Country Club of Detroit. They planned to raze Dodge's Rose Terrace and the club buildings and construct a new mansion. Once more Mizner completed detailed drawings, only to lose the job to Horace Trumbauer of Philadelphia, who designed the Dillmans' Louis XV chateau on the shores of Lake St. Clair.[34]

In 1931 Mizner designed his last large house, a mansion set on Boca Ciega Bay in St. Petersburg, Florida. Byron Simonson, a Mizner draftsman in the mid-twenties, rejoined the firm and supervised construction of the Florida west-coast house. Known as Casa Coe da Sol, or house of the setting sun, it was commissioned by William J. Williams, the founder of the Western Southern Life Insurance Company of Cincinnati.

Mizner's plan centered on a two-story rotunda entered through sliding glass doors from an east-facing open terrace (Fig. 143). A double-curved flying staircase of poured artificial quarry key stone, called Keyite, led to a second story balcony supported by cast Doric columns. Smaller cast Ionic columns supported the round blue glass ceiling (Fig. 144). Skylights in the rotunda roof allowed light to filter through the blue glass, lighting the circular fountain in the center of the rotunda. On the right of the entry Mizner detailed a paneled library with large windows framed by trefoil Gothic tracery and a pointed, domed ceiling with decorated exposed groins. Opposite the library he used a guest suite to balance the entrance facade (Fig. 145). From the arcade surrounding the rotunda, large arched doorways on both the north and south sides led to formally arranged gardens. Three arches opposite the entry defined the gallery facing the western patio and the bay. The southern wing on the bay side contained a 37-by-20-foot living room and a coffee or cocktail room; in the north wing were the dining room, breakfast room, dining loggia, and kitchen and service rooms. In both wings the rooms had two and three exposures and water views. Mizner gained a Moorish effect in the coffee room with a triple domed ceiling and glazed wall tiles (Fig. 146).

Perhaps in recognition of changing styles, Mizner used art

deco decoration for the major guest bedroom and bathroom (Fig. 147). Williams asked the architect to incorporate a recently remodeled cottage on the grounds into the new house. Mizner installed the cottage over the dining room where it became the master bedroom suite. Although smaller in scale than his largest Palm Beach mansions, in the Casa Coe da Sol Mizner created one of his most dramatic houses.[35]

When the Florida East Coast Railway removed its tracks in 1931, Palm Beach redesigned Main Street and changed its name to Royal Poinciana Way. The new plans called for a widened roadway with a broad median park planted with royal palms to extend from the lake to County Road. A proposed post office building on County

145. Casa Coe da Sol, entrance facade.

146. Casa Coe da Sol, coffee room.

Road provided the focal point for the new road. Mizner submitted detailed plans for a Spanish-style post office, only to have the government deny him the contract. In 1931 he also remodeled and redecorated an apartment for Oscar G. Davies on the second floor of Davies's *Palm Beach Daily News* building on South County Road.[36]

In 1932 Mizner completed his last house in Palm Beach. He designed the small, three-bedroom villa at 323 Brazilian Avenue for Kenneth D. Alexander, a West Palm Beach auto dealer, who built the

147. Casa Coe da Sol, bathroom.

house as an investment. Mizner sited the narrow one-story house on the east side of the lot, orienting the living room and dining room to a small protected court on the west (Fig. 148). Only a large double door surrounded by glazed tile and two small grilled windows faced the street (Fig. 149). Mizner placed the living room, with its high, beamed ceiling, in the middle of the house. A stained glass window protected the privacy of the room on the east, while three French doors led to the loggia and the court. William F. Bonsack, a Miami contractor, built the house, the smallest of Mizner's Palm Beach

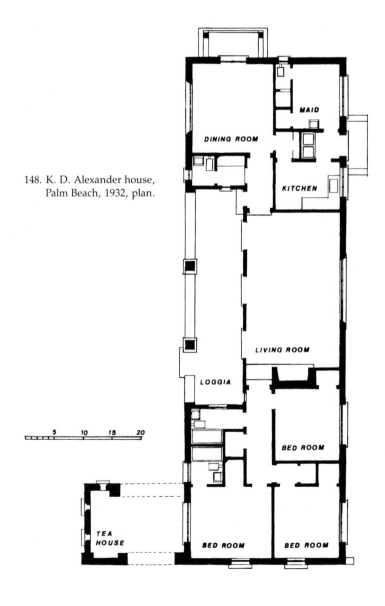

148. K. D. Alexander house, Palm Beach, 1932, plan.

149. K. D. Alexander house.

designs. During the preceding year Mizner had designed both a house and a small shopping center for Bonsack in Miami Beach. Bonsack, a carpenter turned small builder, probably failed to secure financing to construct the shopping center on his lot at Dade Boulevard and Alton Road. He did build a house in Miami at this time, though not from Mizner's plans.[37]

Mizner's last known completed commission was a movie theater for Herman Gold in Belle Glade. Gold and his son-in-law, Abe Dubros, opened a Palm Beach clothing store on Main Street in 1925. In 1926 a bank failure connected to the land bust practically bankrupted the men, who decided to leave Palm Beach for the "frontier" of Pahokee where they invested their remaining money in a group of stores and a small 300-seat movie house. With the success of their Pahokee theater they asked Mizner to design a larger movie house in Belle Glade. The simple wooden framed structure with an art deco facade had 410 seats on the main floor and an additional 190 in the balcony, which was reached by two sets of exterior stairs. Mizner placed two small rental stores on either side of the lobby entrance to the auditorium. Herman Gold named the movie house the Everglades Theater. Mizner, who began his Florida architectural career with the fashionable Everglades Club of Palm Beach, ended it with the Everglades Theater in rural Belle Glade.[38]

Byron Simonson took responsibility for design work in the last years of the Mizner firm, while the architect, his health continuing to decline, wrote his memoirs. In the fall of 1932 Sears Publishing Company of New York issued the first volume of *The Many Mizners*. One reviewer, while saying Mizner lacked literary technique, called his book "one of the most rollicking, rowdiest pieces of humor that any reader will encounter." Without question, Mizner wished to entertain and sell books. The professional career of an architect received slight attention, as the author lightly traced his life from his birth to the death of Ella Mizner in 1915. He pictured a carefree childhood as a younger son in a large and indulgent family which encouraged and rewarded precocity. Although he mentioned many of the events and influences that produced the mature man—his accident, the gift of watercolors from brother Henry, the beauty he found in Guatemala, and his inability to function in the formal academic setting—all of these became secondary to the tales of high and low adventure that pictured the architect as more interested in his next party invitation than in his next commission. Yet for the man who called formal wear his "fishing clothes," the memoirs give an accurate picture of at least part of his life. He believed his readers had no interest in the details of his architecture. Thus when he mentioned clients he used a social setting: a weekend party at Bourke Kochran's estate, or Mrs. I. Townsend Burden arriving in her Rolls for an afternoon visit after his 1917 accident. He told the stories of the sophisticated social architect, the anecdotes that amused and interested those clients who wished to be included in this select company.

Palm Beach eagerly awaited Mizner's second volume which the Sears Company announced for the 1933 season. Those familiar with his wit and "Rabelaisian humor," suggested the architect might "wait in California while it comes off the press." Certainly Palm Beach, which had heard Mizner's many stories and knew his love of gossip, expected him to write an exposé of fashionable society. Mizner never finished the second volume. In fact, the 128 pages of typescript that he completed would have disappointed Palm Beach. In writing about the years from 1918 to 1924, the architect told of the building of the Everglades Club and the beginnings of Mizner Industries, of his pride in designing the Cosden house, of his problems with a few clients, and of his life among the wealthy and social resorters. When he mentioned a former client, he praised or told a lighthearted anecdote. Could Mrs. Stotesbury object to Mizner's account of his carefully training an Italian-speaking artist to pronounce her name "Strawberry"? The famous, and sometimes cruel, Mizner wit came out in stories of non-Mizner clients. The "peerless Irene," so fat that even a Mizner armchair was too small, lacked taste: an obvious explanation for her choice of a rival architect. The typescript disappoints the reader wishing more information about Mizner's architecture, his clients' demands, his design problems and solutions, and his sources of inspiration.[39]

Throughout the years following the collapse of Boca Raton Mizner continued to live in the Villa Mizner. Completely dependent on his professional fees and the profits from Mizner Industries for his livelihood, after 1929 neither source could support the Mizner style of life. Several friends gave financial assistance: Mrs. Henry Rea, who had purchased Lagomar from John Magee, often paid his servants' salaries and his grocery bills, and Edward S. Moore, who owned Mizner's old house at 1800 South Ocean Boulevard, once slipped Mizner's secretary $10,000 in cash. A heart attack claimed Mizner's life on 5 February 1933. Hours before his death, his brother Wilson wired from Hollywood: "Stop dying. Am trying to write a comedy." Mizner's answer characterized his view of life: "Am going to get well. The comedy goes on."[40]

The failure of the Mizner Development Corporation devastated Mizner's personal fortune; it did not end his professional career. Following the collapse of Boca Raton the Mizner firm continued to design and complete projects in many areas of the country. Nonetheless, Mizner never regained the success he had known in Palm Beach. The small, ill-proportioned houses copied from his style during the land boom made Spanish architecture less fashionable for Palm Beach trend-setters. As a successful society architect, Mizner designed for an elite clientele. Their houses, and their social prestige, brought him a steady stream of new commissions. His lack of Palm Beach projects during the Boca Raton years broke this continuity. Newcomers to the resort no longer automatically assumed they needed Mizner to assure their social success. The competition in the late twenties from Maurice Fatio, Howard Major, and John

Volk also hurt Mizner's practice. The collapse of the land boom had little effect on building activity in Palm Beach, though both the hurricane of 1928 and the collapse of the stock market a year later slowed construction. Finally, Mizner's declining health accounted for his inability to promote his firm.

The era of the great Palm Beach Spanish mansion ended shortly after Mizner's death. Although few regular resorters found their incomes seriously affected by the Great Depression, they often "didn't want to make a show of their money." Howard Major's Alley had introduced the more modest British colonial style to the island. He, and the other architects of the era all designed in this style, and by the end of the thirties they also accepted many commissions for Georgian houses. Mizner's hollow-tile and stucco buildings had proven popular because they were less costly and more easily constructed than the elaborately crafted mansions of Flagler and Deering. Now architects argued that the British colonial and Georgian styles saved home builders the expense of "hand-wrought beamed ceilings, grill-work, and stained glass." Soon acres of white roofs dotted a landscape that earlier had known only red tile.[41]

Mizner's reputation as an architect reached its lowest ebb with the publication of Alva Johnston's *The Legendary Mizners* in 1953. The book, a dual biography of Addison and Wilson that originally appeared as a series in the *New Yorker,* was a deliberate compound of half-truths and fiction. Johnston said he had to make Addison's life more colorful because Wilson ran away with the story. A later writer claimed Johnston conducted his research in Palm Beach bars where the patrons vied to tell anecdotes. Of course, in many cases they only repeated Mizner's own stories. From these sources, Mizner became a con man with no architectural training or license. All the cocktail gossip that had entertained Palm Beach for years found its way into Johnston's pages. The result was a lively, witty, and completely delightful volume. Unfortunately, its authority codified and sanctified the Mizner myths.[42]

The book amused Palm Beach; it did not amuse everyone in the architectural profession. In a virulent *Architectural Record* review, Frank G. Lopez attacked Mizner as a "slight architectural talent," a "shady 'architect,' " and a "never-legitimately-frocked architect," and called his architecture the mere copying of "Latinesque precedents." Finding Mizner's "architectural principles . . . appalling," Lopez expressed concern about the image the "uninformed public" received of the profession from Johnston's book. Moreover, Lopez's review reflected the architectural establishment's opinion. Eclectic historical styles like Mizner's no longer found favor in a profession dedicated to functionalism.[43]

Palm Beach's "barefoot" era following World War II did little either to help Mizner's reputation or to preserve his buildings. Many habitués now spent most of the year in town. They demanded greater informality, and particularly the comfort of air-conditioning. In this period many owners of Mizner's houses "modernized," tearing out heavily beamed ceilings, blocking up fireplaces, and painting walls and paneling a uniform flat white. Other owners saw their Mizner houses as anachronisms, too large to air-condition, too expensive to maintain, and too hard to staff. In a few short years Playa Riente, El Mirasol, Casa Bendita, The Towers, Casa Florencia, Casa Joseto, and La Fontana were destroyed, making way for housing developments and new high-rise condominiums.

Several events of the seventies combined to create new interest in Mizner, his architecture, and in architectural preservation in south Florida. The founding of the Boca Raton Historical Society meant a renewed interest in the architect's accomplishments and plans for the city. The publication of Barbara D. Hoffstot's *Landmark Architecture of Palm Beach*, with its appeal "to fight when necessary!" to save the town's architectural heritage, convinced many to take seriously the resort architecture of Palm Beach. The sameness of the unending rows of developer houses constructed during the sixties also prompted a new look at the older, more gracious styles. Finally, Christina Orr's Mizner show at the Norton Gallery, the Society of the Four Arts, and the Henry Morrison Flagler Museum, brought together a collection of Mizner drawings, photographs, and products of his industries which allowed a reevaluation of his work.

These events led to the saving of one of Mizner's last remaining great mansions. When the owner of the William Gray Warden house asked town officials for permission to raze the structure in 1977 and construct townhouses on the land, the new interest in Mizner's architecture helped decide the town council to deny his request. After two years of litigation in which the courts found for the owner, the house was saved at the last moment when Robert Eigelberger received permission to restore the mansion and convert it into six condominium units. Moreover, the controversy over the Warden house also led the town council to adopt a landmarks preservation ordinance.[44]

Interest in Mizner's architecture has influenced a revival of the style in south Florida. Unfortunately, "Spanish," "Mediterranean," or "Mizner style" developments often feature the usual tract-house design with a few cosmetic touches: an arched entrance, a grilled window or gate, and red-tiled roof. On the other hand, Mizner and the Spanish style have also served as inspiration for several unusual south Florida projects. Johnson & Burgee's Miami Cultural Center, a large complex that includes the Miami-Dade Public Library, the Historical Association of Southern Florida Museum, and the Center for Fine Arts grouped around an immense patio; Gee & Jenson's additions for the Boca Raton City Hall and the city's public libary; and many smaller projects have, in the style of the postmodernists, incorporated specific references to Mizner's architecture without attempting to re-create a 1920s Spanish building. Mizner, who served as an inspiration for his own era, has once more become a model for a new generation of architects.

Notes

CHAPTER 1

1. The most scholarly published account of the Mizner family is J. Camille Showalter, "The Mizners in Perspective," J. Camille Showalter, ed., *The Many Mizners: California Clan Extraordinary*, pp. 11–26. See also, Alva Johnston, *The Legendary Mizners*, pp. 3–20; Edward Dean Sullivan, *The Fabulous Wilson Mizner*, pp. 29–53; Addison Mizner, *The Many Mizners*, pp. 1–26. Complete authors' names and full titles will be cited only on first use in each chapter.

2. "The Wreck of the Ill Fated Steamer *Independence*," Showalter, ed., *The Many Mizners*, pp. 5–9.

3. Warren A. Beck and David A. Williams, *California: A History of the Golden State*, pp. 156, 162; Semple first named his town Francisca in honor of General Vallejo's wife. When Yerba Buena changed its name to San Francisco, to avoid confusion Semple substituted Señora Vallejo's second name: Benicia. See also Robert Bruegmann, *Benicia: Portrait of an Early California Town*.

4. *New York Times*, 30 March 1889.

5. Mizner, *Many Mizners*, p. 48.

6. Mary Patricia Chapman, "The Mission of Lansing Bond Mizner to Central America," *The Historian*, August 1957, pp. 388–89.

7. Mizner, *Many Mizners*, p. 56; Elizabeth P. Benson, *The Maya World*, pp. 7–10.

8. Sullivan, *Fabulous Wilson Mizner*, p. 64; Mizner, *Many Mizners*, p. 49; Johnston, *Legendary Mizners*, p. 5; Chapman, "The Mission of L. B. Mizner," p. 390 f.n.

9. Mizner, *Many Mizners*, pp. 57–58; Chapman, "The Mission of L. B. Mizner," p. 391.

10. Chapman, "The Mission of L. B. Mizner," pp. 394–95; Warren Albert Beck, "American Policy in Guatemala, 1839–1900," Ph.D. diss., Ohio State University, 1954, pp. 93–99.

11. Chapman, "The Mission of L. B. Mizner," p. 398; Mizner, *Many Mizners*, pp. 62–64.

12. Mizner, *Many Mizners*, p. 63.

13. Ida Tarbell, "Addison Mizner, Appreciation of a Layman," *The Florida Architecture of Addison Mizner*, n.p.

14. Mizner, *Many Mizners*, p. 64.

15. Ibid., p. 65; Harold Gilliam, *The San Francisco Experience*, p. 33; Roger Olmstead and T. H. Watkins, *Here Today: San Francisco's Architectural Heritage*, p. 330. See also, Frederick Hamilton, "The Work of Willis Polk and Company," *The Architect and Engineer*, April 1911, pp. 35–77; and Richard Longstreth, *On the Edge of the World: Four Architects in San Francisco at the Turn of the Century*.

16. Mizner, *Many Mizners*, p. 74.

17. Tarbell, "Appreciation," n.p.

18. Mizner, *Many Mizners*, pp. 84–85; Johnston, *Legendary Mizners*, pp. 7–8. In 1893 Mizner visited the Columbian Exposition in Chicago. The fair buildings of McKim, Mead & White, George B. Post, Richard M. Hunt, and Louis Sullivan captivated the young man, who said he spent three months "absorbing architecture." He also met Richard Harding Davis at the fair. Mizner claimed that his tale of spiriting Barriose from jail and the country gave Davis the "underlying plot" for his novel *Soldier of Fortune*. Mizner, *Many Mizners*, pp. 67–69.

19. Mizner, *Many Mizners*, pp. 119–20, 151.

20. Ibid., pp. 178–182; Mizner Scrapbook, "Portraits," Society of the Four Arts Library, Palm Beach, contains seventeen photographs of paintings from the royal collection identified on the reverse in Mizner's hand. See also photograph, Showalter, ed., *Many Mizners*, p. 28.

21. Mizner, *Many Mizners*, p. 183.

22. Oliver Herford, Ethel Watts Mumford, and Addison Mizner, *Cynic's Calendar of Revised Wisdom*. Paul Elder and Company of San Francisco and New York published at least seven editions of the bound calendar. In 1907 the company also published a set of "Cynic's Post Cards." Johnston, *Legendary Mizners*, p. 11.

23. Mizner, *Many Mizners*, pp. 201–5.

24. Ibid., p. 217.

25. Ibid., pp. 222–23.

26. Ibid., pp. 224–25.

27. Ibid., pp. 228–29.

CHAPTER 2

1. Addison Mizner, *The Many Mizners*, pp. 233–35; Alex Waugh (see chapter 4, note 39) said that Mrs. Oelrichs and her sister displayed Mizner's Central American pieces in their houses, helping to make them fashionable. Alex Waugh, untitled typescript (Boca Raton Historical Society), chap. 3, p. 6.

2. Marie Dressler, *My Own Story*, passim; Alice Mizner Lewitin to author, 28 December 1981.

3. Mizner, *Many Mizners*, pp. 252–53; Walton J. Ferguson, *Rosecliff*, passim; Charles C. Baldwin, *Stanford White*, pp. 279–80.

4. Mizner, *Many Mizners*, pp. 262–63.

5. Ibid., pp. 265–66; Allen Churchill, *The Splendor Seekers: An Informal History of America's Multimillionaire Spenders, Members of the 50 Million Dollar Club*, pp. 185–96.

6. Mizner, *Many Mizners*, pp. 252–53; *New York Times*, 4 February 1909, 21 July 1917. The Brown house, at 154 East 70th Street, is today the Lenox School. See also Christopher Gray, "Neighborhood," *Avenue*, 20 September 1982, pp. 58–62.

7. Mizner, *Many Mizners*, p. 284; Joan Kent, "The Baxter Homestead: Busy Past, Busy Present," *Cow Neck Historical Society Journal*, October 1970, pp. 12–14; *Plain Talk*, 4 July 1914.

8. "Old Cow Bay Manor House," *Architectural Record*, March 1917, pp. 259–66.

9. *Plain Talk*, 11 November 1911, 23 December 1911, 6 January 1912.

10. Ella Watson Mizner to her sisters, 26 September 1912, to Sister Elsie Watson, 4 July 1912, and to Margot and Henry Mizner, 29 December 1913. Privately owned.

11. Mizner, *Many Mizners*, p. 284. There is no evidence that Mizner was literally Burbank's godson; to Mizner all Californians became Burbank's godchildren. *Plain Talk*, 16 September 1911; *Port Washington News*, 30 November 1912; Ralph C. Martin, *Jennie: The Life of Lady Randolph Churchill*, vol. 2, p. 308.

12. Alva Johnston, *The Legendary Mizners*, pp. 18–19.

13. *Plain Talk*, 25 November 1911.

14. Ibid.; it has been impossible to determine if the house was built as designed. Mrs. Monson owned two lots on Upper Drive in Huntington Bay Estates in 1914; see "Assessment Roll of Town of Huntington, Suffolk, 1914," p. 116. A survey of this lot dated 3 March 1950 shows a house in outline that approximates Mizner's sketch. A fire destroyed this house in the mid-1950s. Neither immediate neighbors nor the town historian can recall the original house. Records of Huntington, L.I., and personal interviews conducted by Mrs. Henry Petronis, 14 and 15 November 1981.

15. *Plain Talk*, 14 October 1911. The Thomas estate (now 235 Middle Neck Road) was sold c. 1925 and a large Beaux-Arts mansion erected on the site of the tennis house, which was moved to a location directly on the beach. At that time a two-story wing was added to the south end and the original brickwork overlayed with stucco. It is now used as a guest house. A large two-story garage-stable on the estate retains its brickwork and small diamond-paned windows. Its decoration closely matches that of the tennis house sketch and probably was built at the same time. Interview with current owners, 22 March 1982.

16. *New York Times*, 6 April 1926; see also Nancy Dubner, "National Register of Historic Places Inventory-Nomination Form: White Pine Camp," 1 March 1978.

17. *Plain Talk*, 14 October 1911; *St. Regian: Yearbook of Paul Smith's College of Arts and Sciences*, 1949, np.; James R. Wood, *Paul Smith's College: 1937–1980*, pp. 108, 131–32. In the early 1920s White sold the camp to Irwin R. Kirkwood, publisher of the *Kansas City Star*. In the summer of 1926 President Coolidge made the camp his summer White House, staying on to September. In 1930 Mrs. Edgar Stern and Mrs. David Levy, daughters of Julius Rosenwald, president of Sears-Roebuck Company, purchased the camp. After eighteen years and the growth of their children, they gave the camp to Paul Smith's College in 1948. The college forestry majors used— and abused—the camp until 1975, when the Arab oil embargo made it too expensive to heat the camp during the Adirondack winters. A fire in February 1966 destroyed Mizner's living room cabin, used as a recreation hall by the college. On a 14 October 1981 visit, Neil Surprenant, college librarian, guided me through the closed and derelict camp.

18. *Plain Talk,* 14 October 1911. The posts of the entry gate at Rock Hall are designed in the form of a Japanese lantern. These lanterns, shown in Mizner's sketch for the Monson house, can also be found in his own garden at Port Washington and in the Thomas tennis house garden. See also, William H. Jordy with Christopher P. Monkhouse, "Three Rhode Island Living Halls of the 1920s and 1930s," in Helen Searing, ed., *In Search of Modern Architecture: A Tribute to Henry-Russell Hitchcock.*

19. *Plain Talk,* 30 September 1911; telephone interview with Ralph D. Howell of the E. W. Howell Company, contractors for E. F. Hutton, 20 October 1981. See also, E. W. Howell Company, *Noted Long Island Homes,* n.p., and Liisa and Donald Sclare, *Beaux-Arts Estates: A Guide to the Architecture of Long Island,* pp. 138–43, for first floor plans of the remodeled house. The Sclares mention that Charles M. Hart designed the residence for "the site of an older, existing frame house." Today it is the administrative center of C. W. Post College of Long Island University. Blueprints for later additions, but not the remodeling, are in the collection of the college's service department. Mizner's plans, Historical Society of Palm Beach County, Palm Beach, hereafter HSPBC.

20. *Plain Talk,* 17 February 1912; Ella Watson Mizner to Sister Elsie Watson, 4 July 1912. Detailed plans for completed house and drawings of entire project, HSPBC.

21. *Plain Talk,* 8 June 1912.

22. Ella Watson Mizner to Margot Mizner, 24 August 1914; Louise Tompkins to author, 1 June 1982; colored sketch, "Detail Deitrich [*sic*] Ceiling," Mizner Scrapbook, "Ceilings, Murals, Paneling and Doors" (Society of the Four Arts Library, Palm Beach). The house, which has only been used for vacations and as a hunting lodge, has never been remodeled or redecorated. Most of Mizner's original Spanish furnishings remain. Although it is impossible to date the house from records, the evidence points to construction in 1912/13.

23. A. J. Weise, *History of the City of Troy,* pp. 78–79; *New York Times,* 11 August 1949; complete plans, HSPBC. Today the house is the admissions building for the New York Institute of Technology.

24. Wayne Andrews, *The Vanderbilt Legend: The Story of the Vanderbilt Family 1794–1940,* pp. 251–53, 286.

25. Ibid., p. 286; see also Augusta Owen Patterson, *American Homes of Today,* p. 15, for a photograph of Beacon Towers, Mrs. Belmont's Sands Point house; Mizner's sketches, HSPBC.

26. Johnston, *Legendary Mizners,* p. 19; plans for beach house, HSPBC. Hunt & Hunt did design a Chinese tea house for Mrs. Belmont on the grounds of Marble House in Newport in 1913. After Mrs. Belmont's death William R. Hearst purchased her Sands Point estate. In 1938 Beacon Towers was razed, although the main gate with its impressive towers remains as an entrance to a small compound of houses. *Port Washington News,* 14 September 1972.

27. Stephen Brown died shortly after completing the house, which Mrs. Brown then sold in December 1919 to Gordan H. Balch. Mrs. Caro Richardson (the Browns' daughter) to author, 2 March 1982. Mrs. Richardson remembers Mizner as "fat and jolly." By 1921 Charles Stone owned the house which had already been remodeled. "The Home of Charles A. Stone, Piping Rock, L.I.," *House and Garden,* October 1921, pp. 32–33; the article credits Wilson Mizner as the original architect. Photographs and plans in sales brochure, Weekes & Weeks of Oyster Bay, c. 1922 (Society for the Preservation of Long Island Antiquities). Over the years the Brown house has been remodeled several times. When the current owner decided to add a library wing to the house he found the foundations for the old living room wing which

had been destroyed earlier. The present house thus appears similar to that built in 1917. Interview with current owner, 22 March 1982.

28. *House and Garden*, April 1916, p. 41, October 1916, p. 38, January 1917, p. 34.

29. Addison Mizner, typescript autobiography (HSPBC), pp. 2–4, 17–20.

CHAPTER 3

1. Addison Mizner, typescript autobiography (Historical Society of Palm Beach County, Palm Beach), pp. 17–20.

2. Ruth Brandon, *A Capitalist Romance: Singer and the Sewing Machine*, pp. 216–22; Isadora Duncan, *My Life*, p. 333; for some reason, standard south Florida practice describes Singer as "the illegitimate son of Isaac M. Singer." Although Isaac did have illegitimate children, Paris was not one of them. The rector of St. John's Episcopal Church married his parents in January 1863.

3. *Palm Beach Post*, 29 July 1918; Mizner TS., pp. 24–27.

4. Amy Lyman Phillips, "The Everglades Club," *Palm Beach Life*, 16 January 1945, p. 90; *Palm Beach Post*, 7 September 1918; Mizner TS., p. 27.

5. A. J. and Kathryn Abbey Hanna, *Florida's Golden Sands*, p. 367; this McCormick has often been confused with Colonel Robert R. McCormick, publisher of the *Chicago Tribune*, who came to Palm Beach in the 1920s. See also "The Work of Messrs. Carrère and Hastings," *The Architectural Record*, January 1910, pp. 1–120.

6. Sidney Walter Martin, *Florida's Flagler*, pp. 142–43; Hanna and Hanna, *Golden Sands*, p. 265.

7. *Palm Beach Weekly News*, 6 February 1920; *The Henry Morrison Flagler Museum*, pp. 3–8; Hanna and Hanna, *Golden Sands*, p. 266.

8. The Junior League of the Palm Beaches, Inc., *Palm Beach Entertains: Then and Now*, pp. 7–8.

9. Ibid., pp. 13–17.

10. Ibid., pp. 9–13; Cleveland Amory, *The Last Resorts*, pp. 399–440.

11. Mizner TS., pp. 30–31.

12. "Our War Work," *The Touchstone*, August 1918, pp. 371–80.

13. Mizner TS., pp. 27–31.

14. Ibid., pp. 36–39.

15. *Palm Beach Post*, 2, 3, 6 August 1918.

16. "Our War Work," *Touchstone*, p. 379.

17. Ibid., p. 379; *Palm Beach Weekly News*, 1 November 1918; Amy Lyman Phillips, "The Everglades Club," *Palm Beach Life*, 14 February 1951, p. 34.

18. Mizner TS., p. 40.

19. *Palm Beach Post*, 24 July 1918, 14 September 1918.

20. Mizner TS., p. 75.

21. Ibid., pp. 37, 44; *Palm Beach Post*, 24 July 1918.

22. See *Touchstone*, pp. 373–74, and Historical Society of Palm Beach County for plans.

23. Phillips, "Everglades" (1951), p. 34; *Palm Beach Post*, 4 April 1920.

24. Phillips, "Everglades" (1951), p. 35 and (1945), p. 98.

25. Mizner TS., pp. 40, 52; Phillips, "Everglades," (1951), p. 45.

26. *Palm Beach Post*, 16 February 1920.

27. Ibid., 18 April 1920, 12 January, 27 April 1923.

28. Phillips, "Everglades," (1951), p. 45; *Palm Beach Post*, 19 December 1919, 18 April 1920.

29. Although the Everglades Club has been remodeled continuously since Mizner's day, his work can be traced though two publications. Plans for the original clubhouse appeared in *Touchstone*, August 1918. In 1929 Clifford C. Wendehack published new plans in *Golf and Country Clubs: A Survey of Planning, Construction and Equipment of the Modern Club House*. It can be assumed that these plans represent the extent of Mizner's additions and remodelings.

30. *Palm Beach Post*, 8 January 1926; Alice De Lamar to author, 4 December 1981.

31. Mizner TS., p. 56.

32. *Palm Beach Daily News*, 13 December 1918; Mary Fanton Roberts, "Exotic Beauty of Palm Beach Homes," *Art and Decoration*, December 1923, pp. 23–24; "Prospectus, Mizner Industries," typescript, n.d., HSPBC. The workmen never shaped the tiles over their thighs as Palm Beach legend claims. This legend probably is a product of the name Las Manos, implying "handmade," which only meant the products of the pottery were not made by machine.

33. Don Morris, "Mizner Industries: Details of the Palm Beaches' Greatest Manufactory," *The New Palm Beaches*, p. 1; "Pottery of Character," Mizner Industries brochure, n.d., HSPBC.

34. Mizner Industries brochures, n.d., HSPBC; Alex Waugh, untitled typescript (Boca Raton Historical Society), chap. 6, p. 5. For a recent overview of Mizner Industries, see Christina Orr-Cahall, "The 'Total Environment' of Addison Mizner," *Antiques World*, December 1980, pp. 74–81.

35. Waugh TS., chap. 7, p. 14; Alva Johnston, *The Legendary Mizners*, p. 60; Mizner Industries brochures, n.d., HSPBC.

36. Steven A. Seiden, "The Mizner Touch," senior thesis, Yale University, 1958, p. 46; Don Morris, "Woodite, Incorporated: The Palm Beaches' Newest Industry," *The New Palm Beaches*, n.p.

37. Seiden, "The Mizner Touch," pp. 43–44; Morris, "Mizner Industries," n.p. When used on oceanfront houses, the cast stone work often deteriorated with age. In order to make the casting sturdy, Mizner added too much steel. Salt water, seeping through the cement, rusted and expanded the steel which caused the cement surface to crack.

38. Mizner File (Henry Morrison Flagler Museum Archives, Palm Beach), contains a series of 1929 letters detailing leasing arrangements between Mizner Industries and the Florida East Coast Railway.

39. *Palm Beach Post*, 29 August 1975; *Palm Beach Daily News*, 15 December 1969; Mizner Industries financial report, 1929, HSPBC.

40. John Taylor Boyd, "The Florida House: Mr. Addison Mizner, the Architect, Recounts the Birth of the New Florida Architecture at Palm Beach in an Interview," *Arts and Decoration*, January 1930, p. 80; David Gray, *Thomas Hastings*, p. 32; see also "Work of Messrs. Carrère and Hastings," *Architectural Record*, pp. 1–120; and Charlton Tebeau, *A History of Florida*, pp. 117–21.

41. "Vizcaya Guide Book," n.d.; Merrill Folsom, *Great American Houses*, pp. 232–45.

42. Mizner TS., p. 56.

CHAPTER 4

1. James H. R. Cromwell, "Palm Beach Past and Present," *Country Life*, January 1935, p. 58; *Palm Beach Daily News*, 8 January 1920; see also Barbara D. Hoffstot, *Landmark Architecture of Palm Beach*, passim.

2. *Palm Beach Post*, 3 May 1921; Augusta Owen Patterson, *American Homes of Today*, np.; Hoffstot, *Landmark Architecture*, pp. 76–77, 212–13.

3. *Palm Beach Post*, 8 July 1919; see also *Florida Architecture and Allied Arts* (Yearbook of the South Florida Chapter of the American Institute of Architects), 1937 through 1941, for Geiger's later work.

4. *Palm Beach Daily News*, 14 November 1919, 13 January 1922, 12 January 1923, 16 March 1981, 7 February 1982.

5. *Palm Beach Post*, 12 July 1920, 10 May 1923, 26 April 1929, 7 April 1942; see also *Florida Architecture and Allied Arts*, 1940–1941.

6. Addison Mizner, typescript autobiography (Historical Society of Palm Beach County, Palm Beach), p. 45.

7. *Philadelphia Evening Bulletin*, 1 February 1940.

8. Nathaniel Burt, *The Perennial Philadelphians: The Anatomy of an American Aristocracy*, pp. 162–63; "The Stotesburys," *Fortune Magazine*, February 1936, pp. 111–12.

9. Mizner TS., pp. 47–48; Burt, *Philadelphians*, pp. 537–38; *Palm Beach Post*, 27 January 1920.

10. *Palm Beach Weekly News*, 7 November 1919; *Palm Beach Daily News*, 7 January 1920; "The Edward T. Stotesbury Home," Ruby Pierce Papers, HSPBC; sales brochure, "El Mirasol," n.d., HSPBC.

11. *Palm Beach Post*, 27 January 1920, 31 March 1923.

12. *Palm Beach Daily News*, 15 February 1926, 27 February 1925.

13. Cleveland Amory, *The Last Resorts*, p. 359; Mizner TS., p. 47. After Edward Stotesbury's death at age ninety in 1939, Mrs. Stotesbury closed Whitemarsh Hall, thereafter dividing her time between Washington, D.C., and Palm Beach. At her death in 1946 the Phipps interests purchased El Mirasol, subdivided the land west of North County Road, and sold lots along Wells Road from County Road to the ocean. The oceanfront house, with twelve acres, was placed on the market at "a fraction of its reproduction cost." After remaining on the market for over a decade, the house was razed in 1959 by a developer who built El Mirasol Estates, a new subdivision of fourteen lots, on the site. *Philadelphia Evening Bulletin*, 1 February 1940; *Miami Herald*, 12 October 1964.

14. Marshall B. Donaldson, *The American Heritage History of Notable American Houses*, p. 348; R. W. Sexton, *Spanish Influence on American Architecture and Decoration*, photograph, n.p.; *Palm Beach Post*, 9 July 1919, 25 January 1920.

15. Mizner TS., pp. 52, 63; *Palm Beach Weekly News*, 7 November 1919; *Palm Beach Post*, 16 March 1920; *Palm Beach Daily News*, 2 February 1980; Wayne Andrews, *The Vanderbilt Legend: The Story of the Vanderbilt Family 1794–1940*, p. 318.

16. Plans for the Kingsley house, HSPBC. Kingsley and Mrs. Slater were longtime residents of Palm Beach. Both houses are still privately owned. A photograph labeled "Moorish Ceiling from Alhambra" in Mizner Scrapbook, "Ceilings, Murals, Panels and Doors" (Society of the Four Arts Library, Palm Beach), shows his source for the Slater dining room ceiling and lighting fixture. During this year Mizner produced plans for a large house for H. C. Clark. As linen and ink drawings remain in the Mizner collection, it was probably built, though it is unlocated.

17. "Spanish Influence at Palm Beach," *Architectural Forum*, August 1924, pp. 73–80; *Palm Beach Weekly News*, 21 February 1919.

18. Christopher Salisbury, "The Mayors of Palm Beach," *Palm Beach Life*, December 1981, pp. 131–32; Mizner TS., p. 76.

19. Interview with L. Draper Babcock, 18 February 1982.

20. Ibid.; Alex Waugh, untitled typescript (Boca Raton Historical Society), chap. 6, p. 13.

21. Babcock interview.

22. Ibid.; telephone interview with Mrs. Vilma Richardson Townby, 28 December 1981.

23. Mizner TS., p. 128.

24. Ibid., p. 63.

25. Childs and Jacobs both established Florida practices during the land boom period. In Palm Beach Jacobs is best known for the elaborate 1928 mansion he did at 860 South Ocean Boulevard for E. Z. Nutting. *Palm Beach Daily News*, 27 December 1928.

26. Early plans for a very large house are dated 1920, HSPBC. The house took its near final form in late season 1920, although in 1921 it was revised and simplified. A later owner installed the large windows on the lakefront facade and removed the terrace steps leading to the lake.

27. Amory, *Last Resorts*, p. 401; *Palm Beach Life*, no month, 1924, clipping, HSPBC.

28. "Residence of H. Caryl Haskins, El Bravo Way," *Palm Beach Villas*, np. Haskins owned the house after Winn, plans in Wyeth Collection, privately held; unlabeled drawings, Mizner Collection, HSPBC; "Robert Jordan Residence, South Ocean Boulevard," *Palm Beach Villas*, n.p., plans also in Wyeth Collection; plans for Woodward house also privately held; John Taylor Boyd, Jr., "The Florida House: Mr. Addison Mizner, the Architect, Recounts the Birth of the New Florida Architecture at Palm Beach in an Interview," *Arts and Decoration*, January 1930, p. 80.

29. *Palm Beach Post*, 30 June 1922, 7 July 1923; George Harold Edgell, *American Architecture Today*, p. 106; James R. Knott, "The Phipps Clan," *Palm Beach Post*, 25 January, 1 February 1981; *Miami Herald*, 8 July 1962; see also Bernard Livingston, *Their Turf: America's Horsey Set and Its Princely Dynasties*, pp. 129–43. During this period the Phipps family and their Palm Beach Company constantly added to their houses or constructed commercial buildings and speculative houses. In 1923 Mizner

added a large wing to Henry C. Phipps's Heamaw. The addition included a two-story living room, loggia, and master bedroom. Mizner plans, Maurice Fatio Collection, HSPBC. Mizner also designed a small store with a second floor apartment which he called Mizner Plaza in 1924 for the Palm Beach Company. This became the first of several projects in Phipps Plaza. Mizner's plans privately owned.

30. Charlotte Curtis, *The Rich and Other Atrocities*, p. 7; *Palm Beach Post*, 24 February 1980; what began as a small ell-shaped house has been added to by Wyeth, Maurice Fatio, John Volk, and Byron Simonson. Today the house stretches for a full block along South Ocean Boulevard and encloses two patios.

31. "Spanish Influences," *Architectural Forum*, pp. 73–80; plans for additions, HSPBC.

32. *Palm Beach Daily News*, 10 January 1923; *Palm Beach Post*, 10 July 1922; Sanborn Insurance Maps, Town of Palm Beach, 1924 (Library of Congress); articles on the Cudahy house appeared in *Palm Beach Post*, 21 March, 28 August 1922, and in *Palm Beach Daily News*, 4 January 1923; the Mitchell house was described in *Palm Beach Post*, 8 September 1922; Warburton became a leading member of the cottage colony and served as town mayor. His house was described in *Palm Beach Post*, 16 March, 14 August 1922, and in *Palm Beach Daily News*, 17 January, 11 February 1923. Plans for remodeling, c. 1926, signed "Addison Mizner, Howard Major, associate architects," Marion Sims Wyeth Collection.

33. *Palm Beach Post*, 8 May, 5 July 1922; Alice De Lamar to author, 18 November 1981; plans, HSPBC.

34. David Freeman Hawke, *John D: The Founding Father of the Rockefellers*, pp. 94–96; *New York Times*, 24 February 1941; Mizner, TS., pp. 71–72; *Palm Beach Post*, 3 July 1922.

35. *Palm Beach Post*, 8 May, 3 July 1922; *Palm Beach Daily News*, 2 January, 9 February 1923.

36. *Palm Beach Post*, 18 March 1923; Mizner TS., pp. 69–70.

37. *Palm Beach Daily News*, 4, 8 January 1924; Matlack Price, " 'Mediterranean' Architecture in Florida," *Architectural Forum*, January 1926, p. 35; "Gulf Stream Golf Club, Palm Beach, Fla.," *Architectural Forum*, March 1925, plates 25–27; Clifford C. Wendehack, *Golf and Country Clubs: Construction and Equipment of the Modern Club House* shows plans. Three small houses built by John S. Phipps on an oceanfront lot in Gulfstream have long been attributed to Mizner. Marion Sims Wyeth designed these houses for Phipps's Palm Beach Company. Wyeth Collection.

38. *Palm Beach Post*, 28 October 1923; *New York Times*, 4, 5, 6 September 1923; *Palm Beach Villas*, n.p. Duke, brother-in-law of Anthony J. D. Biddle, drowned in a boating mishap on 3 September 1923 in Greenwich, Connecticut, and never saw his completed villa. His estate sold the house to Jules S. Bache, the stockbroker. It has been remodeled and rebuilt many times since 1923. All that remains of Mizner's original design is the 45-foot-long living room which gives it the common name of "ballroom house."

39. Waugh, who had served an apprenticeship with an antiques dealer and decorator in England before World War I, came to Palm Beach in 1919 as the house guest of Joseph Riter to recuperate from a war injury. His memoir begins: "I am not Alec Waugh, I am Alex. The difference of only one letter in our names has caused some confusion between the distinguished novelist and myself in the past, so I had better straighten it out at the beginning." Alex Waugh, TS., chap. 1, p. 1; chap. 4, pp. 1–5. Waugh tells the often repeated story of working with Mizner on shopping inventories when a call from the hotel desk announced an unidentified guest. Mizner

twice refused to receive the visitor before a knock sounded at their door. The architect, now furious, prepared to give battle when in walked King Alfonso of Spain to be greeted by Mizner with, "Well, you old son-of-a-bitch, why didn't you say it was you!"

40. In 1928 Wanamaker remodeled the house, adding 15 feet to the living room and building a den and gun room. In 1932 Joseph Kennedy bought the house. He added a sheltered entranceway from the street and a new wing on the south end. Nathaniel Burt, *The Perennial Philadelphians*, pp. 74–75; *Palm Beach Daily News*, 1 January 1929; Maurice Fatio Collection, HSPBC; previews sales brochure, January 1949. The Speidel house was razed in the early 1950s and its ocean-to-lake lot subdivided. Unlike the Thomas house, the lakefront facade of the Claflin house had no Venetian detailing; its interest came from a two-story garage and servants' wing attached to the house by a watergate with a second story arcade. Mizner later added a southern wing and a new stair tower to the house. *New York Times*, 2 February 1939; *Palm Beach Post*, 1 April 1923; original plans and those for remodeling, HSPBC.

41. *Palm Beach Life*, 18 March 1924, p. 18; *Palm Beach Daily News*, 6 January 1924; plans, HSPBC. Mizner placed the kitchen next to the dining room on the oceanfront. When new owners remodeled the house they removed the wall between the two rooms, creating a large new dining room, and extended the living room into the court, doubling its size.

42. *Palm Beach Daily News*, 31 January 1924; original plans and 1931 remodeling plans, HSPBC. A later owner had Wyeth enlarge the dining room, build a new open loggia on the first floor ocean facade, and add new master baths and dressing rooms above. See also Peter C. Newman, *The Canadian Establishment*, vol. I, pp. 10–13.

43. *Palm Beach Life*, 18 March 1924, p. 18; *New York Times*, 1 November 1950.

44. *New York Times*, 25 December 1905, 2 May 1927.

45. *Palm Beach Daily News*, 5 January 1924; Amy Lyman Phillips, "The Everglades Club," *Palm Beach Life*, 16 January 1945, p. 135; *Palm Beach Post*, 10 December 1926. The house was razed in the early 1950s.

46. *Palm Beach Daily News*, 16 January 1924; *New York Times*, 3 February 1926. The Towers gained the reputation as Mizner's most tragic house. Both Wood and its last owner, Robert T. Young, who controlled the New York Central, among other railroads, committed suicide. After Young's death, Mrs. Young razed The Towers and built a new mansion on the site.

47. Interview with L. Draper Babcock, 18 February 1982; plans, HSPBC; Otto Teegen, "Joseph Urban," *Architecture*, May 1934, p. 254; *Miami Herald*, 27 July 1980.

48. *Palm Beach Daily News*, 4 February 1924; plans HSPBC. A later owner remodeled in English Tudor style, installing the two-hundred-year-old "Lord Nelson's Pub," which had been imported complete from England, to the pool complex. No good photographs of the original house are available. The developers of the condominium now on the site saved some stained glass and architectural detailing from La Fontana to decorate the public spaces of their building. *Palm Beach Post*, 30 May 1965, 19 May 1968. See also Merrill Folsom, *More Great American Mansions and Their Stories*, pp. 69–76.

49. *Palm Beach Post*, 10 May 1923; Steven A. Seiden, "The Mizner Touch," senior thesis, Yale University, 1958, p. 35; *New York Times*, 11, 12, 17, 30 September 1924, 9 January 1925; *Palm Beach Post*, 11 February 1923.

50. *Palm Beach Post*, 16 April 1926; *New York Times*, 15 January 1926, 18 November

1940. The Cosdens' Sands Point estate, where they had entertained the Prince of Wales, formerly belonged to Bourke Cockran. They sold it to Vincent Astor.

51. Mizner TS., pp. 77, 87–90; *New York Times*, 17 February 1924. Alex Waugh contrasted Mrs. Cosden's abilities to those of another client who purchased for "astronomic" price furniture represented by the seller as having been owned by Columbus. Waugh concluded it could have belonged to someone from Columbus, Ohio. Waugh TS., chap. 4, p. 2. The size of Playa Riente, and the Cosdens' demand that it be completed for the next season, caused Mizner to depend more on his collection of postcards and photographs for design sources than he usually did for his Palm Beach houses. Steven Seiden points out that although Mizner simplified and adapted the originals to meet his design needs, the great hall and much of the window tracery derived from the Casa Lonja in Valencia, the double stairs from the Cathedral of Burgos. Seiden, "Mizner Touch," pp. 35–40. Mrs. Dodge, angered by the size of her tax bill and the refusal of the town to rezone her property for club or school purposes, held a 12 March 1957 sale of the furnishings and then razed Playa Riente. She gave the Sert murals to the Detroit Art Institute. Emilie Keyes, "Changing Times: 'Playa Riente' Joins Memories," *Palm Beach Life*, 26 February 1957, pp. 63–65; *Palm Beach Times*, 22 December 1957.

52. *Palm Beach Post*, 17 April 1923; interview with L. Draper Babcock, 18 February 1982.

53. *Palm Beach Post*, 10 May 1923.

54. *Palm Beach Daily News*, 8 January 1925.

55. Mizner TS., pp. 91–92.

56. Alice De Lamar to author, 18 November 1981.

57. J. Wadsworth Travers, *Beautiful Palm Beach*, pp. 130–31. Although the first floor of Wilson's house has been completely changed by later remodeling, Wilson's apartment on the second floor has been restored for use as offices. *Palm Beach Daily News*, 21 November 1975.

58. *Architectural Forum*, April 1926, pp. 265–66.

59. *New York Times*, 15 June 1978.

60. In the 1950s new owners subdivided the property into nine building lots and divided the residence into two "townhouses." "Palm Beach, Florida, Magnificent Ocean-Front Villa, 9 Exclusive Residential Plots," previews sales brochure, nd., HSPBC; "Lagomar," *Palm Beach Life*, July 1978, pp. 22–25; *Miami Herald*, 30 March, 29 November 1981.

61. Mizner TS., pp. 122–23; Irving F. Morrow, "The Riviera Revisited," *The Architect and Engineer*, February 1925, pp. 92–95.

62. Interview with Mrs. H. Halpine Smith, 22 December 1981. Throughout the early months of 1926 the Cement Gun Company, owners of the Gunite process of applying stucco with compressed air, used a picture of Riddle's house in their *Palm Beach Post* advertisements. The caption read "Addison Mizner, Architect." See *Post*, 6 February 1926.

63. Waugh TS., chap. 6, pp. 15–16; various versions of proposed plans, HSPBC; During the same year Mizner also designed a large oceanfront house for C. Bai Lihme at South Ocean Boulevard and County Road. Like Mrs. William K. Vanderbilt, Bai Lihme never built the house. Plans, HSPBC. Mrs. George Washington Vanderbilt built a Spanish-style house called The Firth in Biltmore Forest, North Carolina, before her marriage to Peter Gerry in 1925. Although Mizner

often has been credited with this house, Bruce Kitchell, who had designed a Palm Beach house for Mrs. W. Seward Webb, Mrs. Vanderbilt's sister-in-law, signed the plans. Susan Brendel-Pandich, curator of Biltmore House, to the author, 17 April 1981.

64. "Historic American Building Survey: Rasmussen-Donahue House," HSPBC; *Palm Beach Post*, 11, 14, 18 December 1926.

65. Christina Orr, *Addison Mizner: Architect of Dreams and Realities*, pp. 24–25. The Rasmussens sold the house to William Donahue, and in the early 1970s Donahue's son Woolworth glazed the openings in the tower. Helen Adams, "A Palm Beach Original Restored," *Palm Beach Life*, September–October 1972, pp. 42–47. In December 1980 the house sold for $3.2 million, "the top price paid for a single-family home in Florida." *Miami Herald*, 24 December 1980.

66. Howard Major, "A Theory Relating to Spanish and Italian Houses in Florida," *Architectural Forum*, August 1926, p. 103; Dan Parker, "The Kilmer Story," *Weekly American*, clipping, Kilmer family scrapbook; *New York Times*, 13 July 1940; plans, HSPBC. Kilmer's nephew believes the chance to purchase a 1,200-acre horse farm near New Market, Virginia, decided him against building in Palm Beach.

67. Wyeth designed small central patios for the Jenkins house on Barton Avenue (now the Bethesda-by-the-Sea rectory), the Reynolds house at Clark Avenue and South Ocean Boulevard, and his own house on Middle Road. Wyeth Collection. *Palm Beach Post*, 16 February 1926.

68. Boyd, "The Florida House," *Arts and Decoration*, p. 80.

69. Ida Tarbell, *Florida Architecture of Addison Mizner*, n.p.

70. Building Department, Town of Palm Beach; *Palm Beach Post*, 1921–1926, passim.

CHAPTER 5

1. Frederick Lewis Allen, *Only Yesterday*, pp. 272–73; Charlton Tebeau, *A History of Florida*, p. 383; George B. Tindall, "The Bubble in the Sun," *American Heritage*, August 1965, p. 79; Anne O'Hare McCormick, "Mainstreet, too, Winters in Florida," *New York Times Magazine*, 22 February 1925, p. 19.

2. Jane Fisher, *Fabulous Hoosier*, pp. 126–34; Vernon M. Leslie, "The Great Depression in Miami Beach," Master's thesis, Florida Atlantic University, 1980, pp. 20–23; Tindall, "Bubble in the Sun," pp. 78–79.

3. Fisher, *Fabulous Hoosier*, pp. 135–55; Leslie, "The Great Depression," pp. 24–28.

4. Woodrow W. Wilkins, "Coral Gables: 1920s New Town," *Historical Preservation*, January–March 1978, pp. 6–9; Virginia Robie, "A Spanish City in Florida," *International Studio*, May 1925, pp. 107–12; Stuart B. McIver, *The Greatest Sale on Earth: The Story of the Miami Board of Realtors, 1920–1980*, pp. 58–60; Kenneth Ballinger, *Miami Millions*, pp. 21–24; Alfred J. and Kathryn A. Hanna, *Florida's Golden Sands*, pp. 336–38. Martin E. Hampton, a senior member of Merrick's architectural staff, worked with Mizner in Palm Beach. Marion Sims Wyeth designed the "Dutch South African" village for Coral Gables and prepared plans for one which was not built in a Persian theme. Wyeth Collection, privately owned.

5. *Palm Beach Post*, 27 March, 16 June 1925, 6, 11 September 1924.

6. Ibid., 20, 30 March, 10 April 1924, 3 March 1925; John Kenneth Galbraith, *The Great Crash: 1929*, p. 23.

7. "Florida Frenzy," *Harper's*, January 1926, p. 117.

8. *Palm Beach Post*, 21 May 1924, 3 March 1925; *New York Times*, 7 January 1925; John Burke, *Rogue's Progress*, pp. 227–28. Burke's telling of the story is fanciful; among other things, he has Mizner's Mile in Boca Raton.

9. *Palm Beach Post*, 10, 15 April 1925; see also Anona Christina Orr-Cahall, "An Identification and Discussion of the Architecture and Decorative Arts of Addison Mizner (1872–1933)," Ph.D. diss., Yale University, 1979, pp. 59–69. The town spelled its name Boca Ratone or Bocaratone. At first Mizner called the development "Boca Ratone-by-the-Gulf-Stream." He quickly dropped the added "Gulf Stream" and beginning on 28 April 1925 also stopped using the final "e" in Ratone. Local newspapers continued to use the "e" for a few weeks, sometimes distinguishing between the town of Boca Ratone and the development of Boca Raton. Although some local residents objected, within a matter of months the final "e" completely disappeared. The most obvious translation of Boca Raton, or *Boca de Ratones* as it first appeared on early Spanish maps, is "mouth of the rat." Mizner's advertisements never attempted a translation. Later residents, unsatisfied with the obvious translation, have suggested substitutes like "inlet of sharp-pointed rocks." See Jacqueline Ashton, *Boca Raton: From Pioneer Days to the Fabulous Twenties*, pp. 10–11.

10. *Palm Beach Post*, 15 April 1925; *Palm Beach Times*, 15, 20, 22 April 1925. Of all of Mizner's backers, D. H. Conkling is probably the least known. He was publisher of the *Palm Beach Post*. Although this may explain the very good publicity Mizner received from the *Post*, all Florida newspapers treated boom-time developments equally well.

11. "Boca Raton's 'Old' Floresta," *The Spanish River Papers*, February 1977, n.p.; *Palm Beach Post*, 18, 19 June 1925.

12. *Palm Beach Post*, 15 May 1925.

13. Ibid., 17 May 1925.

14. Frank Bowman Sessa, "Real Estate Expansion and Boom in Miami and its Environs During the 1920s," Ph.D. diss., University of Pittsburgh, 1950, pp. 191–92; *Palm Beach Times*, 28 August 1925; Ballinger, *Miami Millions*, p. 94; later the office became a Child's restaurant.

15. *Palm Beach Post*, 5 May 1925. Charles D. Wetmore (1867–1941) and Whitney Warren (1864–1943) usually worked in a Beaux-Arts mode using elements of classicism. Nonetheless, they had designed Eagle's Nest for William K. Vanderbilt II at Centerport, Long Island in Spanish Colonial style. See Frederick Platt, *America's Gilded Age*, p. 282; and Liisa and Donald Sclare, *Beaux-Arts Estates*, pp. 184–89.

16. *Palm Beach Post*, 23, 27 May 1925; Karl Riddle, "Day Book," 30 June 1925, privately owned. Karl Riddle was Mizner's chief engineer. The "Day Book" contains his official diary detailing Boca Raton work.

17. Harry Reichenbach is usually condemned for the excesses of Boca Raton publicity. Johnston says that other promoters directed their attention to the middle class. Reichenbach believed no one wished to be considered middle class, thus his dictum, "Get the big snobs, and the little snobs will follow." Alva Johnston, *The Legendary Mizners*, p. 212; *Palm Beach Post*, 18 May, 2 July 1925 (Mizner Development Corporation advertisements).

18. *Palm Beach Post*, June–November 1925, passim.

19. Riddle, "Day Book," 30 July, 22 September 1925.

20. Riddle surveyed fourteen plats for Mizner. Although ten of these were recorded, three were rejected by Boca Raton authorities as not showing the required easements. One plat, for a black subdivision, lay across the Hillsboro Canal in Broward County. Ritz-Carlton Park was never recorded. Records of the City of Boca Raton. See also Sanford Smith, Donald W. Curl, and Ted Bessette, *Historical, Architectural, and Archaeological Survey, Boca Raton, Florida,* Historic Boca Raton Preservation Board, pp. 28–29.

21. Copies of plat maps, all signed by Mizner as city planner (Boca Raton Historical Society). Although his Palm Beach vias served as the model for several proposed shopping complexes, Mizner also planned a building of ten stores and eight apartments similar to London's Burlington Arcade. *Palm Beach Times,* 11 April 1926. How far plans for the canal proceeded has always been in dispute. Several long-time residents recall a canal with concrete walls; they also remember seeing the gondolas. *Miami Herald,* 4 September 1974. Although only the section between the Intracoastal Waterway and the Dixie Highway was built, the company had signed contracts for the Venetian bridge and made plans to continue the street into the western sections of the city.

22. Riddle, "Day Book," 20, 29 July, 28 October 1925. See also Orr-Cahall, "An Identification and Discussion," p. 61.

23. *Palm Beach Post,* 4 August 1925.

24. Ibid., 18, 19 June, 1, 2, 18 July 1925; Riddle, "Day Book," 30 April, 13 August, 1 October 1925. Riddle opened his office in April with two employees. By October he had sixty-nine workers, almost half of them engineers, on his payroll.

25. *Palm Beach Post,* 7 August 1925.

26. *New York Times,* 3 September 1925. Johnston says that the panels came from a room at the University of Salamanca. After Mizner purchased the panels he produced many Woodite sets, giving rise to a confused idea that "Ferdinand and Isabella issued their historic decrees from twelve sections of Palm Beach." Johnston, *Legendary Mizners,* p. 227; *Palm Beach Post,* 23 August, 1, 5 September 1925; *Palm Beach Times,* 3 September 1925.

27. Kenneth L. Roberts, *Florida Loafing,* p. 22.

28. *Palm Beach Post,* 25 October, 13 November 1925. WFLA did not broadcast until 5 February 1927. By that time no money remained to build conventional studios. Thus the "Voice of Tropical America" originated from a frame structure with its walls and roof covered by palmetto fronds. "WFLA Goes on the Air," *Boca Raton Record,* February 1927, pp. 4–5. The *Record* was a publication of the Mizner Development Corporation.

29. *Palm Beach Post,* 29 October, 25 November 1925. Although Riddle received orders to rush construction of an access road and parking areas for the ship, an executive of the Robinson company told him it "was no doubt another instance of where a thing was being built without proper authority . . . and not to be in any hurry." Riddle, "Day Book," 14 November 1925.

30. *Palm Beach Post,* 7 August 1925; "Bungalows in the Spanish Manner Adapted to Meet American Ideals Designed by Addison Mizner, Architect," *Ladies Home Journal,* February 1927, p. 36; Stella Suberman, "Addison Mizner and the Boca Raton House," *The Spanish River Papers,* October 1978, n.p. Drawings for all of the Old Floresta and Druker houses, Historical Society of Palm Beach County. One of the Druker houses relates very closely to Mizner's "I" model for Old Floresta.

With the collapse of the Mizner Development Corporation the original own-ers of the Old Floresta land recovered their property at a courthouse sale. This group, headed by Chicago architect Hermann V. von Holst (1874–1955), completed the subdivision and gave it the name "Floresta." Von Holst, an 1896 graduate of MIT, taught at the Armour Institute and designed plants for Illinois electric compa-nies. He shared Steinway Hall offices with many of the architects of the Prairie School. When Frank Lloyd Wright abandoned his practice in 1909 he turned over several uncompleted commissions to von Holst, including a Dearborn, Michigan, house for Henry Ford. Marion Mahoney also worked in von Holst's office. In 1932 von Holst retired to Boca Raton where he served as chairman of the town planning board. Local legend says Wright visited von Holst in Boca Raton and expressed approval of Mizner's Old Floresta houses. See H. Allen Brooks, *The Prairie School: Frank Lloyd Wright and His Midwestern Contemporaries*, pp. 85–86; Records of the City of Boca Raton.

31. *Palm Beach Post*, 10 November, 6, 7 December 1925; Riddle, "Day Book," clip-ping, 24 November 1925.

32. *New York Times*, 10, 14 October 1925; Sessa, "Real Estate Expansion and Boom," pp. 288–89.

33. *Palm Beach Post*, 10, 25 October 1925; *New York Times*, 24, 29 November 1925.

34. William H. A. Carr, *The du Ponts of Delaware*, passim.; Johnston, *Legendary Miz-ners*, p. 287; Sessa, "Real Estate Expansion and Boom," p. 147.

35. *Palm Beach Post*, 17, 22 August, 16, 18 September, 10 October 1925; "Florida Frenzy," *Harper's*, January 1926, p. 178; Tebeau, *History of Florida*, pp. 385–87; Homer B. Vanderblue, "The Florida Land Boom," *The Journal of Land and Public Utility Economics*, May 1927, p. 129; Edward Dean Sullivan, *The Fabulous Wilson Mizner*, p. 309.

36. *Palm Beach Post*, 24 February, 10, 14, 25 March 1926; *Palm Beach Times*, 26 March 1926; Riddle, "Day Book," 30 March 1926; Kenneth L. Roberts, *Florida* (Boca Raton edition published by Mizner Development Corporation), pp. 101–4.

37. *Palm Beach Post*, 18 January 1926 (Mizner advertisement); *Distrito de Boca Raton*, Plat 8 (Boca Raton Historical Society). Drawings for several proposed *Distrito* houses including those for Madame Frances Alda, A. T. Herd, and Dr. Maurice Druker, HSPBC.

38. *Spanish River Papers*, February 1976, n.p.; Records of the City of Boca Raton; Harris Allen, "New Spain," *Pacific Coast Architect*, June 1926, p. 6.

39. *Palm Beach Post*, 1 January, 8, 14 February 1926. Every development needed a song. Although Irving Berlin is supposed to have written one entitled, "Boca Raton, You have a Charm all Your Own," history only records "In Boca Raton": "Think of an evening in June/Under a crystal-like moon/Think of an old Spanish tune/You're in Boca Raton./. . . think about old Captain Kidd/Think of a chest that he hid/Dream that you've opened the lid/You're in Boca Raton." *Boca Raton News*, 4 October 1970.

40. Ida Tarbell, *Florida Architecture of Addison Mizner*, n.p.

41. Giles Edgerton, "Great Modern Hotels: Their Architecture and Decoration—The Ritz-Carlton Cloister of Boca Raton, Florida," *Arts and Decoration*, April 1926, p. 57; *Architectural Forum*, November 1926, plates 75–80.

42. Riddle, "Day Book," clipping, 6 February 1926; *Palm Beach Post*, 21, 26 February 1926. Remodeling and rebuilding over the past fifty years have completely changed the character of the hotel. Nonetheless, the particular charm of the inn can be

judged from the Mizner lobby, which remains virtually unchanged and is today used as a registration center for conventions. Although the dining room can no longer be seen on the ground floor, its top half has become the "Mizner Room," a setting for meetings and lectures. The loggia and cloister also remain in near original form. Plans, HSPBC.

43. *Palm Beach Post,* 11, 16 April 1926. Druker completed at least four houses in the southeast area of the city. They were destroyed in the early 1960s when the Arvida Corporation built the Royal Palm Yacht and Country Club development. The Dunagan apartment, on DeSoto Road north of Camino Real, was destroyed to extend the Boca Raton Club golf course. *Boca Raton Record,* February 1927, p. 3; plans, HSPBC.

44. *New York Times,* 29 September 1926.

45. Ibid., 22 June, 21 July 1926, 10 March, 7 November 1927; "Boca Raton's 'Old' Floresta," *The Spanish River Papers,* February 1977, n.p., May 1974, n.p.; Theodore Pratt, *The Story of Boca Raton,* pp. 24–25.

CHAPTER 6

1. *Palm Beach Times,* 3 December 1943; *Palm Beach Post-Times,* 11 May 1958; *Palm Beach Daily News,* 11 December 1928; biographical data, Ruby Pierce Papers; and Fatio Collection, Historical Society of Palm Beach County. In the late 1930s Fatio designed several elegant "neo-Regency" houses. In the period after World War II this style became popular in Palm Beach. These later houses, as produced by lesser hands, gave rise to the popular name "Palm Beach Mausoleum." The sleek International Style house Fatio designed for Vadim Makaroff at 703 North Ocean Boulevard won Treanor and Fatio a gold metal at the Paris Exposition of 1937.

2. J. Wadsworth Travers, *History of Beautiful Palm Beach,* 1928, p. 54; *Miami Herald,* 3 August 1976; *Palm Beach Daily News,* 14 December 1981.

3. *Palm Beach Daily News,* 9 December 1974; *Palm Beach Post,* 10 May 1929; Howard Major, "A Theory Relating to Spanish and Italian Houses in Florida," *Architectural Forum,* August 1926, pp. 97–104; Howard Major, *The Domestic Architecture of the Early American Republic: The Greek Revival,* p. 11. In fairness to Major, his criticism of Spanish architecture in Florida is generally limited to the small carpenter-built houses of the boom, which he called "aberrations." Although in the *Forum* article he never mentions Mizner, in his introduction to the 1929 edition of *Palm Beach Villas* he said: "It would be hardly fitting in a résumé of Palm Beach architecture not to mention the names of Marion Sims Wyeth and Addison Mizner. Both of these very capable architects have designed many of the beautiful homes in Palm Beach." Plans c. 1926 for the remodeling of the Warburton house list Mizner and Major as "associate architects," plans privately owned. For Major's earlier New York work, see *A Monograph of the Domestic Work of Howard Major, Architect* (1922). In this period, Joseph Urban (1872–1933) came to Palm Beach to design Mar-a-Lago for the E. F. Huttons. At first the Huttons asked Wyeth, who had designed Hogarcita and several speculative houses for them on Golf View Road, to plan their new villa. When they decided to engage Urban, Wyeth remained as associate architect. He later disclaimed all responsibility for the house, saying, "I don't want anyone to think I was the architect in charge." *Palm Beach Daily News,* 16 March 1981. Urban designed Palm Beach's most flamboyant and extravagant Spanish mansion for the Huttons. He also planned the Paramount Theater and the Bath and Tennis Club and remodeled the Oasis Club and the Anthony J. Drexel Biddle house. The floridness of the

Urban buildings perhaps contributed to the declining popularity of Spanish architecture in Palm Beach. See Otto Teegen, "Joseph Urban," *Architecture*, May 1934, pp. 251–56.

4. *Palm Beach Post*, 19 February, 6 March 1925.

5. Ibid., 25 March 1925; *Palm Beach Times*, 8 July 1940. This article on the demolition of the hotel included an interview with A.E.R. Betschick, who told of the design process. The salvage company found that half of the steel had deteriorated, that vandals had stolen the plumbing pipes, and that it was impossible to save any of the decorative tiles. Since the expense of demolition exceeded the salvage profits, the company ended its work, leaving the Y-shaped northern section still standing. In the mid-1950s a developer razed this final remnant of the boom-time development.

6. *New York Times*, 10, 30 April 1927.

7. Boynton tax records, 1924–1926, City of Boynton Beach; unidentified newspaper clipping showing sketch of city hall (Boynton Beach Public Library); plans for city hall, HSPBC; Bertha Chadwell, handwritten history of the Boynton Women's Club, n.d.; interview with Mrs. Herbert Keats, 27 October 1981; Historical Building Site Survey, 1978 (Boynton Beach Historical Society); plans for Women's Club, HSPBC.

8. Bruce Kitchell supervised construction in Jacksonville. Interview with L. Draper Babcock, 18 February 1982.

9. Both Mizner and Fatio plans, HSPBC.

10. Albert Ely Ives to H. Rodney Sharp, 23 July 1926; Sharp to Ives, 6 August 1926; 10, 11 January 1927; Ives to Mrs. B. G. du Pont, 31 January 1927; Ives to Sharp, "Tuesday, 1, 1927" (Eleutherian Mills Historical Library). Ives, who had trained at the New York School of Fine Arts and worked as a draftsman for Delano & Aldrich in New York and Fatio in Palm Beach before joining Mizner's office, established a successful practice in Wilmington. Between 1928 and 1930 he designed the additions to Henry Francis du Pont's Winterthur which created "the modified T-shaped [museum] as it is seen today." He later moved to Hawaii where he designed the Hana Mauai Hotel and the Honolulu Academy of Arts. Jonathan L. Fairbanks, "The Architectural Development of Winterthur House," *The Winterthur Story*, pp. 91–92.

11. Hunter S. Frost, *Art, Artifacts, Architecture: Fountain Valley School*, n.p.; plans, HSPBC. Bradley used his 1,700-acre ranch to raise race horses. The thoroughbred stock developed such great stamina in the high mountain altitude that racing officials banned their entry at eastern tracks. In 1930 Bradley sold the ranch. Mizner's house, now known as The Hacienda, formed the nucleus around which Fountain Valley School's campus developed. F. Martin Brown to the author, 27 November 1981.

12. Alice De Lamar to author, 4 December 1981; Curtis Patterson, "A Shelf of New Books: Addison Mizner and Florida," *International Studio*, August 1928, pp. 73–74.

13. Building Department, Town of Palm Beach; some plans for Harris house, HSPBC; Building Department, City of Miami Beach; *Year Book of the Joint Exposition of the Architectural League of Greater Miami and Florida South Chapter, AIA*, 1930, p. 38; plans, HSPBC.

14. Interview, John F. Wymer, Jr., administrator of Good Samaritan Hospital, 1947–1981, 27 October 1981; interview, Marion Sims Wyeth, 27 October 1981. In 1961 John Volk & Associates remodeled the lodge which today is the 278-seat William A. Phillips Auditorium. Although Volk filled in the windows and changed the entrance, the red-tile roof remains as the only reminder of the original complex of

Good Samaritan Hospital buildings. Plans, HSPBC.

15. Complete plans for Gedney residence, HSPBC.

16. Herman Leroy Collins, *Philadelphia: A Story of Progress,* pp. 62–63; *Philadelphia Evening Bulletin,* 23 January 1969; the most complete and detailed of Mizner plans are for the Foerderer house, HSPBC.

17. Matlack Price, "Return to Romanticism," *Arts and Decoration,* October 1930, pp. 49–53, 114. Foerderer sold La Ronda to Villanova University in January 1968. The University subdivided much of the estate. The house is once again in private hands and is being restored.

18. Interview, Alfred W. Jones, Sr., 25 September 1981; Harold H. Martin, *This Happy Isle: The Story of Sea Island and the Cloister,* pp. 41–47.

19. Jones interview; "Your Sea Island Cottage Holiday: Cottage #10," rental brochure.

20. Martin, *This Happy Isle,* pp. 52, 89, 101; "Francis L. Abreu and Fort Lauderdale's Boomtime Architecture," *New River News,* Spring 1982, p. 10. Today only the large Spanish lounge with its great fireplace, tiled floors, and beamed ceilings remains from Mizner's original plans.

21. *Palm Beach Daily News,* 12 December 1928.

22. Ibid., 13 December 1928.

23. Ibid., 24 September 1928; Herb Andree and Noel Young, *Santa Barbara Architecture: From Spanish Colonial to Modern,* pp. 156–57.

24. *Palm Beach Post,* 28 December 1928; *Palm Beach Daily News,* 28 December 1928.

25. *Palm Beach Post,* 21 April 1929; *Florida Embassy Club, Palm Beach,* prospectus, HSPBC. In 1947, a year after Colonel Bradley's death, the Society of the Four Arts purchased the club building. The Society, originally housed next door in the Mizner-designed Singer Building, asked Wyeth to remodel the club. He converted the patio area into an auditorium and added new galleries.

26. *Palm Beach Post,* 27 January 1930; *Palm Beach Daily News,* Historical Number, 1936; *Daily News,* 17 December 1975. Mizner remodeled and decorated an apartment for Oscar Davies in the Daily News Building at Brazilian Avenue and County Road in 1931. See Mizner office list, HSPBC and *Palm Beach Life,* December 1981, p. 158.

27. The original Spingold house, built in 1927, is usually attributed to Mizner. More likely he only completed the additions that converted the small house into a large Spanish mansion. 1929 plans, HSPBC.

28. *Palm Beach Daily News,* 16 December 1929; 10 January 1930.

29. Telephone interview, Helen Mihalick, club secretary, 23 December 1981, 4 February 1982; plans, HSPBC.

30. *Palm Beach Post,* 4 April 1929.

31. *Laws of Florida,* 1915, chap. 6951 (no. 145), pp. 340-46, provides for the establishment of a Florida State Board of Architecture; Mellen C. Greeley, Secretary of the Board to Addison Mizner, 16 July 1930. See Steven Seiden, "The Mizner Touch." For board records, Library of the Schools of Fine Arts and Architecture, University of Florida. Mizner also held registration in New York and Pennsylvania, certificates, HSPBC.

32. Paris Singer, "Foreword," *The Florida Architecture of Addison Mizner;* Alice De Lamar to author, 15 February 1982.

33. Current owners have original blueprints.

34. Various versions of Camp house, HSPBC; Alice C. Dalligan, Chief, Burton Historical Collection, Detroit Public Library, to author, 18 February 1982.

35. "From Zero to Zephyr," *Cincinnati Fine Arts Journal,* February–March 1935, pp. 10–11; untitled frontispiece, *Landscape Architectural Quarterly,* January 1941; *St. Petersburg Times,* 6 January 1980. Although the house had several owners over the years, including General Lacey Murrow, the brother of news commentator Edward R. Murrow, it was never remodeled or seriously altered. The current owners "have patched plaster; repainted; re-silvered-and-gold leafed; replaced decayed structure timbers; replaced broken window panes; stripped down, rewelded and repainted the iron windows and balconies," restoring the house to original condition. Since much of the furniture from Mizner Industries remained, and the present owners have added pieces in keeping, Casa Coe da Sol comes closer than any other existing Mizner house in giving a picture of the intent of the architect.

36. Plans, HSPBC.

37. Plans for the Alexander house and Bonsack projects, HSPBC; clipping, *Palm Beach Post,* nd., HSPBC. Mizner's office also produced various versions of a small house for Blanche and J. A. Ely, pioneer south Florida black educators. The Elys never built on their West Palm Beach lot as both were offered employment by the Broward County School Board. Plans, HSPBC; telephone interview with Mrs. Ely, 13 November 1981.

38. Telephone interview with Jerry Gold, 11 November 1981; *Everglades News,* 4 November 1932. Gold's sons built a larger theater in 1949, selling the Everglades to an oil company which demolished it in 1951 and built a service station on the site.

39. Review of *Many Mizners,* clipping, HSPBC; Addison Mizner, autobiographical typescript, HSPBC, p. 94.

40. Interview with Mrs. H. Halpine Smith, 23 December 1981; Alice De Lamar to author, 4 December 1981; Obituary, *Architectural Forum,* March 1933, p. 38. At the time of his death Mizner had $200 in traveler's checks and no personal bank account. A sale of the architect's personal property at the Villa Mizner, which included odds and ends of china, silver, and some jewelry, netted less than $2,000. On the other hand, claims against the estate amounted to over $200,000. Most of the claims involved the mortgage holders of the Via and Villa Mizner, who asked for nearly $180,000. Among the other petitioners were Irving Berlin, the songwriter, who asked to recover $25,000 he had loaned Mizner in April 1927; the publisher of *Florida Architecture,* who requested $80 for four unpaid copies; and Hudgins Fish Company of West Palm Beach, which demanded $27.34. As is often the case, most of the estate's assets went toward the cost of administration. Palm Beach County Probate, 1933, #201, microfilm #3123.

41. "Palm Beach Aristocrat," *Architectural Digest,* November–December 1972, pp. 16–21. This article, on one of John Volk's early Spanish houses, includes an interview with the architect.

42. Mrs. Alice Mizner Lewitin to author, 28 December 1981; Jacqueline Ashton, *Boca Raton: From Pioneer Days to the Fabulous Twenties,* pp. 189–90 f.n.

43. Frank G. Lopez, "We were having some people in for cocktails," *Architectural Record,* July 1953, pp. 46–48.

44. The Junior League of the Palm Beaches, *Palm Beach Entertains: Then and Now,* pp. 65–66; *Palm Beach Daily News,* 17 April, 27 November 1977, 16 March, 14 May, 10 June 1979, 24 August 1980; *New York Times,* 20 March 1977.

Bibliography

The archives, collections, and records of the following libraries, historical societies, museums, organizations, and cities were consulted for this work:

Avery Architectural Library at Columbia University, New York, for information on William Treanor, Howard Major, Joseph Urban, and Frederick Rhinelander King.

Boca Raton History Society for Mizner Development Corporation history, early city records, the *Boca Raton Record*, the Society's publication *The Spanish River Papers*, and Alex Waugh's typescript of Florida experiences in the 1920s.

Boynton Beach Historical Society for information on Mizner Mile and early city history.

Boynton Beach Public Library for records of Mizner's involvement in the city.

Boynton Woman's Club for history of the clubhouse.

City of Boca Raton for minutes of early town council meetings and building records.

City of Boynton Beach for building and tax records.

City of Miami Beach building records for Harris brokerage office information.

Delray Beach Public Library for *Delray Beach News* and history of Gulfstream.

Eleutherian Mills Historical Library, Greenville, Delaware, for material on Mrs. Bessie Gardner du Pont's house.

Henry Morrison Flagler Museum Archives, Palm Beach, for information on Whitehall and Mizner Industries.

Historical Association of Southern Florida for updated 1924 Sanborn insurance maps of Palm Beach and Mizner files.

Historical Society of Palm Beach County, Palm Beach, for Mizner Collection which includes the architect's office tracings and some blueprints, photographs, records, and materials from Mizner Industries, and a typescript copy of Mizner's second volume of memoirs. The society also owns a collection of Maurice Fatio office tracings and a complete collection of *Palm Beach Life*, which was consulted from 1915–1982. Individual articles are cited in the Notes.

Library of Congress, Division of Maps, for 1919 and 1924 Sanborn insurance maps of Palm Beach, general collection for periodicals.

Miami-Dade Public Library, Florida Room, particularly for early editions of *Florida Architecture and Allied Arts*, published by local chapters of the AIA.

The Nassau County Museum for property maps of Nassau County and photographs.
The New-York Historical Society for material on clients and Mizner during his New York years.
Pennsylvania Historical Society, Philadelphia, for biographical information on Mizner's clients.
Port Washington Public Library for *Plain Talk* and *Port Washington News*, and information on Baxter homestead.
Society of the Four Arts Library, Palm Beach, for Mizner's scrapbooks and the architect's own library.
Society for the Preservation of Long Island Antiquities, Setauket, for property maps, Mizner holdings.
Town of Palm Beach building records for information on permits.
West Palm Beach Chamber of Commerce for complete collection of Palm Beach city directories.
West Palm Beach Public Library, Florida Room, for information on local history in the 1920s.

PERSONAL (P) AND TELEPHONE (T) INTERVIEWS AND CORRESPONDENCE (C):

Miss Alice De Lamar (C)
Mrs. Alice Mizner Lewitin (C)
L. Draper Babcock, 18 February 1982 (P)
Alfred W. Jones, Sr., 25 September 1981 (P)
Mrs. Herbert Keats, 27 October 1981 (P)
James Mannion, 13 January 1982 (P)
Mrs. H. Halpine Smith, 22 December 1981 (P)
Marion Sims Wyeth, 27 October 1981 (P)
John F. Wyner, Jr., 27 October 1981 (P)
Mrs. J. A. Ely, 13 November 1981 (T)
Jerry Gold, 11 November 1981 (T)
Mrs. Helen Mihalick, 23 December 1981, 4 February 1982 (T)
Mrs. Vilma Richardson Townby, 28 December 1981 (T)

NEWSPAPERS:

Boca Raton News, passim
Delray Beach News, 1925–1926
Miami Herald, passim
New York Times, passim
Palm Beach Daily News, 1918–1933, and passim
Palm Beach Post, 1918–1933, and passim
Palm Beach Times, 1922–1933, and passim
Palm Beach Weekly News, 1918–1919
Plain Talk, 1911–1914
Port Washington News, 1907–1917

PUBLISHED BOOKS:

Allen, Frederick Lewis. *Only Yesterday.* New York: Harper and Brothers, 1931.
Alpern, Andrew. *Apartments for the Affluent.* New York: McGraw-Hill, 1975.
Amory, Cleveland. *The Last Resorts.* New York: Harper and Brothers, 1948.
Andree, Herb, and Noel Young. *Santa Barbara Architecture: From Spanish Colonial to Modern.* Santa Barbara: Capra Press, 1980.

Andrews, Wayne. *The Vanderbilt Legend: The Story of the Vanderbilt Family, 1794–1940.* New York: Harcourt, Brace and Co., 1941.

Area Planning Board of Palm Beach County. *Historic Preservation Study.* May 1979.

Ashton, Jacqueline. *Boca Raton: From Pioneer Days to the Fabulous Twenties.* Boca Raton: Dedication Press, 1979.

Baldwin, Charles C. *Stanford White.* New York: Dodd, Mead & Co., 1931.

Ballinger, Kenneth. *Miami Millions: The Dance of the Dollars in the Great Florida Land Boom of 1925.* Miami: Franklin Press, 1936.

Baltzell E. Digby. *An American Business Aristocracy.* New York: The Free Press, 1958.

Beach, Rex. *The Miracle of Coral Gables.* New York: Currier and Harford, 1926.

Beck, Warren A., and David A. Williams. *California: A History of the Golden State.* Garden City, NY: Doubleday & Co., 1972.

Benson, Elizabeth P. *The Maya World.* Rev. ed. New York: Thomas Y. Crowell Co., 1977.

Birmingham, Stephen. *The Right People: A Portrait of the American Social Establishment.* Boston: Little, Brown and Co., 1968.

Bottomley, William Lawrence. *Spanish Details.* New York: William Helburn, 1924.

Brandon, Ruth. *A Capitalist Romance: Singer and the Sewing Machine.* Philadelphia: J. B. Lippincott Co., 1977.

Brooks, H. Allen. *The Prairie School: Frank Lloyd Wright and His Midwest Contemporaries.* New York: W. W. Norton and Co., 1976.

Bruegmann, Robert. *Benicia: Portrait of an Early California Town.* San Francisco: 101 Productions, 1980.

Burchard, John, and Albert Bush-Brown. *The Architecture of America: A Social and Cultural History.* Boston: Little, Brown and Co., 1961.

Burke, John. *Rogue's Progress.* New York: G. P. Putnam's Sons, 1975.

Burt, Nathaniel. *The Perennial Philadelphians: The Anatomy of an American Aristocracy.* New York: Arno Press, 1975.

Bush-Brown, Harold. *Beaux Arts to Bauhaus and Beyond.* New York: Whitney Library of Design, 1976.

Byne, Arthur, and Mildred Stapley. *Provincial Houses in Spain.* New York: William Helburn, 1925.

Carr, William H. A. *The du Ponts of Delaware.* New York: Dodd, Mead & Co., 1964.

Churchill, Allen. *The Splendor Seekers: An Informal History of America's Multimillionaire Spenders, Members of the 50 Million Dollar Club.* New York: Grosset & Dunlap, 1974.

Collins, Herman Leroy. *Philadelphia: A Story of Progress.* New York: Lewis Historical Publishing Co., 1941.

Curtis, Charlotte. *The Rich and Other Atrocities.* New York: Harper & Row, 1976.

Donaldson, Marshall B. *The American Heritage History of Notable American Houses.* New York: American Heritage Publishing Co., 1971.

Downing, Antoinette, and Vincent Scully. *The Architectural Heritage of Newport, Rhode Island, 1640–1950.* New York: Clarkson N. Potter, 1967.

Duncan, Isadora. *My Life.* New York: Liveright, 1955.

Edgell, George Harold. *The American Architecture of Today.* 1928. Reprint. New York: AMS Press, 1970.

Edwards, George Wharton. *Spain.* 1926.

Ferguson, J. Walton. *Rosecliff.* Newport: The Preservation Society of Newport County, 1977.

Fisher, Jane. *Fabulous Hoosier.* New York: Robert M. McBride and Co., 1947.

Florida Architecture of Addison Mizner. Foreword by Paris Singer, "Appreciation of a Layman" by Ida M. Tarbell. New York: William Helburn, 1928.

Florida: "The East Coast." Miami: The Miami Herald, 1925.

Florida Revival and "Theme-Town" Architecture: 1880–1929. Tallahassee: Florida State University Art Gallery, 1977.

Folsom, Merrill. *Great American Mansions and Their Stories*. New York: Hastings House, 1963.

———, *More Great American Mansions and Their Stories*. New York: Hastings House, 1967.

Frost, Hunter S. *Art, Artifacts, Architecture: Fountain Valley School*. Colorado Springs: Tiverton Press, 1979.

Galbraith, John Kenneth. *The Great Crash: 1929*. Boston: Houghton Mifflin Co., 1961.

Gilliam, Harold. *The San Francisco Experience*. Garden City, NY: Doubleday & Co., 1972.

Gray, David. *Thomas Hastings: Architect*. Boston: Houghton Mifflin, 1933.

Hallenbeck, Cleve. *Spanish Missions of the Old Southwest*. Garden City, NY: Doubleday, Page & Co., 1926.

Hamlin, Talbot F. *The American Spirit in Architecture*. New Haven: Yale University Press, 1926.

Hanna, Alfred J., and Kathryn A. *Florida's Golden Sands*. Indianapolis: Bobbs-Merrill Co., 1950.

Harner, Charles C. *Florida's Promoters: The Men Who Made It Big*. Tampa: Trend House, 1973.

Hasbrouck, Frank, ed., *The History of Dutchess County, New York*. Poughkeepsie: S. A. Matthieu, 1909.

Hawke, David Freeman. *John D: The Founding Father of the Rockefellers*. New York: Harper & Row, 1980.

Herford, Oliver, Ethel Watts Mumford, and Addison Mizner. *The Cynic's Calendar of Revised Wisdom*. 7 editions. San Francisco and New York: Paul Elder and Co., 1903–1917.

Herringshaw's City Blue Book of Biography: New Yorkers of 1917. Chicago: Clark J. Herringshaw, 1917.

Hoffstot, Barbara. *Landmark Architecture of Palm Beach*. Pittsburgh: Ober Park Associates, 1974.

Howell, E. W., and Co. *Noted Long Island Homes*. Babylon, L.I.: E. W. Howell Co., 1933.

James, Henry. *The American Scene*. New York: Charles Scribner's Sons, 1946.

Jencks, Charles. *The Language of Post-Modern Architecture*. New York: Rizzoli, 1977.

Johnson, Stanley. *Once Upon A Time: The Story of Boca Raton*. Miami: E. A. Seemann Publishing for Arvida Corp., 1979.

Johnston, Alva. *The Legendary Mizners*. New York: Farrar, Straus & Young, 1953.

The Junior League of the Palm Beaches, *Palm Beach Entertains: Then and Now*. New York: Coward, McCann & Geoghegan, 1976.

Kavaler, Lucy. *The Private World of High Society*. New York: David McKay Co., 1960.

Kimball, Fiske. *American Architecture*. 1928. Reprint. New York: AMS Press, 1970.

Lewis, Oscar. *The Silver Kings*. New York: Alfred A. Knopf, 1947.

Livingston, Bernard. *Their Turf: America's Horsey Set and Its Princely Dynasties*. New York: Arbor House, 1973.

Longstreth, Richard. *On the Edge of the World: Four Architects in San Francisco at the Turn of the Century*. New York: The Architectural History Foundation, co-published with The MIT Press, 1983.

Loos, Anita. *Kiss Hollywood Good-bye*. New York: Alfred A. Knopf, 1974.

McGinniss, Joe. *Going to Extremes*. New York: Alfred A. Knopf, 1980.

McIver, Stuart B. *The Greatest Sale on Earth: The Story of the Miami Board of Realtors, 1920–1980*. Miami: E. A. Seemann Publishing, 1980.

———, *Yesterday's Palm Beach*. Miami: E. A. Seemann Publishing, 1976.

Major, Howard. *The Domestic Architecture of the Early American Republic: The Greek Revival*. Philadelphia: J. B. Lippincott Co., 1926.

———, *A Monograph of the Domestic Work of Howard Major, Architect*. New York: Architectural Catalog Co., August 1922.

Major, Nettie Leitch. *Mar-a-Lago, Palm Beach, Florida*. Palm Beach: 1969.

Marshall, Virginia D. *Port Washington Recalled*. Port Washington, L.I.: Port Printing Service, 1967.

Martin, Harold H. *This Happy Isle: The Story of Sea Island and the Cloister*. Sea Island, Ga: Sea Island Co., 1978.

Martin, Ralph C., *Jennie: The Life of Lady Randolph Churchill*. 2 vols. Englewood Cliffs, N.J.: Prentice-Hall, 1971.

Merz, Charles. *The Great American Band Wagon*. New York: The John Day Co., 1928.

Mizner, Addison. *The Many Mizners*. New York: Sears Publishing Co., 1932.

Morris, Don. "Mizner Industries: Details of the Palm Beaches' Greatest Manufactory," and "Woodite, Incorporated: The Palm Beaches' Newest Industry" in *The New Palm Beaches*. West Palm Beach: Palm Beach Press, 1929.

Murdock, Luke S. *Palm Beach and West Palm Beach: The Palm Beaches, "Where Summer Spends the Winter."* West Palm Beach: Long and Murdock, 1926.

Newcomb, Rexford. *Mediterranean Domestic Architecture in the United States*. Cleveland: J. H. Jansen, 1929.

———, *Spanish-Colonial Architecture in the United States*. New York: J. J. Augustin, 1937.

———, *The Spanish House for America: Its Design, Furnishing, and Garden*. Philadelphia: J. B. Lippincott Co., 1927.

Newman, Peter C. *The Canadian Establishment*. Toronto: Seal Books, 1979.

Ney, John. *Palm Beach: The Place, The People, Its Pleasures and Palaces*. Boston: Little, Brown and Co., 1966.

Noffsinger, James Philip. *The Influence of the Ecole des Beaux-Arts on the Architects of the United States*. Washington: Catholic University of America, 1955.

O'Connor, Richard. *The Golden Summers*. New York: G. P. Putnam's Sons, 1974.

Olmsted, Roger, and T. H. Watkins. *Here Today: San Francisco's Architectural Heritage*. San Francisco: Chronicle Books, 1968.

Orr, Christina. *Addison Mizner: Architect of Dreams and Realities (1872–1933)*. West Palm Beach: Norton Gallery and School of Art, 1977.

Palm Beach Villas. Introduction by Howard Major. Vol. 1. Palm Beach: R. O. Davies Publishing Co., 1929.

———. Introduction by Howard Major. Vol. 2. Palm Beach: R. O. Davies Publishing Co., 1934.

Patterson, Augusta Owen. *American Homes of To-day: Their Architectural Style, their Environment, their Characteristics*. New York: Macmillan Co., 1924.

The Plan of Palm Beach prepared under the Direction of the Garden Club of Palm Beach approved by the Town Council. 1930.

Platt, Frederick. *America's Gilded Age: Its Architecture and Decoration*. New York: A. S. Barnes and Co., 1976.

Powell-Brant, Evanell K. *Debauched Proverbs and Other Miznerisms of Addison Mizner and Wilson Mizner*. Tampa: 1979.

Pratt, Theodore. *The Story of Boca Raton*. St. Petersburg: Great Outdoors Publishing Co., 1963.

Recent Florida Work by Treanor and Fatio, Architects. Palm Beach: Davies Publishing Co., 1932.

———, 2nd edition. Palm Beach: Davies Publishing Co., 1938.

Roberts, Kenneth L. *Florida*. Boca Raton: Mizner Development Corporation, 1926.

———. *Florida Loafing*. Indianapolis: Bobbs-Merrill Co., 1924.

St. Regian: Yearbook of Paul Smith's College of Arts and Sciences. 1949.

Sclare, Liisa, and Donald. *Beaux-Arts Estates: A Guide to the Architecture of Long Island*. New York: Viking Press, 1980.

Scudder, Janet. *Modeling My Life*. New York: Harcourt, Brace, 1925.

Scully, Vincent L., Jr. *The Shingle Style: Architectural Theory and Design from Richardson to the Origins of Wright*. New Haven: Yale University Press, 1955.

Searing, Helen, ed. *In Search of Modern Architecture: A Tribute to Henry-Russell Hitch-cock.* New York: The Architectural History Foundation, copublished with the MIT Press, 1982.

Sexton, R. W. *Spanish Influence on American Architecture and Decoration.* New York: Brentano's, 1927.

Showalter, J. Camille. *The Many Mizners: California Clan Extraordinary.* Oakland, Ca.: The Oakland Museum, 1978.

Sirkis, Nancy. *Newport Pleasures and Palaces.* New York: Viking Press, 1963.

Smith, Sanford, Donald W. Curl, and Ted Bessette. *Historical, Architectural, and Archaeological Survey, Boca Raton, Florida.* Historic Boca Raton Preservation Board, 1980.

Sordo, Enrique. *Moorish Spain: Cordoba, Seville, Granada.* New York: Crown Publishers, 1963.

Starr, Kevin. *Americans and the California Dream, 1850–1915.* New York: Oxford University Press, 1973.

Stockbridge, Frank Parker, and John Holliday Perry. *Florida in the Making.* New York: deBower Publishing Co., 1926.

Strange, Michael. *Who Tells Me True.* New York: Charles Scribner's Sons, 1940.

Street, George Edmund. *Some Account of Gothic Architecture in Spain.* 1914. 2 vols. Reprint. New York: Benjamin Blom, 1969.

Sullivan, Edward Dean. *The Fabulous Wilson Mizner.* New York: The Henkle Co., 1935.

Tallmadge, Thomas E. *The Story of Architecture in America.* New York: W. W. Norton and Co., 1927.

Tebeau, Charlton. *A History of Florida.* Coral Gables: University of Miami Press, 1975.

Thomas, Dana L. *Lords of the Land: The Triumphs and Scandals of America's Real Estate Barons.* New York: G. P. Putnan's Sons, 1977.

Travers, J. Wadsworth. *History of Beautiful Palm Beach.* West Palm Beach: Palm Beach Press, 1928.

20th-Century Decorating, Architecture and Gardens: 80 Years of Ideas and Pleasure from House and Garden. New York: Holt, Rinehart and Winston, 1980.

Van Pelt, John V. *Masterpieces of Spanish Architecture: Romanesque and Allied Styles.* New York: Pencil Points Press, 1925.

Villiers-Stuart, Constance M. *Spanish Gardens: Their History, Types and Features.* New York: Charles Scribner's Sons, 1929.

Wecter, Dixon. *The Saga of American Society: A Record of Social Aspiration, 1607–1937.* New York: Charles Scribner's Sons, 1937.

Weigall, T. H. *Boom in Paradise.* New York: Alfred H. King, 1932.

Weise, A. J. *History of the City of Troy.* Troy, NY.: William H. Young, 1876.

Wendehack, Clifford C. *Golf and Country Clubs: Construction and Equipment of the Modern Club House.* New York: William Helburn, 1929.

Whittlesey, Austin. *The Renaissance Architecture of Central and Northern Spain.* New York: Architectural Book Publishing Co., 1920.

The Winterthur Story. The Henry Francis du Pont Winterthur Museum, 1965.

Wood, James R. *Paul Smith's College: 1937–1980.* Paul Smiths, NY: Paul Smith's College, 1980.

Year Book of the Joint Exposition of the Architectural League of Greater Miami and Florida South Chapter, AIA. 1930.

PERIODICAL ARTICLES

Allen, Harris. "New Spain." *Pacific Coast Architect* 29 (June 1926): 5–33.

Ash, Agnes. "Those Colorful Palm Beach Collectors." *Antiques World* 3 (December 1980): 82–87.

"Barrio De Los Palmeras, Palm Beach Florida." *The Architect* 5 (March 1926): 624–34.

Bliven, Bruce. "Mr. Croesus, His Paradise." *The New Republic* 38 (9 April 1924): 176–78.

"The Boca Influence." *Boca Raton* 1 (October 1981): 22–24.

Boyd, John Taylor, Jr. "The Florida House: Mr. Addison Mizner, the Architect, Recounts the Birth of the New Florida Architecture at Palm Beach in an Interview." *Arts and Decoration* 32 (January 1930): 37–40, 80, 102.

"Bungalows in the Spanish Manner Adapted to Meet American Ideals Designed by Addison Mizner." *Ladies Home Journal,* (February 1927): 36.

Calhoun, Charles. "Gold Coast Architect." *Arts and Antiques* (July–August 1981): 72–75.

Chapman, Mary Patricia. "The Mission of Lansing Bond Mizner to Central America." *The Historian* 19 (August 1957): 385–401.

Cromwell, James H. R. "Palm Beach Past and Present." *Country Life* 67 (January 1935): 57–60, 80.

Davis, Mollie. "Epilogue to Swimming." *Arts and Decoration* 38 (April 1933): 12–14, 60.

Edgerton, Giles. "Great Modern Hotels: Their Architecture and Decoration—The Ritz-Carlton Cloister of Boca Raton—Florida." *Arts and Decoration* 24 (April 1926): 57–59, 111.

"Francis L. Abreu and Fort Lauderdale's Boomtime Architecture." *New River News* 20 (Spring 1982): 2–10.

"From Zero to Zephyr." *Cincinnati Fine Arts Journal* 7 (February–March 1935): 10–11.

George, W. L. "Humanity at Palm Beach." *Harper's* 150 (January 1925): 213–22.

"A Glimpse of the Via Mizner." *Arts and Decoration* 32 (January 1930): 36.

Gray, Christopher. "Neighborhood." *Avenue* 7 (20 September 1982): 53–62.

"Gulf Stream Golf Club, Palm Beach, Fla." *Architectural Forum* 42 (March 1925), plates 25–27.

Hamilton, Frederick. "The Work of Willis Polk and Company." *The Architect and Engineer* 24 (April 1911): 35–73.

Holley, Lillian Harlow. "Creator of Castles in Spain." *The Hollywood Magazine* 1 (September 1925): 32–35.

———. "Palm Beach Homes of Distinction." *The Hollywood Magazine* 1 (April 1925): 10–17.

"The Home of Charles A. Stone, Piping Rock, L.I." *House and Garden* 40 (October 1921): 32–33.

Howe, E. W. "The Real Palm Beach." *Saturday Evening Post* 192 (17 April 1920): 42.

Isman, Felix. "Florida's Land Boom." *Saturday Evening Post* 198 (22 August 1925): 14.

Kay, Jane Holtz. "Mizner's Eden." *American Preservation* 4 (1981): 35–48.

Kent, Joan. "The Baxter Homestead: Busy Past, Busy Present." *Cow Neck Historical Society Journal* (October 1970): 12–14.

Kent, William Winthrop. "Domestic Architecture of California." Parts I, II. *The Architectural Forum* 32 (March 1920): 95–100, 151–56.

Lopez, Frank G. "We were having some people in for cocktails." *Architectural Record* 99 (July 1953): 46.

Major, Howard. "A Theory Relating to Spanish and Italian Houses in Florida." *Architectural Forum* 45 (August 1926): 97–104.

Morrow, Irving F. "The Riviera Revisited." *The Architect and Engineer* 80 (February 1925): 44–109.

"A New Influence in the Architecture of Philadelphia." *Architectural Record* 15 (February 1904): 3–121.

"No One Swims in the Ocean in Palm Beach." *Country Life* 67 (February 1935): 36–38.

"Obituary of Addison Mizner." *Architectural Forum* 56 (March 1933): 38.

"The Old Cow Bay Manor House." *Architectural Record* 41 (March 1917): 259–66.

Orr-Cahall, Christina. "Palm Beach: The Predicament of a Resort." *Historic Preservation* 30 (January-March 1978): 10–15.

———. "The 'Total Environment' of Addison Mizner." *Antiques World* 3 (December 1980): 74–81.

"Palm Beach." *Fortune* 13 (February 1936): 56.

"Palm Beach Aristocrat." *Architectural Digest* 28 (November–December 1972): 16–21.

Patterson, Curtis. "A Shelf of New Books: Addison Mizner and Florida." *International Studio* 40 (August 1928): 73–74.

Price, Matlack. " 'Mediterranean' Architecture in Florida." *Architectural Forum* 44 (January 1926): 33–40.

———. "Returning to Romanticism, 'La Ronda'—A Castilian Villa Set in a Lovely Spanish Garden, at Bryn Mawr in Pennsylvania." *Arts and Decoration* 33 (October 1930): 49–53, 114.

Rainey, Lillian Fryer. "The Rich Majority." *Century* 115 (April 1928): 713–15.

"Residence of Mr. and Mrs. F. C. Williams." *Landscape Architecture* 30 (January 1941): 1.

"Ritz-Carlton Cloister." *Architectural Forum* 36 (November 1926): plates 75–80.

Roberts, Kenneth L. "The Time Killers." *Saturday Evening Post* 194 (1 April 1922): 68.

Roberts, Mary Fanton. "Exotic Beauty of Palm Beach Homes." *Arts and Decoration* 20 (December 1923): 22–25.

———. "Lake Worth at Twilight: Where Our Returned Wounded Men Will Find Peace and Health." *The Touchstone* 4 (October 1918): 52–55.

———. "Our War Work: By Paris Singer." *The Touchstone* 3 (August 1918): 371–80.

Robie, Virginia. "A Spanish City in Florida." *International Studio* 81 (May 1925): 107–12.

Shelby, Gertrude M. "Florida Frenzy." *Harper's* 152 (January 1926): 177–86.

"Spanish Influence at Palm Beach." *Architectural Forum* 41 (August 1924): 73–76, plates 25–28.

Story, Walter Rendell. "Old Spain Enters the American Home." *New York Times Magazine* (7 March 1926): 12.

"The Stotesburys." *Fortune* 13 (February 1936): 111–12.

Teegen, Otto. "Joseph Urban." *Architecture* 69 (May 1934): 251–56.

Tindall, George B. "The Bubble in the Sun." *American Heritage* 16 (August 1965): 76–83.

Townsend, Reginald T. "Along the American Riviera." *Country Life* 49 (January 1926): 35–42.

Vanderblue, Homer B. "The Florida Land Boom." *Journal of Land and Public Utility Economics*, part I. 3 (May 1927): 113–31, part II. 3 (August 1927): 252–69.

Wilkins, Woodrow W. "Coral Gables: 1920s New Town." *Historic Preservation* 30 (March 1978): 6–9.

"Winter Refuges in Florida." *Travel* 36 (March 1921): 16–17.

"The Work of Messrs. Carrère and Hastings." *The Architectural Record* 27 (January 1910): 1–120.

Youngman, Elmer H. "Florida, the Last Pioneer State of the Union." *Bankers' Magazine* 112 (January 1926): 7–51.

UNPUBLISHED MATERIALS

Akin, Edward Nelson. "Southern Reflections of the Gilded Age: Henry M. Flagler's System, 1885–1913." Ph.D. dissertation, University of Florida, 1975.

Beck, Warren Albert. "American Policy in Guatemala, 1839–1900." Ph.D. dissertation, Ohio State University, 1954.

Leslie, Vernon M. "The Great Depression in Miami Beach." Master's thesis, Florida Atlantic University, 1980.

Mizner, Addison. Autobiographical typescript (1933). The Historical Society of Palm Beach County.

Orr-Cahall, Anona Christina. "An Identification and Discussion of the Architecture and Decorative Arts of Addison Mizner (1872–1933)." 2 vols. Ph.D. dissertation, Yale University, 1979.

Riddle, Karl. "Day Book" (1925–1926). Privately owned.

Seiden, Steven Arnold. "The Mizner Touch." Senior thesis, Yale University, 1958.

Sessa, Frank Bowman. "Real Estate Expansion and Boom in Miami and its Environs During the 1920's." Ph.D. dissertation, University of Pittsburgh, 1950.

Waugh, Alex. "The Mizner Industries." January 1963, typescript, Historical Society of Palm Beach County.

———. Untitled typescript. Boca Raton Historical Society.

List of Buildings and Projects

All items on this list have been verified by consulting Mizner office tracings and blueprints in the collections of the Historical Society of Palm Beach County and in private hands, his office inventory list, newspaper articles at the time of construction, building department permits, Sanborn insurance maps and city directories, letters written by Ella Watson Mizner, and visits to the buildings when possible. The date is year of construction, or in case of projects, year designed. Palm Beach and West Palm Beach are abbreviated P.B. and W.P.B.

1906   Garden and garden furniture, Farmholme, Stonington, CT.

1907   Remodeling of Hotel Rand, 142 W. 49th Street, NYC.

Completion and decoration of town house for Stephen H. Brown, 154 E. 70th St., NYC (now Lenox School).

Additions and remodeling for Addison Mizner, Baxter Homestead, 15 Shore Dr., Port Washington, L.I.

1910   Gardens for Raymond Hitchcock, 22 Sunset Rd., Kings Point, L.I.

Additions for Archibold S. White, White Pine Camp, Paul Smiths, NY (now Paul Smith's College).

Tennis house for Ralph Thomas, 235 Middle Neck Rd., Sands Point, L.I.

1911   Garden and amphitheater for William Bourke Cockran, The Cedars, Hempstead Harbor and Shore roads, Port Washington, L.I. (demolished).

Residence for Jerome Alexandre, Colebrook, CT.

Residence for Sarah Cowen Monson, Upper Drive, Huntington, L.I. (demolished).

Residence for William A. Prime, Warburton Hall, Northern Blvd., Roslyn, L.I. Remodeling and additions by Shape & Hart (now C. W. Post Center, Long Island University).

1912   Residence for John Alley Parker, Sands Point Rd., Sands Point, L.I.

235

Two speculative houses for Charles Dodge, Wampage Shores, Port Washington, L.I.

Residence for Alfred Elliot Dieterich, Dutchess County, NY.

1913   Interiors for residence of John Sedgwick Hyde, Bath, ME.

1915   Residence for Mrs. O.H.P. Belmont, Sands Point, L.I., project.

Beach or tea house for Mrs. O.H.P. Belmont, Sands Point, L.I.

1916   Residence for I. Townsend Burden, Jr., Northern Blvd., Greenvale, L.I. (now New York Institute of Technology).

1917   Residence for Stephen H. Brown, Duck Pond Rd., Locust Valley, L.I., altered.

1918   Everglades Club, villas, and garage, Worth Ave., P.B. (villas and garage demolished, club remodeling and additions by Mizner, Wyeth, and Volk).

1919   Shops and apartments, Maisonettes, Worth Ave., P.B. (interiors designed by Martin L. Hampton, demolished).

Residence or tea house for E. Clarence Jones, Villa Yalta, 189 Sunset Ave., P.B. (demolished).

Residence for Edward T. Stotesbury, El Mirasol, 348 North Ocean Blvd., P.B. (additions by Mizner, Wyeth, and Fatio, demolished).

Residence for Charles A. Munn, Amado, 455 N. County Rd., P.B. (additions by Fatio).

Residence for Gurnee Munn, Louwana, 473 N. County Rd., P.B. (additions by Fatio).

Residence for Addison Mizner, El Salano, 720 S. Ocean Blvd., P.B. (sold to Harold S. Vanderbilt, additions by Mizner and others).

1920   Residence for Mrs. Elizabeth H. G. Slater, Costa Bella, 111 Dunbar Rd., P.B.

Residence for Dr. Willey Lyon Kingsley, La Bellucia, 1200 S. Ocean Blvd., P.B.

Residence for H. C. Clarke (probably built, unlocated).

1921   Residence for Addison Mizner, Concha Marina, 102 Jungle Rd., P.B. (sold to George Sloane, additions by Wyeth, Fatio, Volk, and others).

Residence for Leonard Thomas, Casa de Leoni, 450 Worth Ave., P.B. (additions, remodeling).

Residence for Captain, the Honorable Charles J. Winn, 121 El Bravo Way, P.B. (additions and remodeling by Mizner and Wyeth).

Residence for O. Frank Woodward, 163 Seminole Rd., P.B. (additions by Wyeth and Major).

Residence for Alfred G. Kay, Audita, 582 S. Ocean Blvd., P.B. (additions by Wyeth).

Residence for John S. Phipps, Casa Bendita, 434 N. County Rd., P.B. (additions by Mizner, demolished).

1922   Residence for Joseph M. Cudahy, 135 Grace Trail, P.B.

Residence for Alice De Lamar, 1426 S. Ocean Blvd., P.B. (designed in Mizner's office, demolished).

Residence for Madame Jeannette Gais, 150 S. Ocean Blvd., P.B. (demolished).

Residence for Willis Sharp Kilmer, P.B., project.

Residence for Walter G. Mitchell, 182 S. Ocean Blvd., P.B. (demolished).

Residence for Barclay Harding Warburton, Casa Maria Marrone, 480 Worth Ave., P.B. (additions by Mizner, Major, Wyeth, and Geisler, now divided).

Residence for William Gray Warden, 112 Seminole Ave., P.B.

Residence for Addison Mizner, Sin Cuidado, 1800 S. Ocean Blvd., P.B. (sold to Edward S. Moore, additions by Mizner).

1923   Residence for Anthony J. Drexel Biddle, El Sarimento, 150 S. Ocean Blvd., P.B. (additions by Mizner and Urban).

Residence for Daniel H. Carstairs, 280 N. Ocean Blvd., P.B. (additions by Fatio).

Residence for Arthur D. Claflin, 800 S. County Rd., P.B. (additions by Mizner).

Residence for Joseph Cosden, Playa Riente, 947 N. Ocean Blvd., P.B. (additions by Mizner, demolished).

Residence for Angier B. Duke, 160 Barton Ave., P.B. (sold to Jules S. Bache, additions, remodeling by Major, Volk, and others).

The Gulfstream Golf Club, Ocean Blvd., Gulfstream (additions and remodeling).

Residence for George Luke Mesker, La Fontana, Royal Palm Way at Ocean Blvd., P.B. (additions and remodeling by Mizner, Fatio and others, demolished).

Office and studio for Addison Mizner, 337 Worth Ave., P.B.

Additions to residence of Henry C. Phipps, Heamaw, 401 N. Ocean Blvd., P.B. (demolished).

Residence for DeGrimm Renfro, Villa Tranquilla, 100 El Brillo Way, P.B. (additions by Mizner and Wyeth).

Remodeling of residence of J. Leonard Replogle, Sunrise Villa, 138 N. Ocean Blvd., P.B. (demolished).

Residence for Edward Shearson, Villa Flora, 110 Dunbar Rd., P.B.

Residence for Dr. Preston Pope Satterwhite, Casa Florencia, 910 S. Ocean Blvd., P.B. (demolished).

Residence for Joseph Speidel, Casa Joseto, 942 S. Ocean Blvd., P.B. (demolished).

Residence for Rodman Wanamaker II, La Guerida, 1113 N. Ocean Blvd., P.B. (additions by Fatio and others).

Residence for William M. Wood, The Towers, 548 N. County Rd., P.B. (demolished).

Store for Henri Bendel, Seminole Ave. and lake, project.

1924   Residence for Addison Mizner, Villa Mizner, 341 Worth Ave., P.B.

Shopping plaza for Addison Mizner, Via Mizner, Worth Ave., P.B.

Shops and apartments for Ocean and Lake Realty Co., Palmway Building, Royal Palm Way and S. County Rd., P.B.

Shop and apartment for Palm Beach Company, Mizner Plaza, 238 Phipps Plaza, P.B.

Shops and apartments for Palm Beach Company, The Plaza Shops, S. County Rd. at Phipps Plaza, P.B.

Residence for John Magee, Lagomar, 1560 S. Ocean Blvd., P.B. (additions by Mizner, subdivided).

Residence for Wilson Mizner, 237 Worth Ave., P.B.

Residence for Paul Moore, Collado Hueco, 1820 S. Ocean Blvd., P.B.

Residence for Ysabel Chase, Seventeen-Mile Dr., Pebble Beach, CA.

Station for Seaboard Railroad, West Palm Beach, project.

1925   Residence and studio for Sir Oswald Birley, Everglades Club grounds, P.B. (demolished).

Residence for H. Halpine Smith, 323 Chilean Ave., P.B.

Residence for Karl Riddle, 1000 Belmont Place, W.P.B.

Office and apartment building for Paris Singer, Singer Building, Royal Palm Way, P.B. (converted by Volk).

Boynton Woman's Club, 1010 S. Federal Hwy., Boynton Beach.

Residence for Mrs. William K. Vanderbilt, Jr., P.B., project.

Residence for C. Bai Lihme, P.B., project.

Shopping plaza and apartments for Paris Singer, Via Parigi, Worth Ave., P.B.

The Cloister Inn, Boca Raton (additions by Wyeth, Schultze & Weaver, and others).

The Administration Buildings, Boca Raton.

Cloister Inn garage, Boca Raton (demolished).

Houses A to J for Mizner Development Company, Boca Raton (twenty-nine completed in section later known as Old Floresta).

Houses for Harry Vought and Company, Spanish Village, Boca Raton.

Residence for Addison Mizner, Castle Mizner, Boca Raton, project.

Boca Raton Housing, Boca Raton, project.

Venetian Bridge for Boca Raton, project.

Office building for E. B. Davis, Boca Raton, project.

Residence for George A. Long, Boca Raton, project.

Residence for A. S. Alexander, Boca Raton, project.

Residence for Anderson T. Herd, Boca Raton, project.

Boynton City Hall, Boynton Beach, project.

1926   Residence for George Rasmussen, Casa Nana, 780 S. Ocean Blvd., P.B.

Blue Heron Hotel for Paris Singer, Palm Beach Ocean development, Singer Island (partially completed, demolished).

Town Hall for Boca Raton (completed by William Alsmyer).

Small speculative houses for Dr. Maurice Druker, SW 18th St., Boca Raton (four or five completed, demolished).

Apartment house for H. W. Dunagan, DeSoto Road, Boca Raton (demolished).

Riverside Baptist Church, Park and King streets, Jacksonville.

Residence for Bessie Gardner du Pont, Chevannes, Kennett Pike, Greenville, DE (completed by Albert Ely Ives).

Water tower, pump houses, golf course, and sewer, Boca Raton (partially completed).

Additions to residence of Dr. H. Marshall Taylor, Riverside Ave., Jacksonville, project.

Las Carreros Jockey Club, Boca Raton, project.

Winter campus for Montemare School for Girls, Boca Raton, project.

Theater for Boca Raton, project.

Pink House, Boca Raton, project.

Residence for Madame Frances Alda, Boca Raton, project.

Residence for Dr. Maurice Druker, Boca Raton, project.

Residence for Porte G. Quinn, Boca Raton, project.

Residence for Harry Reichenbach, Boca Raton, project.

Residence for Radcliffe Roberts, Boca Raton, project.

Residence for Hugh Tevis, Boca Raton, project.

Residence for John McMullen, Boca Raton, project.

Residence for John Whelan, P.B., project.

1927   Residence for John R. Bradley, Casa Serena, Colorado Springs, CO (now Fountain Valley School).

Additions and renovations for Mrs. Glen Hodges, 306-312 Worth Ave., P.B. (additions by Fatio).

1928   Residence for Jerome D. Gedney, 1720 S. Ocean Blvd., Manalapan.

Additions for residence of John F. Harris, 4 El Bravo Way, P.B.

Brokerage office and apartment for John F. Harris, 2629 Collins Ave., Miami Beach (demolished).

Nurses' Lodge, Harris Hall, Good Samaritan Hospital, W.P.B. (converted to auditorium by Volk).

The Cloister, Sea Island, GA (additions by Francis L. Abreu and others).

Residence for Alfred Jones, Sr., E. Spalding St., Sea Island, GA.

Residence for Alfred E. Dieterich, Casa Bienvenita, Park Lane, Montecito, CA.

Residence for Percival E. Foerderer, La Ronda, 1020 Mount Pleasant Road, Bryn Mawr, PA.

Residence for "Mrs. Blank," Mizner Mile, Boynton Beach (partially built, demolished).

Deauville Beach Club, Windsor, Canada, project.

Additions to residence of Dan Murphy, Los Angeles, CA, project.

1929 Embassy Club for Colonel Edward R. Bradley, Royal Palm Way, P.B. (conversion to gallery and auditorium for Society of the Four Arts by Wyeth).

Memorial fountain and plaza, S. County Rd., P.B.

Palm Beach shop for McCutcheon and Co., S. County Rd. and Seaview Ave., P.B.

Palm Beach Shops for Burdine's, 230 South County Rd., P.B.

Additions to residence of Nate Spingold, La Puertas, 152 Wells Rd., P.B. (later additions by Fatio).

Residence for William R. Hearst, P.B., project.

Fox Chapel Country Club, Fox Chapel, PA, project.

1930 Brokerage office for E. F. Hutton, 264 S. County Rd., P.B.

Residence for Hugh Dillman, Grosse Point, MI, project.

Residence for Alex Camp, Dallas, TX, project.

1931 Residence for William J. Williams, Casa Coe da Sol, 501 Park St., North, St. Petersburg.

Apartment for Oscar G. Davies, Daily News Building, S. County Rd. at Brazilian Ave., P.B.

Post Office for Palm Beach, S. County Rd. at Royal Poinciana Way, project.

Bonsack shopping center, Miami Beach, project.

Residence for William F. Bonsack, Miami or Miami Beach, project.

1932 Residence for K. D. Alexander, 323 Brazilian Ave., P.B.

Everglades Theater for Hugo Gold, Belle Glade (demolished).

Residence for J. A. Ely, W.P.B., project.

Index

Figure numbers are given in italics following page numbers. Buildings outside of Palm Beach are cross-referenced under the cities in which they are located.

Sources of Illustrations